Thomas Henry Braim

New Homes

The Rise, Progress, present Position, and future Prospects of each of the Australian Colonies and New Zealand

Thomas Henry Braim

New Homes

The Rise, Progress, present Position, and future Prospects of each of the Australian Colonies and New Zealand

ISBN/EAN: 9783337153717

Printed in Europe, USA, Canada, Australia, Japan

Cover: Foto ©ninafisch / pixelio.de

More available books at **www.hansebooks.com**

NEW HOMES:

THE RISE, PROGRESS, PRESENT POSITION, AND FUTURE PROSPECTS

OF EACH OF THE

Australian Colonies and New Zealand,

REGARDED AS

HOMES FOR ALL CLASSES OF EMIGRANTS.

BY

THOMAS HENRY BRAIM, D.D., F.R.G.S.,

&c., &c., &c.,

LATE ARCHDEACON, DIOCESE OF MELBOURNE, AND NOW RECTOR OF BISHOP'S CAUNDLE, SHERBORNE, AND CHAPLAIN TO THE MOST NOBLE THE MARQUIS OF LOTHIAN.

Profusely Illustrated.

"God blessed them; and God said unto them, Be fruitful and multiply, and replenish the earth, and subdue it."—*Gen.* i. 28.

"God Himself hath formed the earth and made it; He hath established it, He created it not in vain, He formed it to be inhabited.—*Isa.* xlv. 18.

LONDON:
BULL, SIMMONS & CO., 9, WIGMORE STREET.
1870.

TO

His Grace the Duke of Manchester,

WHO,

IN TESTIMONY OF AN ENLIGHTENED DESIRE FOR THE BENEFIT

AND PROGRESS OF ENGLAND AND HER COLONIES,

HAS ACCEPTED THE HONOURABLE POSITION OF

President of the National Emigration League,

THIS BOOK

IS, BY THE KIND PERMISSION OF HIS GRACE,

MOST RESPECTFULLY DEDICATED.

Preface.

So many books have appeared on the Australian Colonies, and amongst them so many of sterling merit, that it might seem presumptuous to bring out another. Those books, however, have generally been limited to one or two particular colonies, and published at a high price. At this moment, when the popular mind is so strongly directed to the emigration of the masses, it was considered by competent judges that if a single and reliable volume could give a bird's-eye view of the whole of the colonies which form the Australasian group, and also of New Zealand, and that at such a price as would bring it within the means of the million, it would supply an acknowledged desideratum.

The Author having been in Australia for more than thirty years, leading there an active life in scenes far removed from literary ease, is quite aware that this little compilation may have serious defects regarded as a mere composition; but he trusts that it will be kindly received, and judged in a friendly spirit, as the production of one who has aimed only at writing what might be useful, and might be depended upon as a truthful description of the several colonies of which it treats.

To the Agents-General of each of the colonies, to the Managers of the Banks connected with Australasia and New Zealand, and to a host of kind advisers and helpers too numerous to be named in detail, he begs to return his sincerest thanks.

THE RECTORY,
    BISHOP'S CAUNDLE, SHERBORNE.

CONTENTS.

	PAGE
CHAP. I.—INTRODUCTION	9
II.—AUSTRALIAN DISCOVERY,—NEW SOUTH WALES	62
III.—TASMANIA	119
IV.—WESTERN AUSTRALIA	169
V.—VICTORIA (FORMERLY PORT PHILLIP)	189
VI.—SOUTH AUSTRALIA	257
VII.—QUEENSLAND (MORETON BAY)	339
VIII.—NEW ZEALAND	363

New Homes.

Chapter I.

IT is, I am told by those who are well versed in the subject, a matter of very general complaint, that there does not exist any one single volume which gives, as it were, a connected view of all the Colonies which form the great Australasian group, including the various provinces of New Zealand. Books almost without number have appeared, treating on one or other of these places. Many of them are written by very able men, and contain a vast mass of most useful information. At this moment, however, public attention is increasingly attracted to the subject of Emigration; and it has been thought that a cheap and popular book would be appreciated. A book such as may be found not only on the Library table, but at our Mechanics' Institutes and Working Men's Reading Rooms, and wherever, in fact, men congregate for the purpose of getting useful and practical information. Such a work must needs be written by a man who speaks from local knowledge, and from personal observation. Having been myself a resident for more than thirty years in three of the

Australian colonies, and having had great opportunities for becoming acquainted with the rest of them, I trust that I may be enabled to write such a sketch of them as may be found to be extensively useful. My object is simply *utility*. I aim at presenting to the enquiring reader, who is looking out for information or thinking of removing to a new home, such an epitome of each colony in succession as may, I hope and believe, assist him in forming a right judgment. And of one thing the reader may rest quite assured, viz., that I wish to bring before him nothing but a candid statement of facts. I have no favourite theories to advocate, and no pet colony to praise at the expense of another. I only wish them all to be better known at home than they are. The more they are known the larger will be the exodus to them. Since my return to England I have been requested to deliver lectures on Australia at several large centres of population. Such lectures have been invariably received with much favour. But those attending them have owned to me their almost entire ignorance of Australian geography and history. I wish to help in removing this ignorance, and to make people in England better acquainted with these great colonies, which are rapidly growing up into a nation of no mean importance. Perhaps by some it may be argued that I shall not be a writer who should be trusted on all points— religious ones, for instance—inasmuch as I am a clergyman of the Church of England, and may be supposed to have peculiar feelings in favour of my own communion, and prejudices against other denominations. I do not hesitate to say that no fault will be found with me on this head at least; although being and glorying in being a clergyman of the Church of England, I have lived so long abroad, where there is no State Church, and where all denominations are on a perfect equality, that I am not likely to err in this respect. Besides which, I know most intimately men of all creeds, and have the greatest respect for all those "who love the Lord Jesus Christ in sincerity," by whatever name they may pass among men.

Having thus given a reason why I think such a book as I am writing should be presented to the public; having stated that I write from no mere hearsay, but as having for so long a time dwelt amid the scenes I describe; and having also removed what might have raised a prejudice against myself as a chronicler of Australian history, I will without further preface address myself to the task before me. And if, within the compass of a small volume, I can take you out to the colonies, travel with you from one to the other of them, tracing by the way "their rise, progress, present condition, and future prospects," and then bring you safely home on a voyage by steam, round that region of storms, Cape Horn, I think you will agree with me that I have beaten the electric telegraph *hollow*. But who shall go on the voyage? For whom are these colonies fit and promising places to resort to as an adopted home? My own lengthened expatriation has made England, and much of what I see in England, quite new to me. The style in which all classes appear to me to live is completely altered. A great deal of the old and charming simplicity which I remember in bygone days has passed away for ever. There is a restlessness among masses of the people; a great amount of competition in every grade of society; all ranks vie with each other in expense of living, of dress, and of equipage; people dress in broad cloth who in my boyish days dressed in fustian; and silks and satins are the attire of people who used to appear in prints. And the puzzle to me continually is arising, How is all this done? How can the people, as a *whole*, make such a display? Of course I know that England is a great and wealthy nation— greater and wealthier than any other nation—but still is all that I see the result of improved circumstances? I fear not. I suspect from all that I see, and from what I am told, that a vast proportion of our population are given to keep up appearances. Men do not like their neighbours to outvie them in the goodness of their houses, the richness of their furniture, the style of their dress, or the quality of their entertainments; and hence there is a continual and most unwholesome competition and rivalry existing. Many a man rides in his carriage who ought to be walking; and many a lady is dressed to receive visitors whose household duties urgently claim her personal superintendence. But this is considered *necessary*, in order to keep up the credit of those who are in business. Surely, however, this is a very hollow, artificial state of society. True, says every one to whom you speak, most true. But so it is; and " when you are at Rome, you must do as Rome does." To my mind it appears quite clear that in this great and famed land every profession and every business is *overcrowded*. The land cannot hold them, and continue to be healthy and vigorous, as of old. The remedy is *emigration*. When we read the word *emigration*, we are apt to confine it to poor labourers and their families; we picture to ourselves an English or an Irish port, with its vessels crowded with hundreds of poor exiles quitting their native land, to seek bread on other and fairer shores. But that is not my idea. I think that new homes should be sought by *all* classes, excepting of course those who by birth or by position are so happily placed as to be above the necessity of working for their subsistence. I have seen around me since my return many a professional man of every kind, many a merchant, farmer, tradesman, and mechanic, as well as the miner, the labourer, and the domestic servant, whose position might be greatly benefited by seeking on other shores that remuneration for his labour which he so richly merits, but which he sees no prospect of here. I think that at all times, but just now especially, the *capitalist* whose attention is drawn to the Australian colonies would reap a return for his money which here he may seek in vain. Without entering upon the dangerous field of speculation, he might invest his money in almost any one of the colonies, and in almost any undertaking, with the certainty of obtaining for it a far better return than he can do in England, where money appears to be a drug, with only a nominal value attached to it. The colonies are expanding so much every year, that *professional* men of average ability will in time work themselves into a position. There is a great want of earnest-minded ministers of religion of all denominations. And I do not hesitate to say that, as a *body*, they are better off than in England. Of course we have no great prizes, no rich deaneries or fat rectories; but then there is none of the actual *want* which is to be found among English curates, nor the necessity for keeping up appearances, which seems so requisite among the occupants of the smaller livings in this country. But it may be objected, "Yes, but who would live in a country where you have to depend on the *voluntary* system—where your own people provide your stipend?" I would. And I have done so, and would not mind doing so again. I believe that the respect shown to the clergy in the colonies is quite equal to what they receive here; and that if a man does his duty, he will be properly provided for without any violence being done to his feelings. In many of those new townships which are continually springing up, the *merchant* and the *tradesman*, if they will but be content to creep before they walk, and to walk before they run, will find an opening which year by year will go on improving. I have been living a good deal in the country since my return. I find the *small tenant* farmer gone, and the country parcelled out into large farms, held by men who are in many cases only struggling against a host of difficulties. Look at the Australian farmer, and compare his position with the English tenant-farmer, and I am sure you will see the superiority of the former over the latter. If he have a little capital he may select his own virgin soil, have a large farm direct from the Government, **pay a mere trifle for it as rent or interest for a few years**, and after that it becomes *his own for ever*, without the payment of any price at all. If he have a family, every one is a help, and not an encumbrance. Of course, such a man must go through a great deal of hard work; he must take off his coat, and work with a will; his wife must not think so much of her dress as of her household duties; but then they are working for themselves and for their children. Every year their property is increasing in value; and if they will be but true to themselves, they will, God blessing their industry, reap a rich reward. A story is told of two professional men who, worn out with anxiety and crushed down by competition, and by keeping up hollow appearances, often talked together of trying to better their lot, and getting rid of the mockery by which they were surrounded. At last it was arranged that one should go out first and report progress. He went and got some land, and reared his hut and got some corn. Little by little you might see fences rising round you, and crops going in; and though the new farmer had no money, he had money's worth in his cleared *freehold* land and his increasing stock. Then came out his friend, a man of another stamp, and when he visited the farmer, he found the lady who when last he saw her was dressed in satins, presiding at the piano in a handsome drawing-room, now with her gown sleeves tucked up making her butter; and the husband's axe in the distance telling fearfully on some giant in the forest. And he was disgusted. It would never do for him. But the lady told him that she had never known what comfort was till then; they worked hard and slept well; they were making a home for themselves, and for their children after them; if they were spared for two or three years more the worst of their toil would be over; and above all, she said, we have no " Mrs. Grundy " here. Yes, in all the colonies there are hundreds of families, many of them gentlemen and ladies by birth, and many more who are nature's noblemen, who have thus, in the wilds of Australia, raised themselves to positions of comfort and independence. The desire to possess a "bit of land," which he can call *his own*, seems to be a desire implanted in the human heart. I know of no countries where this most reasonable ambition can be more easily gratified. I have spoken of the farmer as having *capital*. And a little capital is a great advantage; nay, is almost necessary. But then, I do not mean such a capital as is required for a large farm in England. Many a labouring man, knowing what he is about, will become a servant on a farm for a year or two. Whilst in that capacity he will keep his eye about him, spy out a bit of good land, save up his large wages, get it, and commence operations in a small way. Such a man nearly always succeeds if he have but common prudence. The *mechanic* may emigrate with great advantage. Some trades are more in demand than others; and we shall hereafter be able to speak more to the point on this subject. There are times when mechanics are less in demand than at others; and in new countries, with a shifting population, it is not easy to give advice to this class of persons. They sometimes have to go long distances before they get their work; and at others they are without work. But as you will see as you read further the wages are very high. The hours of labour are, as a rule, eight hours. This class generally manage as soon as possible to put themselves up a little house of their own, so as to save the landlord's demands, and the tax-gatherer does not so frequently make his calls upon them. It has always appeared to me that the great fault of such persons is clinging to the large towns, and being too particular as to what they do. If the towns are full, strike out into some country place. If your own occupation is at the moment overcrowded, take labourer's work—any work, for a short time. All will come right presently. Get into *work* of some kind. Work brings money, and time brings experience. If emigrants pursued this plan, and met the difficulties inseparable from a settlement in a new country with a hearty good will, and laughed at, instead of grumbling over, the discomforts of the first few months, we should hear less of that discontent which arises at times from those who will not be satisfied unless they can see all the appliances of an old and artificial state of society transplanted ready to their hand in their new homes. There is a difficult class to be dealt with, who are very ready for emigration, but who perhaps are most unfitted for it. I mean *young men* brought up in offices. Men who can write and read and cast accounts, and nothing else; whose hands are white, and who physically are not equal to any exertion, even if they were disposed to work at rough employments. There are now so many natives of the soil whose parents have a connection and a certain amount of local interest, that they generally get a preference in our banks, insurance, merchants', and other offices. And if a young man of this class, arriving at any one of the great centres of population, can do nothing else but office work, he may, and I know he often does, meet with great disappointment. But the number of *such* young men is, I trust, on the decrease. In these days of *athletic* exercises, when Oxford and Cambridge, and all our great schools, vie with each other in muscle as well as in brain, this race of "do nothings" will gradually disappear. Our ablest men now, with the pen and with the tongue, are also our best at the oar, the bat, and the leaping bar. Send out such a man. If he did not get into an employment which was most congenial to him, why he would take off his coat and "turn to" at anything that was honest, however hard, till his time came. And of a man made of such material there is no fear eventually. There is one view of the Australian colonies which is not, I think, presented to the English reader with sufficient prominence. I mean as a home for those of *delicate constitutions*. Medical men are beginning to turn their attention to these countries. How many are there who are constitutionally quite unfitted for living in England, to whom its moist and foggy winters produce the worst results, and whose early death may be expected, who might be greatly benefited by a change to one or other of this great group of colonies. Dr. S. Dougan Bird, in his excellent work on Australasian Climates, and their Influence in the Prevention and Arrest of Pulmonary Consumption, says:—"In these colonies we have good examples of all the varieties of climate, air, and soil required for the treatment of pulmonary consumption, whether in winter or summer. Thus Launceston, in Tasmania, (24 hours by steamer from Melbourne) fulfils every condition which we should require for the class of persons to which Pau is beneficial. It is in a moist, clayey soil, in a valley at the junction of the North and South Esk, about 40 miles from the sea, protected from all winds but the north by high ranges of mountains, whilst the heat and dryness of these winds are obviated by their passage across the Bass's Straits. The atmosphere is usually still, moist, and equable, and to healthy persons relaxing, as the ozoniferous west and south-west winds cannot reach the valleys. Count Strzelecki compares the winter climate of Launceston to that of Lisbon, while in summer it is not warmer than Cheltenham. There are excellent hotels and lodging-houses in the town, and living is not dearer than in any English watering-place, whilst the scenery is highly picturesque, and there is no lack of society and the amusements which can be expected in a provincial town. There are other parts of the northern coast of the island whose winter climate is identical with that of Algiers or Sicily, considerably warmer, and less damp and relaxing than Pau, without the dry and stimulating air of the mainland. Hobart Town and the southern coast may be looked upon rather as a summer climate for invalids than as a winter residence, although in Europe it would take a high rank amongst the latter, its coldest month having a mean temperature of 45·82° Fahrenheit, that is to say, considerably warmer than the winter of Pau, and on a level with most winter climates in the south of Europe. The whole of Tasmania is very salubrious and well suited to European constitutions, particularly those exhausted by residence in India or other hot climates." The mortality of Hobart Town is far lower than any town mortality in Europe. "But," continues Dr. Bird, " the climate, *par excellence*, of these colonies is that of Moreton Bay and its neighbourhood, in Queensland, not far from the southern limit of the tropics. Here the average winter temperature on the coast is 62° or 63°, warmer even than Madeira—an air soft and soothing, without being relaxing, and sunny brilliant weather. This, of all climates that I ever heard of, is the one most likely to prolong the life of an advanced case of consumption in an irritable constitution, whose bronchial membrane resents any fall in the temperature. A considerable number of instances are familiar to the inhabitants of the more southern colonies of persons, apparently in a hopeless stage of disease, recovering sufficiently in Queensland to follow their ordinary avocations."

The climate of South Australia is dry, warm, tonic, and stimulating. "The soil for many miles around the city of Adelaide is a light sandy loam, in which the vine, the orange, and the geranium flourish in great vigour and beauty. In the matter of temperature, South Australia may be compared with Malta, or even Tunis, but in general salubrity they will bear no comparison.

"Many of the northern districts of Victoria, on the frontiers of New South Wales, and still further north, have winter climates which present admirable modifications of this type—dry, warm, and tonic—but not so stimulating as that of South Australia. But besides the decided antitheses of climate, we have others which, without such positive characteristics of soothing or stimulating air, are suitable to that numerous class of consumptive patients who require simply a warm, bright, and salubrious climate in winter, and have not any special requirements beyond this. Sydney, and the coast of New South Wales in general, differ very considerably in climate from that of Victoria. It is several degrees nearer the Equator, and out of reach of the west and south-west winds. The result of which is, that the average temperature is higher both for the year and in winter, the air is less ozoniferous and stimulating, the changes are fewer and not so rapid, and have more regularity. The winter temperature at Sydney is about 53°. The winters are warm, light, and pleasant during the day, but chilly at night. Taking it all in all, there is perhaps no climate in the world so generally suitable to consumptive cases at all seasons of the year as Melbourne and its neighbourhood. With the winter temperature of Rome or Barcelona, the southern littoral of Victoria is not hotter in summer than Paris; less moist and boisterous than New Zealand, it equally falls short of the excessive dryness of South Australia, and the close damp heat occasionally experienced at Sydney."

Since my return to England, observing how numerous is that class of persons who are obliged to seek out some mild retreat, at least for the winter, it appears to me important that the peculiar advantages presented by the different Australian colonies should be brought prominently before the public. And it must be borne in mind that the voyage is now, as compared with what it used to be, more like a pleasure excursion, and is most generally of the greatest benefit to the invalid. I believe that when the climate of Australia is better known at home, there will be a far greater number of persons seeking it than at present. And it is not only in cases of consumption that it appears to be so beneficial. But when persons go out at an advanced period of life, they seem to renew their youth, and to take a fresh lease of life—like trees transplanted into a more congenial soil.

There is another class of persons to be found pretty frequently in all parts of England, and in the continental towns. I mean those who are in possession of small fixed incomes arising from property. These incomes are so small, that there is a perpetual struggle going on to "make both ends meet." Such persons often leave their native land and go amongst foreigners, not that they like their surroundings, but simply led to do so by motives of economy. I cannot but think that they would feel themselves more at home in the Australian colonies, and far more comfortable. They would enjoy a fine climate, have all the comforts and conveniences of life in the midst of a society which is thoroughly English, and not have to exercise such rigid economy as they are obliged to do now. But such an one may say to me, "Is it really so? What kind of places are your towns? What are your houses like? What is the state of society? Have you the same or worse trouble with your servants? Are the means of grace within your reach? What is the state of education?" All the cities and large towns are very like English towns. Fine broad streets, handsome shops—as handsome as those in Regent Street—crowds of well dressed people and numbers of well appointed carriages meet you at every turn. These cities have, in most cases, parks and botanical gardens; and the same amusements are to be found in them as in England. The houses are built after the English plan, except that they are frequently to be found with the broad verandah to keep out the rays of the sun. House rent is high, but is falling every year; and the rates and taxes are very small compared with those at home. The various building societies which are in existence enable persons of small means to become their own landlords on easy terms, whereby those who are obliged to live in towns soon escape from the necessity of paying rent. The state of society is of course varied. It depends upon the locality in which you are placed. But if your lot be cast in any of the great centres of population you will find really good society. It was formerly considered rather exclusive. This arose from the necessity of the case in the early days of the different colonies, but the cause for it is dying out.

But it is not only in the large towns that you are privileged to meet with thoroughly well educated men and women, but in the remotest parts of the various colonies. In travelling in the interior I have often come upon the settler's hut at night, and been received with that warmth of welcome which characterizes that class. And though the house was perhaps nothing but a slab hut, if only it were blessed with a mistress, you would see signs of refinement all about you. The master receiving his periodicals and his reviews by each mail, and first-rate standard books; and the evening often enlivened by music and by song. And hardly ever through all my travelling, and mixing as I have done with all kinds of people, have I been obliged to retire to my room for the night without the host and hostess and the members of the family joining with me in reading the word of God, before we bent the knee to Him who watcheth over us by night and by day. Nay, if the settler knew beforehand of my approach he would generally send round to the out-stations and to his neighbours, if he had any, so that I frequently found a large gathering to join in the evening sacrifice of prayer and praise. I have often joined in worship in the stately cathedrals of England, and much as I have enjoyed our services in those venerable piles and listened to the peal of the fine organ and the sweet voices of the choristers, I never yet have found anything so enjoyable as these little bush services, composed of people hastily drawn together from all quarters. The Christian minister has much to be thankful for in these colonies, for his message is ever gladly received and he is himself cordially welcomed. Of course he sometimes has to put up with somewhat strange quarters, but then he does not mind that. I remember on one occasion, after travelling all day, I came upon a remote station late at night. It happened to be on the last night of the year. I found that the settler was a Scotchman, and that there was a great gathering of his clan to dance the old year out and the new one in. I was glad to escape to my little crib or bunk. But tired as I was I could not sleep, for the music and the dancing and the singing and the shouting came to my room. During the darkness of the night I heard a scuffle at my door, and great confusion as

OPOSSUM.—*page 27.*

from men who perhaps had taken a little too much whiskey. But it shortly ceased. In the morning I was told that one Highlander in his cups had become so smitten with his fair partner that he proposed to her then and there, and determined on rousing up the parson to get him to marry them off the reel. All his friends joined with him; but the settler himself, mindful of the rites of hospitality, got some to stand by him, and his party proving to be the stronger they protected my room from being invaded. At another time I slept in a little cooking hut with a broad open chimney made of wood. And down this chimney came opossums, and got on to my bed and came smelling about me, causing me like a frightened child to hide my head beneath the clothes. And often, if inclined to study astronomy, I could do so without fatigue, as I could watch the stars quite well between the openings in the roof. Perhaps the funniest night's accommodation I ever had was in the colony of Victoria, many years ago. I was desirous of visiting a new village, at a distance of about 60 miles from the town in which I had been staying. There was no road, and only a track here and there. A clergyman, to whom I stated my difficulty, kindly agreed to drive me to it. We started, and travelled, as we thought, 60 miles with the same horses. Night came on and we saw no signs of the village. Ten at night came and we were still out. Quite dark. No food. Nay, we had not even a lucifer match with us, wherewith to strike a light. By-and-bye my friend said, "I am sure there is a shepherd's hut within a mile or two of this spot. Will you go and hunt for it, or will you stay and mind the horses?" The expedition appeared so Quixotic that I preferred staying by the horses. And off he went. I was thus left in the darkness of the night with two strange horses in the grim forest alone. What if he should lose himself and not return? What should I do? Should I raise a loud "coo-ee"? If I did some of the natives might come, and it might not be over safe to be found under such circumstances. After two hours—which seemed to me like two days—he came back, accompanied by a man with a lantern. He had discovered a shepherd's hut by a light placed in the window. We went to the hut, having previously tied our horses to gum-trees with their bridles. They thus, after a journey of 60 miles, picked up what little grass they could for themselves, and were ready to start fresh with us next morning. What would an English groom think of this? The shepherd's wife kindly gave us the invariable mutton-chop and damper, and some post and rail tea. And then we thought of bed. Yes, bed in the *singular number*. For there was but one in the whole hut, for the two clergymen, the shepherd and his wife, and their three children. However, they most politely gave us the bed, put the children across at the bottom, and slept underneath themselves. In the morning you can easily imagine that we got up *rather early*.

Then comes the question of domestic servants. This and the weather seem to form the two grand subjects of discourse in England. Therefore you cannot be surprised that it should be a trouble also abroad. But I really do not think we have more annoyance on this head there than here. Wages are much higher, of course. In days gone by there was a very different state of things. All our servants then were convicts. I have lived in the country and had eleven or twelve of them in the house. And capital servants they were. They were assigned to you by the Government. You fed and clothed them. They could not leave your premises after certain hours without a "pass" from you, or they were liable to be taken up by the constables. Going into Hobart Town to dinner, from Boa Vista, where I then resided, I requested a prisoner footman to come and walk home with me through the bush. During our dark and dreary walk I said, "John, why were you sent out?" And he then told me that he was a baker by trade, and that in a passion he had stabbed his master with a carving knife, and only just escaped the gallows. Not a very pleasant revelation to be made to one under the peculiar circumstances in which I was just then placed. But he was a very faithful fellow, and I parted from him with great regret. In fact you had these people so much under your control—so much of their little comforts depended upon you, and your report had so great an influence on the time at which they obtained their tickets-of-leave, that, unless they were radically bad, you got on very well with them. Now and then, however, you were left without servants. This happened just after our arrival in the colony. We had a baby in the house, and no "help" of any kind. I could nurse the baby, and that was pretty well all I *could* do. But what about dinner? My wife knew nothing about cooking. But there happened to be hanging up a fine-looking piece of beef. She came to me in great trouble, hoping but hardly expecting that I should be able to start some valuable suggestion. She said she had tasted a dish called "bubble and squeak," which appeared to be made of slices of beef mixed with cabbage, and she thought she could manage to cook that very well. To show my sympathy I put down the baby and went into the garden and cut some fine cabbages. And so I left it. After a time I was told that dinner was ready, and I went down to it and helped first my wife and then myself. But our knives and forks were soon put down, and we looked most comically at each other. The meat was *raw* and the cabbage *hard*. We had to dine off bread and butter. Now, we afterwards discovered that the meat should have been previously cooked and the cabbage boiled. My wife resolved from that day that if she ever had any daughters they should not be educated, as she herself had been, in utter ignorance of all culinary arts. And this pledge she fully redeemed, bringing up her children so that they were initiated at an early period in all such domestic duties.

As regards the ordinances of religion, they are now dispensed far and wide through all the colonies. The village must be very small and the neighbourhood very scattered which does not now enjoy the means of grace. All denominations of Christians have ministers. And I do really believe that these men will compare satisfactorily with their brethren in this highly-favoured land. How different is all this from what it was when I first went to Australia! Then, my ecclesiastical superior was the Archdeacon of Australia (Dr. Broughton), and my bishop was the Bishop of Calcutta—the well-known and much beloved Daniel Wilson. Just imagine one man having the spiritual oversight of the whole of the vast continent of Australia, Tasmania, and New Zealand, and acting under a bishop as far off as Calcutta. Dr. Broughton became the first Bishop of Australia, and afterwards Bishop of Sydney and Metropolitan. In order to obtain the help of suffragan bishops, he generously gave up a large portion of his own income. After a long life of labour the aged bishop went on a visit to England. He lost his life from his unremitting attention to some of the passengers who had yellow fever, and just as he closed his eyes in death it was evident that his thoughts were dwelling on the land he had left behind him—that land which he had loved so well—for he was heard to whisper these words, "The earth shall be full of the knowledge of the Lord, as the waters cover the sea."

And no one need be afraid respecting the education of his children. I knew the time when the want of it was sorely felt, when the best boarding-school in one of the colonies was kept by a prisoner; when even young ladies were taught by that class of persons. But that is completely a tale of days gone by. There are now excellent schools to be found in every town and village, available for the children of all denominations alike. The teachers hold their certificates from the respective governments; they are well paid, and the schools are inspected by the officials most regularly. In the large towns, there are besides first-rate colleges and grammar schools, presided over by men of mark from the English and Scotch universities; and the more advanced colonies of New South Wales and Victoria have universities, with their affiliated colleges, and a curriculum of study similar to that laid down by the home universities, and with the power of granting degrees in law, medicine, and arts.

I often hear the complaint made in England that it is a non-marrying age. The young men like their liberty. They do not marry. Those in the upper classes prefer the luxury of their clubs to the comforts of a home; and men in the middle ranks of life seem afraid of commencing housekeeping. A lady at the West-end of London told me lately, that the men were so fond of their club-life that you had to tempt them with the best of dinners and the choicest wines or they were deaf to your invitations. What is the cause of all this? Does it arise from the expensive style in which all classes are now living? Are the young women of the present day less domesticated in their habits, so that men shrink from incurring obligations which they may be unable to fulfil? It would seem to me that these causes have a great deal to do with the non-marrying propensities of the present day. And it is a subject of such grave importance as to be well worthy of careful consideration. When I was a youth myself, it was very common for a professional man to feel that he could prudently marry so soon as he had a very moderate income, some two or three hundred a year; and many of my compeers did so, and brought up their families respectably on such incomes. And if you went a step lower in the social scale, there were numberless marriages on incomes of £150 a year, or even less than that. But it is not so now. It seems to be considered necessary to have fine houses, handsome furniture, means of getting about for holiday trips, ability to entertain, and to dress expensively, or you must not entertain the idea of matrimony. I think this is all very wrong and greatly to be deplored. And I am sure that it is *felt* much by young people of both sexes. Some time ago I was travelling, and at a house where I was staying we were talking on the subject, and a lady of a certain age, the burden of whose song was "Nobody coming to marry me, nobody coming to woo," took an opportunity of asking, "If I thought there would be a probability of her getting settled in life if she went to Australia." And the same thought probably passes through the mind of many a woman as she sees her years creeping on, and finds the hair beginning to turn, and the prospect as far off apparently as ever of obtaining a home of her own. There can be no doubt at all that the number of marriages in the colonies, as compared with those in England, is greatly in favour of the former. People are on the whole better off there, and they are not so tied down by the rules of society as to feel themselves compelled to live at the same expensive rate. I am a great advocate for early marriages generally, and especially in the colonies. Many a young couple who may have been engaged for years in the mother country waiting for something to turn up which may give them a fair start in life, and thus encourage them to settle, might do so safely abroad, and find their prospects improved as well as their comforts vastly increased by the step.

But if these colonies are well adapted to all the classes of whom I have been speaking, they present peculiar advantages to the labouring population. I am living in Dorsetshire, and I see before my eyes every day the state in which the labourers here are obliged to live. The wages are from nine to ten shillings a week, and the man pays rent for his cottage and has to purchase fuel and keep his family entirely out of that sum. Mr. Bonwick, in his timely little publication on Emigration, says:—" A fortnight ago I had the folly to ask a Devonshire cottager the price of beef. She fairly laughed at me for thinking that she, that never tasted such a luxury, could tell its price. I wonder whether she has heard the tune of 'The Roast Beef of Old England.' Poor soul! *Old England* was the time of her father and grandfather. How she did stare when I spoke of farm labourers getting meat three times a day in Australia." As we proceed with our work, the labouring man will find under the head of each separate colony the wages which are to be obtained. Many of them in addition hold out inducements to emigrants in the shape of grants of land. Here the labourer as a rule remains a labourer for life, there he only continues in that position until he has gained colonial experience, and saved a little money, and after that he has every chance of becoming his own master, and very probably an employer of labour himself. But it is, remember, the country for hard work. "The hand of the diligent maketh rich." There are loads of idle, dissipated fellows—"loafers," as they are called—to be found there as everywhere, and these men are loud in their condemnation of the colony. But the fault is in themselves. The men to whom our colonies hold out inducements are the able-bodied and the willing workers. Persons devoid of energy and without physical powers are not adapted for roughing it in a new country. But, strange to say, you find the masses of the agricultural population anything but inclined to move from home. And this arises in a great measure from the want of energy produced by poor living. Go amongst the intelligent artisan class, or those engaged in mining pursuits who work hard and live well, and they readily lend an ear to any proposition which may be made to them of improving their position. The great drawback to success is very often *drink*. Men earn money more, readily, and unless they are strong-minded and set some great object before them, they are apt to give way to habits of intemperance. These habits are a curse anywhere, but if in a warm climate a man gives way to this soul and body destroying vice, there is little hope of him. The governments hold out all facilities to the labouring classes. There are savings' banks in every township, and in most places mechanics' institutes or rooms of some kind, where, when the short day's work is done, the workman may pass a portion of his time in wholesome relaxation.

For female servants of every class—if only they know their work—this is indeed just the country to go to. Such persons will, as in the case of men, find under the head of each colony the rates of wages which are given. When a cook or a laundress can get from £30 to £40 a year, a parlour-maid £30, and a general servant from £25 to £30 a year, such a country may well be regarded as the place to which good servants may resort. It is true that dress is rather more expensive, perhaps 20 per cent. dearer. But still this leaves a large margin in favour of Australia. The only thing of which the employers of labour have to find fault is, that they cannot keep their servants. Only get a nice girl who knows her work and is prudent, and she soon gets married. For a long time every servant in my own house only left our employ as, by marriage, she went to a house of her own. Why, here in England, girls " walk " with their young men, and never dream of anything but " walking," till they have worn out more pairs of shoes than would have bought a farm in Australia. But the servants must not only know their work but be of truly respectable character, or there is no hope of their getting into good families. A continuous supply of such women would be a great boon to all the colonies. It would not be easy to glut the market, for the servant of to-day is the mistress of to-morrow.

When I talk to such people about going out, they say they dread the voyage. " It is so long. It is so dangerous." It used to be long and it was formerly more dangerous. But now it is neither the one nor the other. Nautical men tell us that it is the safest voyage that can be made. After the first few days—and *all* people do not even suffer for that short period—it is a most enjoyable life, and if you were to see immigrants after a three months' voyage, you would agree with me in thinking that it certainly had done them no harm. The Victoria Government at this moment are contemplating the establishment of a line of large steamers which shall sail monthly round the Cape of Good Hope, carrying 500 passengers at each trip, on reasonable terms. If this be done it will be a great boon to all classes of emigrants. Do not think 500 too many. I came home in the noble steamer the *Great Britain*, and there were nearly 900 of us on board. Everything was managed most admirably: the living like that in a large hotel, a German band played upon the deck, and music and singing and dancing and private theatricals seemed to enable the passengers to pass the time right merrily. But the labourer and the female servant may say to me, "Suppose all this to be true, and that we should like to go, but how are we to get out? We have not the money wherewith to pay our passages." *Free* passages are granted to single female servants of good character, from eighteen to thirty-five years of age. And on your arrival at your destination you are not cast adrift but received for a time into a "Home," which is carefully supertended, until you have the opportunity of obtaining employment.

A new company has just been formed under most flattering auspices, which promises to be of material service. We subjoin its prospectus for the information of the intending emigrant:—

"EMIGRANT and COLONIST'S AID CORPORATION (Limited). Incorporated under the Companies Acts, 1862–1867. Capital £250,000, in shares of £1 each, with power to increase. 10s. to be paid on application and 10s. on allotment. The shares will thus be fully paid up, with no further liability.

TRUSTEES.

His Grace the Duke of Manchester.
The Viscount Bury, M.P., President Royal Colonial Society.
R. R. Torrens, Esq., M.P.
R. N. Fowler, Esq., M.P.

DIRECTORS.

His Grace the Duke of MANCHESTER, Chairman, 1, Great Stanhope-street, W., Kimbolton Castle, St. Neot's, and Tandragee Castle, Ireland.
The Rev. Henry Alexander, B.A., The Vicarage, Shelford, Notts, Chaplain, R.N.
H. G. Ashurst, Esq. (of H. A. Smith and Co., Merchants), 9, Fenchurch-street, E.C., Chairman English Assurance Company.
J. Bergtheil, Esq., 48, Clifton-gardens, Maida-hill, W., late Member of the Legislative Council, Natal.
Sir George Bowyer, Bart., D.C.L., Radley-park, Abingdon, Bucks, and 14, King's Bench-walk, E.C.
S. J. Cooke, Esq., 47A, Moorgate-street, E.C., late Commissioner of Crown Lands, Victoria.
C. W. Ligar, Esq., F.R.G.S., Westminster Palace Hotel, S.W., Managing Director, late Surveyor-General of Victoria.
Captain Bedford Pim, R.N., 11, Belsize-square, N.W., Chairman Central American Association.

(With power to add to their number.)

BANKERS.—Messrs. Dimsdale, Fowler, and Bernard, 50, Cornhill.
SOLICITORS.—Messrs. Kimber & Ellis, 79, Lombard-street, E.C.
SECRETARY.—Colonel Francis C. Maude, R.A., V.C., C.B., F.R.C.S., F.S.A., F.R.G.S., Member of Council, National Emigration Aid Society.
OFFICES.—5, Queen-square, St. James's-park, S.W., and 47A, Moorgate-street, E.C.

"ABRIDGED PROSPECTUS.

" This Corporation has been formed for the purpose of securing the success of the emigrant and colonist, without making him an object of charity, paying a fair return for the capital employed on his behalf, and at the same time carrying out the designs of the benevolent and philanthropic.

" It is proposed to effect these objects in the following manner :—

" By obtaining concessions of land, by purchase or otherwise, on terms which will enable the Corporation to subdivide it, and make grants of intermediate portions thereof to settlers, either gratuitously or on easy terms ;

" By providing passages for approved persons and their families, and advancing money for that purpose ;

" By procuring for the settlers a suitable reception in the colony they may select; forwarding them from the port to their homesteads ; advising them as to the best mode of procedure; giving them such aid towards social organisation as shall be best calculated to secure to them a successful career in their new home ; and assisting them in money and kind towards erecting their dwellings and cultivating their land ;

" By assisting emigrant colonists of vocations other than agricultural to obtain employment suited to their respective capacities ;

" By making arrangements between colonial employers and mechanics and labourers for their mutual advantage.

" In apportioning the land, it is proposed to adopt a plan of temporarily reserving, as nearly as possible, intermediate allotments between the locations of the different settlers, which in course of time must become valuable, from the mere fact of the adjoining land being settled; opportunities will thus be afforded to the prosperous settler of extending his borders, and to the Corporation of realising profit.

"A strong inducement will thus be presented to capitalists to settle on the unoccupied land of the Corporation, since families with capital desiring to settle thereon can calculate on agricultural assistance in its immediate vicinity among the emigrants sent out by the means of the Corporation itself.

"The Corporation proposes to repay its shareholders in the following manner :—

"By the repayment by the settler, with interest, of moneys advanced to him on security of his allotment ;

"By the allotment to the shareholders of parcels of land to be specifically reserved for them as after mentioned ; and

"By the sale, at advanced prices, of reserved lots, townships, villages, and business sites, rendered valuable by the settlement of adjoining lots.

"As soon as a sufficient number of shares have been taken to enable the Directors to send out a first batch of emigrants, arrangements will be made to do so without waiting for the subscription of the whole capital ; shareholders will then have the right, in a certain order, of nominating a family or individual emigrants, duly approved, to be sent out by the Corporation.

"The Directors will receive the shares of the subscribers at par, in whole or part payment of passage-money and advances, according to circumstances—thus relieving the settler of a like amount of indebtedness to the Corporation.

"The Corporation proposes to ensure the life of every head of a family emigrating, for the amount of advances made to him. The premium on the policy to be included in such advances. By these means the widows and children of settlers will have their heritage free from the debt created by the head of the family. The Corporation, on the other hand, will recover its advances without injuring those whom it desires to protect.

"The Directors propose, when acquiring grants of land, to set aside a certain number of acres to the shareholders, to be allotted and conveyed at so much land for every share held. By these means the shareholders will have real estate as security for their capital, with the prospect of a considerable and continually increasing value being put upon it. To prevent such land, however, becoming waste by non-occupation, the Corporation reserves to itself the right to manage such allotted lands, if unoccupied, and to let them, or to call upon the shareholders to sell them at certain minimum rents or prices, which will be announced on each allotment.

"The Corporation will also undertake to contract with Colonial or other Governments for the management of emigration, or with private persons wishing to send out emigrants.

"The Corporation has received several offers of land in eligible situations and at moderate prices, which are under consideration.

"The Directors have also been informed by competent authority that it may be fairly assumed that the respective colonial Governments will afford liberal assistance to the Corporation; and they believe that certainly one, and probably others of them, will undertake the collection, and guarantee the repayment of the advances made by the Corporation to emigrants settling in their colonies.

"The Directors will endeavour to select land in such localities as will offer the greatest advantages in point of soil, climate, facility of access from the coast, &c., and the probability of an early re-sale at advanced prices.

"The Corporation will accept loans, on security of its land or otherwise, on terms to be agreed upon, from any persons desirous of forming a memorial town or village on its lands, or for any other of its objects. Money will also be accepted on deposit from settlers themselves, or clubs, which will be allowed to bear interest, and be appropriated as the depositors may think fit, for promoting the emigration of relatives or friends, &c.

"Full prospectuses and any further information may be

obtained on application to the Secretary, at the Offices of the Corporation, or from its Solicitors."

And a few married couples may be helped out, but this will do but little towards relieving that immense body of people in England, who, destitute of work, are craving for food. It is an *exodus* which is required to be of material benefit to this country and of essential service to the colonies. There, their waste lands are waiting for the hand of man; and here, every occupation is overcrowded. The state of our pauper population is the most important question of the day. Some writers are proposing emigration on a large scale, to be carried on at the expense of the government or of the board of guardians; that on arrival at their destination they should have work guaranteed to them for at least twelve months on new railroads or some such public works; that thus the colonies would be opened up and an increased value given to the waste lands at least equal to the expenditure incurred. This matter of *expense* is just the question. It is hard to say how it is to be overcome. We heartily trust that some scheme may be devised by all the parties who are interested, whereby this country may be relieved of its surplus and the colonies correspondingly benefited. I own that I am not at all sanguine of Imperial help in the matter. The Ministry of the present day seems disposed to ignore all colonial claims. Nay, there appears to be a desire to throw off the colonies altogether. On this subject a very able paper was lately read before the Society of Arts by Mr. John Robinson, F.R.G.S., an excellent analysis of which is to be found in that admirable paper the *Australasian*, from which we give the following extract:—

"Mr. Robinson, in a bold yet careful generalisation, discusses the commercial, social, and political condition of the colonial empire, and in an able argument, supported by full and carefully compiled statistical tables, shows *how ill England could afford to lose any portion of a state so magnificent and powerful.* Forty years ago the Australasian group had practically no existence. New South Wales in 1836 was a penal settlement, and New South Wales was Australia. In 1850, the import trade was two millions, and the export trade two millions and a third. In 1866 its imports were nearly nine millions, and its exports eight and a half. The imports of Victoria—startled into life by the gold discoveries—had advanced during the same period from £744,000 to more than £14,000,000. The exports of the whole Australian colonies in 1850 amounted to £4,648,178. In 1866, they had advanced nearly 700 per cent., being more than £31,000,000. The export of gold in 1866 amounted to £11,708,397, of which Victoria contributed more than half. The wool shipments advanced from five to nine millions sterling; and coal, coke, flour, grain, hides, horses, cattle, copper, gum and timber, have been shipped from her many ports. In sixteen years, the trade of the group had increased from £9,027,894 to £67,164,616, and of this £30,500,000 was done with the United Kingdom; and the population of the seven dependencies, which in 1861 was 1,266,432, is now 1,662,063, while a public debt of £24,000,000 has been incurred on account of railways, public works, and immigration. Such has been the rapid rise of the Australian empire. In twenty years a city has arisen out of the wilderness, and a people possessing a marine, a press, and distinct nationality, has grown up almost in a night.

"It is with this 'nation' as it now exists that English legislators have to deal; and in treading on this delicate ground, Mr. Robinson shows as much modesty as courage. Pointing out the claims of the colonies to self-government, and crediting the colonists with every wish for the maintenance of colonial governors in a style befitting their position, the lecturer strongly animadverts upon the Imperial selfishness which too often saddles a young colony with the burden of self-defence. To permit the privilege of self-government and enforce the penalty of self-protection is a one-sided system of policy, the effects of which have been lately made manifest. A young colony is like a young man, and at the best it is scarcely fair for the wealthier, older, and wiser nation, to impose upon feeble shoulders the whole burden of a responsibility so heavy and galling. On one point Mr. Robinson speaks with an earnestness which we can appreciate—the necessity for naval defence. While a part of the British Empire, a colony can claim such assistance as a right. As an independent state, obscurity, distance, and insignificance would at once combine to shield it from aggression; but as a vulnerable part of a great empire it offers a tempting inducement to attack. Yet, if the claims of her colonies upon England are heavy, the gain is worth the cost. The colonial empire, more especially that portion of it which is termed Australasia, is the Jason arisen out of the cauldron. England, with her multitude of struggling workers, her thousands of suffering poor, seeks for an outlet for her superfluous population, and finds it in a new land, where there is room for countless homes and work for unnumbered hands. There is no exile, no banishment. The same tongue is spoken, the same laws protect, the same God is worshipped; and the time will surely come when England will find herself no effete nation sinking into her second childhood, but the wise, revered, protecting, and protected centre of a vast system of states, whose interests, language, laws, and religion shall be one.

"'Here,' says Mr. Robinson, 'in this old and thickly-crowded land, it may be that men find it hard to stem the torrent of competition, or to rise to higher levels of social life or public usefulness. But there, in those fifty dependencies, openings abound for every kind of effort and every grade of ambition. There, the farmer can acquire by slight outlay and by indisputable title breadths of soil that in Europe would almost make a principality. There, the honest working man can live on his own freehold, and work his way on by rapid steps to a condition of honourable independence. There, the earnest youth who looks to public life as the proper field of patriotic aims, can find the object of his aspirations within ready reach. There, the distinctions may be less dazzling, the sphere of public recognition may be obscurer and less prominent, but the chances of attaining them are incomparably more abundant, and the influence exerted, when viewed in its bearing on the future that is now being shaped and foreshadowed, is, if anything, more direct and more enduring.'"

It is very encouraging to see the subject of the "colonies" taken up, as it has been of late, so ably by the *Times*. Several letters, showing great acquaintance with the subject, have just appeared. One of them, "H. D. W.," closes with the following remarks:—

"We are not, in the continental sense, a military nation. Our horror of a conscription prevents it. We are not invariably successful in dealing with subject races. We find in the fields of industry and commerce formidable competitors. But there are two points in which we are signally predominant—our navy and our colonies. In these we have never failed.

"In all human institutions there is a crisis; but wise nations, like brave men, overcome it. They do not abandon a great future for a transient obstacle. If there are defects in our colonial system we will remedy them. If we have overlooked opportunities we will utilize them. To abandon the colonies would be as suicidal as to suppress our navy rather than substitute iron for wooden ships.

"Everything points to the continuance of colonial prosperity, and knits us closer to our colonies. Telegraphs bring daily tidings to our homes; the Suez Canal opens a nearer track for our commerce and emigrants. A visit to the colonies has become the complement of a polished education. Colonists are holding the highest posts in our Government and foremost places in our legislature, our literature, and science.

"Is this the moment to sacrifice a great career for a utilitarian chimera? Are we to enrich others by the wealth we reject, and to subside into a second-rate European State, or to continue at the head of a confederation of free nations?"

An "Australian Colonist" closes a pamphlet on the subject thus:—

"I cannot see what the English legislators are about to waste so much breath and money about things not affecting the masses of the country, and quite ignore matters, like emigration, essential to the vitality of the nation. The English Government should at least help the colonist to pay the passage, as both ends get an advantage. Despots might wish to keep men as 'food for powder;' but a Christian community must, and will soon, help the poor to better quarters."

We know not from what source the help may come, but that some well-devised scheme of emigration may speedily be set on foot is greatly to be desired.

Having thus glanced at the different classes to whom emigration would be of advantage, let me beg you to accompany me on my own voyage to

Australia, as it took place in the year 1835. I was but a stripling, just fresh from St. John's College, Cambridge, when the offer of an important post in the colony of Tasmania was made to me, which I saw fit to accept. My ship was selected, my outfit economically prepared, my cabin fitted up, and all things secured. The day for sailing, in the month of August, came at last. I shall never forget the feelings with which I saw the shores of dear old England vanish from my sight. The man who takes a short trip to the continent, or even to the American colonies, cannot realise the feelings of one who, especially in those days, was going to the other side of the globe, to a land whence in all human probability he would never return. Whatever may have been his feelings in the days that are past, however unkind circumstances may have been to him, and however bright the future may appear; however in the days gone by he may, like an Englishman, have grumbled and found fault, yet when he catches the last view of his native land, he cannot but feel, if he does not say, "England, with all thy faults I love thee still, my country!" In the days I refer to, nearly thirty-five years ago, a voyage to Australia was no joke. From five to six months were required for it. The only really good vessels that went out were the convict ships. There was no P. and O. Company in existence then, making a kind of pleasure trip of it, and landing you in less than fifty days; there was no Panama route dreamt of then. There was no calling for passengers at Plymouth, no joining your ship at Marseilles. No, no! Gravesend was the place. A sad name, and sad were the associations connected with it. Having gone on board late at night, I was told that we should sail with the tide about two in the morning. I awoke then and heard the water splashing against the side of the ship, and feeling quite well I began to think that going to sea was very pleasant. About eight o'clock the steward came into my cabin, and in my simplicity I ventured on some remark to that effect. What was my surprise and disappointment to find that we were still lying quietly at anchor, and my fancied immunity from the ills the voyager is heir to was premature. During the day the good old ship did weigh anchor, and all was favourable until we arrived in the Bay of Biscay— that sad meeting of the waters, where so many a good ship, like the ill-fated *London*, has foundered, and her passengers have met with a watery grave. This bay I have seen as smooth as a pond. But on my first visit to it a storm arose, a fearful jumble of a sea—that thing which sailors so greatly dread— quickly got up; all that we could do was to "lay to," all progress was out of the question, for wind and wave were alike against us, and thus

"We lay, till the next day,
In the Bay of Biscay, O!"

And it was unmitigated misery to almost everything

on board. Old sailors felt qualmish, none could keep their feet, all mirth was hushed, even in the forecastle. As for the passengers, let me draw a veil over their misery. It can be *felt*, but it cannot be described.

"Ye gentlemen of England, who live at home at ease,
O little do ye know of the troubles of the seas."

The next day rose bright and clear. The sea went down. We soon began to get on deck, forgetting the misery of the past in the pleasure of the present. We bowled along, just catching sight of the cloud-capped peak of Teneriffe; then met with nothing till we crossed the Line, and had all the exciting scene of Neptune coming on board and claiming toll from the passengers. In good time we rounded the Cape of Good Hope and saw such seas as I think are seen in no other part of the world's oceans. They tell us that the height of a wave seldom if ever exceeds forty feet. But that is quite enough. Imagine, not only being unceremoniously lifted up forty feet on the crest of a wave, but then—and it is far worse—going down head foremost into the trough of the sea. And this agreeable process repeated continually. One good thing is, that the sea and the winds are generally in your favour there. The huge waves come tearing after your ship, and a landsman would think it impossible to escape being swallowed up. Sometimes, as with us, the wind dropped, but the sea kept chasing us still. And then in the dead of the night grim-looking monsters, dressed up in peajackets and sou'-westers, with lanterns in hand, like so many Guy Fawkes, came unceremoniously into our stern cabin to put in the "dead lights," lest the sea should strike the windows and fill the cabin if not endanger the whole ship.

"Sail O!" Ay, what excitement that was. The monotony of your life broken, the constant inspection of sea and sky interrupted by a homeward bound ship heaving in sight. The pleasure of speaking, sending letters on board to loved ones at home, was quite an event.

To the southward of the Cape, but before you near it, and right in the track of vessels outward bound to Australia, lies the island of Tristan d'Acunha, with which quite a romantic story is associated. The island was so named after the Portuguese navigator who discovered it in 1506. It is about five miles square, and rises perpendicularly about 3,000 feet out of the sea. The highest mountain is said to be more than 8,000 feet above the sea level. It is very remote from any settlement, more so in fact than any other place. St. Helena, which is the nearest place to it, is about 1,200 miles from it. It was formally taken possession of by the English in 1817, and a guard was kept there during the earlier part of Napoleon's captivity at St. Helena. But it was soon abandoned. A corporal named Glass obtained leave to remain behind with two other men. And by degrees a little colony was formed, and the inhabitants were a most interesting people. When we sighted it in 1835, the weather was clear, the sea smooth, and the captain in a good humour. And it was agreed that we should endeavour to get supplies of pigs, poultry, eggs, vegetables, and milk. Governor Glass came off to us in a fine whale boat, and took some of us on shore. The first thing we saw as we landed through the heavy surf was sea-lions basking on the shore. The cottages at the base of the hill were neat, and the people exceedingly simple and urbane. Whaling ships sometimes call off there for supplies and for purposes of traffic, but there had been none there for a long time. And so the island ladies had not a single pin or needle or bit of thread left. The school-master, who acted as chaplain, showed me his only book of sermons, actually in tatters from constant perusal. All these wants we were able to supply. But whilst we were admiring everything around us, behold we cast our eyes towards our ship, and we saw her drifting in to the iron-bound shore. The wind under the influence of the mountain had dropped, and the current was setting us on to the rocks where so many a brave ship had been wrecked before. The captain hurried us on board, sent out a boat ahead to tow us off, but apparently in vain, so that shipwreck stared us in the face. But man's extremity is God's opportunity, and presently, just as we could almost have thrown a biscuit on the shore, a slight cat's-paw was seen on the waters, the upper sails filled, and we were saved. And here I may just mention a curious coincidence that happened with reference to this island. Eleven or twelve years after I had been settled in the colony, a gentleman's yacht came to Sydney on a cruise from England, a beautiful yacht, which had only to be seen to be admired. Its owner, Mr. B. Boyd, was kind and hospitable, and invited a large party of gentlemen on board to dine. I was one invited, and sat on my host's left hand. After dinner, he was requested to give us an account of his outward voyage, which he did in a most agreeable manner. In the midst of his remarks he said, "By-the-bye I must not forget to tell you of one of the most pleasant days I ever spent in my life. It was on the little island of Tristan d'Acunha. The day I arrived there, old Governor Glass's wife was confined of a daughter, and he was of course highly delighted. I asked him if he would yield his power to me for one day, and let me be governor instead of him. To this he assented. I proclaimed a holiday for every one, and got all kinds of good things from the vessel and invited all the islanders to dinner. And a right glorious dinner we had. After dinner I made a speech; and in drinking the health of the 'baby,' I said, 'Who amongst you has got any good sheep for sale?' I bought some fine ewes, and handed them over to trustees to watch over them and their increase, giving them power to sell and invest, and to hand the entire proceeds over to the young lady when she came of age; so that, if the trustees be faithful, she will have a nice dowry to bring to the man of her choice, if God should spare her. In the evening we had service, and after it the schoolmaster chaplain showed me his books and tracts—all well thumbed, and some of them tattered and torn—and he said, 'It is now twelve years since we had a new book, and then these were given to us by a young gentleman who was on his way to Australia.'" I was enabled to corroborate the truth of this, for by a somewhat strange coincidence I, sitting at the speaker's side, was the young gentleman referred to. Now that I think of it, that young lady must be now about twenty-one years of age. And in these days of sordid calculation this may be a hint to some young man desirous of getting settled if he could see his way clearly. Just look at the advantage of the whole thing. There would be "love in a cottage," near a wood, or perhaps *in* a wood; no rent, no taxes, and no Christmas bills, for there are no shops.

Poor Benjamin Boyd! In his love of adventure he travelled from place to place, visiting many a remote savage island of the sea, and on one of them, as he and his crew were on shore getting a supply of water, he was cruelly fallen upon and tomahawked. And thus his bones are bleaching on a far off shore.

His Royal Highness the Duke of Edinburgh visited the island of Tristan d'Acunha in the *Galatea*, and was exceedingly kind to the people. The old governor had gone to his rest. A handsome white marble headstone bears the following inscription:—

"WILLIAM GLASS,
Born at Kelso, Scotland,
The founder of this settlement at
Tristan d'Acunha,
In which he resided 37 years,
And fell asleep in Jesus
Nov. 24, 1853. Aged 67 years."

" Asleep in Jesus: far from thee
Thy kindred and their graves may be;
But thine is still a blessed sleep,
From which none ever wake to weep."

The chaplain of the steamer, and author of "The Cruise of the *Galatea*," went on shore and baptized sixteen children. And he would gladly have performed other duties if the parties had only been willing. "The remarkable coincidence of there being seven unmarried girls in the place—one of them remarkably pretty—and just seven equally eligible bachelors, naturally suggested to the chaplain the propriety of offering them an opportunity of pairing off then and there in the orthodox way. He therefore expressed his willingness to remain among them two hours to perform the ceremony, if any should be so inclined. But the maidens were coy and the swains were slow, and no advantage was taken of the offer. Possibly the much vexed question of Married Life *v.* Celibacy, which among us appears just now to incline to the disparagement of the former state, had got imported into the place with the crinolines and elastic boots, and the youth in this far away spot espoused the views of our West-end club houses, giving in their adhesion to the order of the Benedicts. At any rate, the chaplain's offer found no favour, and Hymen no votaries."

But to return to our voyage. By-and-bye we were becalmed. The sea was as glass, and near us there was another island—Amsterdam. We had heard that the sea close in shore was literally alive with fish, and that if we stepped ashore there was a boiling spring, like those in Iceland, where we could cook them. Off we went, only too glad to escape from our prison walls, and indeed I never saw such fishing in my life. We were all intent on throwing over our lines with nothing but a bit of red rag on them, and the fish almost jumped out of the water to be caught. It was the most exciting sport of the kind I ever saw. One after another we pulled the huge fellows in, till presently the captain called out, "Stop, look at the boat!" And then we found that we had filled it so full that we were just level with the water, and we had to throw overboard part of our prizes. Back to the ship, where the next day the rigging was covered with fish hung up to dry, and the ship's company had fish to their heart's content till we reached Australia. And at last, thank God, the man on the look-out aloft cried, "Land on the larboard bow, sir!" And sure enough there lay the land of our adoption looking like some fantastic cloud. It was the southern coast of Van Diemen's Land—now called Tasmania—which we had sighted. By-and-bye we entered d'Entrecasteaux Channel, where we were delighted to see, here and there, a cottage with a trim little garden, and the smoke curling up amongst the trees of the forest. Presently an officer came to the captain and reported, "A boat coming off, sir." "Back the main-yard! Throw a rope over the gangway!" A boat came alongside, and a little old man jumped aboard, took no notice of the captain, gave his orders to the man at the helm, and acted as if he were in full command. Our captain did not like this, and he went up to him in no very pleasant mood, but the little man pushed him aside, and went on giving his orders. In about five minutes he took the captain to the side of the ship and showed him a reef of sunken rocks, not laid down in the charts of those days, right on to which he had seen that we were running. Being an old pilot, "who had coiled up his ropes and anchored on shore," he had observed our ignorance of the danger, and had been the means under God of saving us from a watery grave. And so our voyage ended. We had grown so fond of the old ship that we went down and dined on board two or three times a week, and when she sailed it seemed like parting from an old friend; besides which, it was the connecting link between us and our fatherland.

And what is the effect of a long voyage on the mind? That depends on how the time is spent. To very many it is a sad ordeal. All kinds of idle and expensive habits are formed which are not easily got rid of; but to the well disciplined mind there is something profitable in a long voyage. There is but a step—there is but a plank—between you and death. You realize the presence of God, and the frail hold you have on life more I think on board ship than anywhere else. And many an one has found that it has been good for him, in a spiritual point of view, to have voyaged on the mighty deep. I would earnestly recommend every emigrant to set himself to some definite work for his voyage, and to avoid especially the habit of drinking, which is so very common, and for which there are far too great facilities furnished by the ability to purchase spirits at a low rate. And it behoves the voyager to be very careful what friendships he forms—perhaps his after-life will be greatly influenced thereby—and it is not easy to shake off intimacies formed under such circumstances. When we landed we bid farewell to many of our fellow passengers, and we have never met since. About one of them, however, I must just say a word. One day on board I observed a venerable white-haired old man sitting quite apart from the rest. I got into conversation with him. He told me his story. He was nearly seventy years of age. His wife was nearly his own age. They had one only son who was very dear to them; he had been an apprentice in London, and had gone astray through the influence of bad companions. He had been sent out to the convict settlement. The poor parents were distracted. They knew not what to do. They could get no rest. They felt that they could not go down to their graves in peace and leave their boy to perish. And so, in the hope of saving him from the evil influences by which he was surrounded, and leading him, if it pleased God, to Him who is "the sinner's Friend," these old people agreed to part. There were no free passages in those days, and they could not muster money enough to pay for both; and so the old man tore himself away from the wife of his youth and the stay of his declining years, and undertook the long voyage to Australia. On landing in the colony, I found that the lad had been re-convicted and was working in chains on the roads, and thus the poor father's hope of getting him assigned to him was out of the question. He was provided with a home, a solitary room over our coach-house, in which he delighted, and there he lived for years. Time rolled on, and at length, by the exercise of a little interest, the son's ticket-of-leave was obtained, and the old man went into the bush to live with him.

I then lost sight of him for more than twenty years. For old people in going to the colonies frequently take as it were a new lease of life, and enjoy "a green old age." Shortly before I sailed for England, when making an archidiaconal tour to the gold-fields near Ararat, the clergyman of the district told me of a venerable patriarch, nearly a hundred years of age, who was held in the deepest reverence by all around him and who was most anxious to see me. On enquiry I found that it was my old friend. His son had married, and was a respectable member of society, and the father's wishes had I trust been gratified. Shortly after this "he fell asleep in Jesus," full of years, full of blessings, full of faith in God, as a God who *hears* and a God who *answers* prayer.

And now, after this general introductory chapter, we must proceed to describe one after another each of the colonies which form the Australasian group. And to whichever of them you may give the preference, resolve to go to it in a right spirit, and turn neither to the right hand nor to the left, and depend upon it success will eventually crown your efforts. Do not be over anxious about making money. "A man's life consisteth not in the abundance of the things which he possesseth." Of course I do not mean that you should not endeavour to better your condition, for that probably is the very object for which you leave your native country. But there is so much of speculation, so many are not content to reach the top of the ladder step by step, but want to spring up all at once. They *may* succeed: the probability is that in the long run they will fail. Whereas by steadily feeling your way and going on gradually, you will, with God's blessing on your honest endeavours, reap a rich reward.

Chapter II.

AUSTRALIAN DISCOVERY.—NEW SOUTH WALES.

FOR a long time before anything was known of the Australian continent, it was the settled opinion of astronomers and geographers that there must be some great continent in the southern hemisphere as a balance to Asia and Europe. The coast-line from the north-west round by the east to the south shore was known to the Portuguese in 1542. In 1606 Luis Vaez de Torres sailed through the strait between New Guinea and Australia, and it was afterwards called "*Torres Straits.*" In 1642 Tasman anchored in Frederick Henry's Bay, to the south of the island of Tasmania, and landed there. He hoisted Prince Frederick Henry's flag, and named the land in honour of his master, Anthony Van Diemen. He also went to the north of the great continent and explored the Gulf of Carpentaria, so called by him in honour of Carpenter, the president of the Dutch East India Company. In consequence of these discoveries the Dutch assumed to themselves a national property in this vast continent and gave it the general name of "New Holland."

CONFLUENCE OF THE NEPEAN AND WERA GAMBIA.—*page* 62.

The first of our countrymen who saw any part of Australia were Dampier and Cook (not the renowned navigator). They cruised along the west coast, landed at several places, careened and watered their ships, and then started again on their privateering expedition. Ten years after this Dampier published a very exaggerated account of his discoveries. In the year 1768, Cook, the great circumnavigator, set out on his first voyage of discovery round the world, chiefly with a view of determining the existence of a great southern continent. After having discovered parts of New Zealand, he steered westwards towards the "terra incognita Australis," that land the shape of which had been for nearly two hundred years baffling the skill of the scientific world. He passed Cape Howe, and named it after his admiral—Howe. He anchored, and saw many natives on the shore, who went on quietly with their occupations, taking no notice of the movements of those on board the "big canoe." But as soon as they attempted to land they were in arms, and brandishing their clubs and spears rushed upon them. A musket was discharged in self-defence, which wounded one of them, whereupon they all took to flight. At the spot where Cook first landed, the Philosophical Society of Sydney have placed a plate of copper with a suitable inscription. It bears the date of April 28, 1770. And as a century will soon have elapsed since that period, steps are now being taken in Sydney to erect a statue to commemorate the circumstance of his first setting his foot upon the shores of Australia. When Cook went on shore, Banks and Solander accompanied him. They found the land covered with beautiful flowers, hence Cook named it "Botany Bay," a name which in after years struck terror into the hearts of very many. The soil in the neighbourhood is very sandy and barren, and up to this day it remains almost in a state of nature. It is about six miles from Sydney, through a track of sand. But a fashionable hotel, tea and zoological gardens have been established there, and the place is frequented as a retreat for newly married people to spend their honeymoon in. Cook stayed a week in Botany Bay, and left it on a Sunday morning with a fair wind, and keeping within two or three miles of the land. Whilst the captain was at breakfast, the look-out at the mast-head—a man named Jackson—reported that he saw the entrance to what appeared to be a good anchorage, and so the captain, half in derision, named it "Port Jackson;" that beautiful bay at the head of which the city of Sydney was afterwards built. On went the good ship towards the north until they entered the tropical sea near Moreton Bay (which now forms part of the great colony of Queensland). Here it was that Cook first fell in with the wild turkey, and he named the place "Bustard Bay." Here they also found plenty of turtle and saw kangaroos. They gladly ate its flesh but found it somewhat insipid. They had not then learned how

KANGAROO.—*page 64.*

to dress it as a "steamer," nor did they know that the tail makes capital soup. They also found fish in abundance. The finest kinds are the guard-fish of the mainland, and the trumpeter of the Derwent, in Tasmania. They also found some enormous cockles, some of them, they say, having 20 lbs. of meat in them. The insects, the plants, the animals, were all of the deepest interest to the naturalists who accompanied the expedition. When Cook, after many narrow escapes from coral reefs, reached Cape York, at the entrance of the Gulf of Carpentaria, he hoisted English colours and took possession of the whole eastern coast by the name of New South Wales, in right of his Majesty King George III. And thus England, with the tacit consent of Europe, became possessed of this magnificent country, comprising nearly one-half of the vast island continent.

At first it was thought that Van Diemen's Land formed part of the mainland; but Bass, in 1798, discovered a passage through, thus proving it to be an island. From an examination of the south coast of New Holland, and the north shore of Tasmania, it is quite evident that originally they were united. Bass' Strait is studded with large and picturesque islands. These were formerly inhabited by runaway convicts and their sable partners, but they have now been let on lease by the government as sheep and cattle stations.

From the very earliest days of the settlement of

Sydney in Port Jackson, instructions were constantly sent out to its governors to fit out expeditions for exploring the adjacent bays and rivers, and surveying ships were dispatched from time to time to ascertain the latitude and longitude of every cape and headland. And the sons of the soil have been noted for their indomitable perseverance in making discoveries inland. From the Windmill Hill in Sydney a fine view was obtained of the country in the distance. To the westward a glimpse could be got of some high mountains, which from their colour they called the Blue Mountains. For a lengthened period these were only looked at, and speculations were rife as to what there was beyond them. A strong desire grew up to find out. In 1812, Mr. Oxley was appointed Surveyor-General, and Mr. Evans Deputy-Surveyor of Lands; and they found on enquiry that two enterprising colonists, Wentworth and Blaxland, had penetrated into the interior and found there well-grassed plains beyond the barrier of the Blue Mountains. Further exploration brought to light a beautiful country. Convict labour formed a capital road, and the spot was subsequently visited by Governor Macquarie, who fixed the site of what is now the flourishing city of Bathurst, near to which, nearly forty years afterwards, the great gold discovery took place. Bathurst is a large and prosperous place, 120 miles from Sydney, and is situated about 2,000 feet above the level of the sea. The grandson of the venerable Marsden, so well

VIEW OF THE ENTRY TO PORT JACKSON.—*page 66.*

known at Parramatta, and who was styled the "Apostle of New Zealand," has just been appointed as its first bishop, and if he only make as good a bishop as he has proved himself an able parish priest, he will prove a great blessing to his diocese.

In the year 1817 Evans traced the Macquarie and Lachlan rivers till they lost themselves in the marshes of the interior. The great want of Australia is navigable rivers. The greatest of them, however, the Murray, and which is now of the utmost value to the settlers of the interior, enabling them to get up their stores and to send down their wool by steamers, runs a course of nearly 1,500 miles.

Next to Evans and Oxley as explorers come Hovell and Hume, two settlers, who followed the Murrumbidgee and Yass rivers to their junction with the Murray, and thence to the western shores of Port Phillip—now called Victoria. Then came poor Allan Cunningham, who discovered a fine grazing country, but died in the bush. He was followed by Captain Sturt, the "Father of Australian exploration," as he is called, from his having penetrated furthest inland towards the centre of the continent. Then came Sir Thomas Mitchell, whose well-known book details at length his discoveries. And then a Polish nobleman, Strzlecki, penetrated the dense forests of the Australian alps, and gave the name of Mount Kosciusko to the highest peak—6,500 feet—in memory of his country's national patriot. And then we find poor Ludwig Leichhardt, whom I had the great pleasure of knowing well, and who, being an enthusiast in the study of botany, resolved on undertaking the fearful task of crossing the continent from the east to the west coast. Starting in 1844, they explored tropical Australia for 1,500 miles, to Port Essington. They were so long absent that they were mourned as lost. A second time, in the year 1848, they started, and have never returned. Even to this day great interest is felt as to their fate, and once more it is proposed to send out another expedition to discover some traces of them. Kennedy, a government surveyor, failed in his endeavour to explore the eastern flank of the Australian cordillera within the tropics. The poor leader was speared by a black and died. He had with him a friendly native guide who describes the sad scene in touching terms, thus : "He said, Jackey, give me paper and I will write. I gave him paper and pencil and he tried to write, and he then fell back and died; and I caught him as he fell back and held him, and I then turned round myself and cried. I was crying a good while until I got well; that was about an hour, and then I buried him. I digged up the ground with a tomahawk and covered him over with logs, grass, and my shirt and trousers. That night I left him near dark."

The attention of the Royal Geographical Society was, after this, directed to the desirability of ascertaining the true nature of central Australia. Mr.

Gregory was in England at this time (1854), and as he had had some experience in exploration he was entrusted with the command of an expedition, whose object was to try and reach the centre from the north-west coast. He ascended the Victoria river of Stokes, and after penetrating 300 miles into the interior found that it was a desert.

In 1858, the Victorian government offered a reward of £1,000 to the first party who should cross the central region from south to north, or *vice versâ*. And in the meantime, John McDouall Stuart, a South Australian colonist, penetrated 500 miles north-west from the head of Spencer's Gulf, and discovered some available country. In 1860, he crossed the centre of the country, and reached 18° 40′, but was driven back by the blacks. A mountain in the centre of the land bears his name. Again he went forth and manfully fought his way till he reached the shores of Van Diemen's Gulf, which is washed by the waters of the Arafura Sea, a distance of 1,500 miles in a straight line.

But Stuart was not the first to make this journey from sea to sea. Twelve months before he arrived at Van Diemen's Gulf, Burke and Wills had achieved the work. They started from Melbourne, and crossed the central region some 300 miles east of Stuart's track, and reached the Gulf of Carpentaria. But Burke and Wills both died within a short distance of the settled districts. Their bodies were brought to Melbourne, and a public funeral was decreed to their remains. A handsome monument has been erected to their memory in a prominent part of Collins Street.

In 1862, Landsborough followed up the Flinders River and traced its source in the mountains of Queensland, and discovered the source of the Thomson River. And McKinlay started from the Leichhardt River and traversed an immense tract of unknown country in the centre of the continent. Now, then, we know that the land is about 2,500 miles from east to west, about 1,900 from north to south, and contains nearly three millions of square miles.

Before New South Wales was taken up as a place of banishment for convicts, offenders against the laws were sent to Virginia, in America. When the American colonies gained their independence, in 1783, Cook's account of the salubrity of the climate of Australia determined the government on sending their prisoners to it.

Their doing so was opposed by a well known writer of the day, who said, "If you form a colony in New Holland it will soon throw off the yoke of England and become dangerous to it, for it will be nothing but a nest of pirates." Not very complimentary this to the Australians, who through good report and evil too have ever been noted for their loyalty to the British crown, and who are anything rather than piratically inclined.

It was in 1787 that the first fleet was dispatched.

At first they went to Botany Bay, but subsequently removed to Port Jackson. The voyage out took eight months. On the 26th of January the people were landed, the British flag was hoisted, and the first steps taken towards forming a settlement on the shore—a day still regularly kept as a holiday by all classes of the people. Compare the wild forest of that day, with a silent stream of water running through it into the bay, with the present noble city of Sydney, and it seems to have been the work of magic.

The first governor of the infant settlement was Captain Phillip; the chaplain, an officer who was almost forgotten in the arrangement of the expedition, was Mr. Johnson; the whole population, 1,030. The entire stock consisted of one bull, four cows, one horse, three mares, and three colts. Now, this single colony, reduced so vastly as it has been of late years in its area, contains 14,000,000 of sheep, 1,728,427 horned cattle, 280,201 horses, and 173,168 pigs.

The prisoners soon began to be troublesome. In the very earliest days there were rumours of the discovery of gold. The convicts broke up quartz yielding gold and paved the streets of Bathurst with it. Each governor from the very first knew that it was an auriferous country, but the fact was carefully concealed, for had it been known when the whole population or nearly so were prisoners, nothing but anarchy and confusion could have arisen.

The troubles of the early settlers were great indeed. Famine frequently stared them in the face. They were reduced to the greatest straits. So short were they of bread on one occasion that when the officers were invited to dine at Government House each guest was requested to bring his own bread; and so one waggish lieutenant stuck his piece on his sword, and marched with it thus to the governor's quarters, greatly to the amusement no doubt of the soldier who presented arms to him as he passed.

The convicts soon tried to escape into the bush. One man—an Irishman of course—said he wanted to get away to China, a distance of 5,000 miles, but he went travelling round and round in a circle—as you are very apt to do in the bush—and never got more than fifteen miles from Sydney.

The next governor was Grose. Phillip, on his return to England, represented to the government the advisability of inducing free settlers to go to the infant colony. But it was very difficult to persuade people, although tempting offers in the shape of land and convict labour were held out to them. Some of the officers on duty, when their time of service was expired, accepted the government offers and remained; and among them the father of Australian sheep farmers, John Macarthur.

The prisoners were dressed in yellow—hence called " Canary Birds "—and, chained together, were marched to their work on the roads, which they performed under a guard of soldiers with loaded muskets. They formed the fine roads which exist in the colony, and particularly the one between Sydney and Parramatta; and much as we may decry the system, they by their labour did the work of a century in a very few years. In fact to convict labour and to the discovery of gold Australia owes its present commanding position. With roads came of course traffic; commerce, industrial pursuits, and manufactures flourished.

Hunter succeeded Grose as governor, and to him the colony was indebted for its first printing press. It was introduced in the year 1795. The first newspaper was published in the time of Governor King, in 1803. Funny things those early newspapers were. Even later than that a good deal, we have seen copies of newspapers in Tasmania printed on the blue paper in which grocers wrap up their tea; and in the early days of Port Phillip, John Pascoe Fawkner brought his out in manuscript.

Then came Captain Bligh as governor. In those days, 1806, the governors had almost absolute power. Bligh cruelly persecuted Captain Macarthur. This exasperated the military, who went to Government House, under the command of Colonel Johnson, where the governor was found hid under a feather bed, whence he was taken and marched down to his ship. Bligh, you will remember, commanded the *Bounty* when the crew mutinied and escaped to Pitcairn Island.

In 1810, Governor Macquarie came to the colony;

F

an excellent governor, and a great friend to the prisoners. Hitherto the expenses of New South Wales had been enormous. In 1823 it was found that between five and six millions of money had been spent in the colony for Imperial purposes; but from that time it became gradually self-supporting. The country was rapidly becoming rich. In 1815 the export of wool was 30,000 lbs.; in 1867 it exported 21,708,902 lbs. As soon as the fineness of the wool and the adaptability of the country for sheep was discovered then commenced the era of free immigration. Numberless younger sons of good families, having a younger son's slender portion, which was as nothing at home, went out and turned their capital to great advantage as "squatters" on the government lands. The new comers were the pioneers of the wilderness, pushing out farther and farther into the unknown regions. And it was soon discovered that the land was not only fit for sheep and cattle and horses but for grain, and in fact almost all the products of the world can be grown in some part or other of Australia. Tasmania, the southern parts of Victoria, and New Zealand, agree with everything English, and the northern parts of Victoria, New South Wales, Queensland, and South Australia, with almost everything tropical. Very early orange groves were planted at Parramatta, near Sydney, and we read of a single grove producing an annual income of £1,000. Wine was soon made by Macarthur, under the management of some Greek convicts who were assigned to him. The Australian wines are improving every year, and there can be no doubt that they will become great wine countries. This colony alone has now 1,483 acres of vineyard, which produced last year 993,863 gallons of wine and 13,582 gallons of brandy.

The two next governors were Sir T. Brisbane and General Darling. Then, in 1831, came Sir R. Bourke, a very popular governor, who was liberal in his views, an encourager of religion, of education, and of manufactures. And he was succeeded by Sir George Gipps, who commenced his term of office in 1838 and continued until 1846. During his governorship the upset price of land was raised to £1 an acre. There was extravagant speculation everywhere; this was followed by general embarrassment. A calamitous drought extended over three years. Wool fell greatly in price, and was reduced both in quality and quantity. Boiling down sheep for their tallow commenced. Transportation was discontinued, the corporation of Sydney was formed, and the " old legislative council" sat for the last time in 1843. On the 1st of August, 1843, the first representative assembly took place, and many important acts were speedily passed. Sir George Gipps had a most trying time of it. Political parties ran very high and caused him no little anxiety. This was to be fully expected under the new system of government which was introduced. His enemies complained that there was a want of courtesy in his manners, but those who knew him well did not think so. But, however many persons differed from him, all were agreed as to "the talent, unremitting labour and integrity of purpose with which his Excellency discharged the arduous duties devolving upon him." In June, 1846, Sir George Gipps, broken in health and spirits, left for England, and died very shortly after his arrival.

Sir Charles Fitzroy, the brother-in-law of the Duke of Richmond, was the ninth governor of New South Wales. During his term of rule the discovery of gold took place, and in the midst of all the turmoil that arose therefrom it was very fortunate for the governor that the colonial secretary, Mr. E. Deas Thomson, was at hand, whose great ability and long experience were of the utmost benefit to the colony. Lady Mary Fitzroy met with an accident in the colony which caused her death. The most important circumstance which occurred during his administration was the foundation of the Sydney University. Up to this time the Sydney and Australian Colleges, the College of Lyndhurst, the King's School at Parramatta, and a few private grammar schools, were the only places where the upper classes could provide anything like a suitable education for their sons. As the colony advanced in wealth something more was felt to be necessary. Here and there a young man was sent to Oxford or to Cambridge, but the risk was very great, and the outlay enormous. The government granted a valuable building site of 130 acres, ample assistance was offered by the legislature, and thus arose the Sydney University, "an association of students without respect of religious creeds." The Church of England and the Roman Catholics erected colleges in connection therewith. Degrees in arts, law, and medicine are conferred; and, by royal charter, the same rank, style and precedence were granted to its graduates as are enjoyed by those of the English Universities. It is endowed with £5,000 a year. The first provost was Mr. E. Hamilton, a Cambridge wrangler of high standing. He was succeeded by Sir Charles Nicholson, who has been a most liberal patron of the University. Dr. Woolley, the professor of classics, was lost in the ill-fated *London* steamer on his return to the colony. The building is a magnificent edifice, comprising all that is necessary for the conduct of the institution. Eighteen scholarships of £50 a year have been provided for out of the University funds.

Sir W. Denison, vacating his post of lieutenant-governor of Tasmania, became the tenth governor of New South Wales. He was a man of great administrative talent, and a most healthy tone was given to society by himself and by Lady Denison. Responsible government having been conceded to the colony for so short a time, there was a constant change of Ministry. Like a set of nine-pins, they were no sooner in their places than they fell. It is said that Sir William was so continually bowing one set of ministers in and another out that he did it like an automaton. Mr. afterwards Sir Stuart Donaldson was the first minister under responsible government. The colony is governed now, 1870, by the Earl of Belmore.

It was in the year 1851 that the discovery of gold took place, which has of course altered everything in the colony—caused a nation to be born in a day—and has exercised, and is still exercising a great influence on the markets of the world. Hargreaves, who had just returned from California to Bathurst, discovered gold. The place was named the "Valley of Ophir." Great excitement at once prevailed, especially when a poor black fellow, knowing nothing of its value, found a mass of quartz containing 106 lbs. of gold. From that moment madness seized the whole community; shepherds left their flocks untended; the crops were left unreaped upon the ground; merchants and shopkeepers closed their stores; clerks and civil officers threw up their paltry £500 or £600 or even £1,000 a year, and off they went. Before the year closed nearly 150,000 oz. of gold had been exported. The squatters were in dismay, little thinking of the great advance which would take place in the value of their stock from the influx of new comers to the El Dorado. The regular trade of the colony was for a time paralysed. When a ship arrived in harbour the crew would all desert; and so, in self-defence, the captains, in some cases, agreed to head their crews, and take them for a trip to the diggings. Judge Therry in his interesting work on the colony gives some amusing instances of the state of things in Sydney at this time. House rent, he says, rose 100 per cent.; hay rose from £5 to £20 a ton; a cabbage cost 2s. 6d.; and a man and his wife, as servants, asked £3 3s. a week as wages. Sydney was like a deserted village. Streets of empty houses were sold for a few hundreds of pounds, which in a year's time were re-sold for as many thousands. The Judge gives some marvellous instances of individual success. A retired soldier had saved, during fourteen years' service, £100; he bought with it 100 acres of land, and within two years of the discovery of gold sold it for £120,000. A "lollipop" maker, whose fortune did not exceed £10, kept a public house on the diggings at which he made £6,000 a year, and went home with £20,000, leaving freehold property behind him producing £1,500 a year.

There is a branch of the Royal Mint in Sydney. The yield of the precious metal during the last three years shows a considerable falling off. There were 222,715 oz. sent to the Mint and 12,328 oz. exported. The average wages of the miners last year was £67 4s. 5d. a man.

But New South Wales possesses that which is of greater importance to her than gold. I mean her inexhaustible coal mines at Newcastle, to the northward of Sydney and elsewhere. Last year she exported 473,357 tons, of the value of £253,259. They are able now to ship nearly 4,000 tons a day. Newcastle, the capital of the district, is now an episcopal city, and it is a free port, ranking as the second in the colony. Hence up the Hunter, to Morpeth and Maitland, is a very fine agricultural country, and it is mainly taken up by farmers and settlers.

The Registrar-General of New South Wales has lately issued his statistical reports, of which we largely avail ourselves as the most reliable source of information. The population is 466,739; there had been 3,426 marriages, 18,317 births, and 8,631 deaths. Only 2,179 persons had arrived from Great Britain. In the two lunatic asylums there were 1,061 persons. There are 62 charitable establishments. In the hospitals 4,421 received medical treatment, and 5,825 received outdoor relief. Provision was made in the benevolent asylums for 3,277 inmates. There are 650 churches and chapels, and the average number of persons attending the services is 135,263. The number of ministers of religion was 438. Sunday schools are attended by 39,512 children, being a considerable increase over the past year. There are 651 day schools assisted by the government, and 529 private schools, making a total of 1,180. The orphan and industrial schools are also very largely assisted from government funds. The public schools are now under a "council of education." The legislature provided last year £86,766 13s. 8d. towards their support, and the voluntary subscriptions were £30,719 6s. 8d. The criminal statistics show a decided improvement. In 1860 the ratio per thousand of the population was as 1 in 483; in 1867 it was 1 in 372. Trade and commerce show a great falling off. The returns have not been so low since 1861. The imports are now £6,599,804, and the exports £6,880,715. But still the value of the imports was at the rate of £15 0s. 8d., and the exports £15 13s. 6d. per head of the population. A corresponding decrease has taken place in the shipping, there being 231 less ships than in the preceding year. There are now 155 steam mills, and a total of 188 mills in the colony for grinding and dressing grain. Of late years a great demand has sprung up for colonial tweeds, owing to their great durability. In the last year 175,348 yards of woollens were manufactured. Soap and candles are also largely produced. Both these items show a large increase; there are now 30 establishments in operation. Tobacco manufacture is making slow progress. In 1867, 6,933 cwt. were manufactured. There are 40 boiling-down establishments, and last year 54,862 sheep and 3,842 cattle were slaughtered at these places. The estimated value of all minerals raised at the various mines in 1867 may be thus summed up: gold, £909,812; coal, £342,655; copper, £35,316; and kerosene shale, £17,957; making a total of

£1,305,740. The total number of the occupiers of land on the 31st March, 1868, (excluding those for pastoral purposes) is 25,875, who hold 7,737,651 acres. The increase under this head is very large. The wheat crops average 9 bushels 36 lbs. to the acre; maize, 32 bushels 26 lbs.; barley and oats were below the average. Attention is being drawn to new crops. Thus last year 76 acres were laid out in cotton, which produced 13,680 lbs.; sugar is receiving some attention; and, on the Paterson, 7 acres of rice were put in and produced 1,000 lbs. to the acre. Potatoes were the crop in 15,440 acres, and hay in 74,346. There are nine banks, having liabilities amounting to £6,906,466, and their assets to £10,574,571, showing an excess of assets over liabilities to the amount of £3,668,105. In the savings' banks there are deposits amounting to upwards of £700,000; and in the penny banks nearly £6,000. In 1867, at the Royal Mint, 2,370,000 sovereigns and 62,000 half-sovereigns were coined. Since the opening of the Mint, in 1855, 6,214,391 oz. of gold have been coined, and gold coinage issued to the amount of £24,349,427.

The receipts on account of public revenue in 1867 were £2,012,041, and the payments £2,225,075. The public debt of the country is about seven millions sterling. The total receipts from the railways were about £190,000, and the *net* earnings nearly £72,000. There are 477 post-offices in the country, and nearly 7,000,000 letters were posted in the year. In the twelve months £810,000 were expended in public works; 684 persons became insolvent, whose liabilities united came to £737,789. At the close of 1867 there were 1,537 volunteers on the roll. If the reader has only taken the trouble to go carefully through the long array of figures above, it will show him how great must be the resources of this colony, although the past year has shown a reduction in many of the items—reductions which we trust and believe are only of a temporary character.

The form of government in the colony is known as "responsible." There are two chambers—the members of the Lower House being elected on a residentiary suffrage of six months, and the members of the Upper House are nominated for life. The tendency of the legislation is democratic. The highest offices of the state are within the reach of everybody. The newspapers are the great vehicles for political instruction to the masses of the people. Sydney has two daily papers—the *Morning Herald* and the *Empire*. The former has a circulation of about 12,000. Great ability is displayed in them, and they are remarkable productions for so young a country.

Of the religious bodies, the two largest are the Church of England, numbering 160,000, and the Roman Catholics 100,000. The Presbyterians stand next, at 35,000; and the Wesleyans at 24,000.

Until lately the only training theological college in connection with the Church of England was what is known as "Moore College," which has done and continues to do a great work for New South Wales, and also for Victoria, in the training of young men for holy orders. But now most of the denominations have ceased to depend entirely on England for their clergy, and have established local institutions for this purpose.

Sydney gives you the impression of being a much older town than it is. There are some very fine buildings in it. The Government House is in every respect worthy of the colony. It is a handsome castellated building, from whose massive tower floats bravely the "meteor flag of England," when the governor is in residence. The house is 170 feet long and $40\tfrac{1}{2}$ feet high, and has some noble rooms. The grand staircase is a noble specimen of Australian workmanship, and is built of cedar. The chimney pieces are all of colonial marble. A fine statue by Bailey of Sir R. Bourke stands in the domain. It was uncovered by the then governor in 1842, who declared that the view presented from the spot where he stood equalled in loveliness any scene in the known world. In truth it is a most lovely spot. This leads you to the Botanical Gardens—a very extensive and beautiful promenade overlooking the glorious bay. The fashionable suburb of Sydney is called Woolloomooloo, and is the residence of

VIEW OF SIDNEY COVE, PORT JACKSON.—*page* 84.

many of the colonial aristocracy. Hyde Park is one of the few fine open spaces, which contribute much to the health of the city, and enable the people to get fresh air and the bracing sea-breeze within a few minutes' walk of the busiest parts of the town. Most of the banks have now handsome buildings. There are also three theatres, a school of arts, three clubs, and a very fine museum. A "free library" has just been opened. The churches as a whole are not fine specimens of architecture. We must however make an exception in favour of St. Andrew's Cathedral—I am sorry to say the *only* Church of England cathedral worthy of the name in the southern hemisphere. This was commenced in 1836, and has only been lately opened. It is 155 feet long, 60 feet wide, and 70 feet high. The organ is a very fine one, by Hill and Son, and cost £1,500. Joshua Watson, a great friend of Bishop Broughton's, presented the eastern window. The font is of New Zealand stone, and is considered very handsome. All the principal windows are of stained glass. A recumbent figure of the first bishop in Caen stone, by Lough, is a wonderful likeness of that remarkable man. No less a sum than £30,000 have already been expended on this building. It is said that the completion of the towers will cost £5,000 more; and that bells and clock will require about £1,200 in addition.

The Roman Catholics had their cathedral in

Hyde Park, but it was destroyed by fire. With the energy which characterises that body they are erecting a new one, which it is said will far surpass the former one.

There are two dry docks, two patent slips, and one floating dock. The high rate of wages keeps back the shipbuilding trade. The government have however of late been manufacturing on the spot goods' trucks for the railways and the bodies of passengers' carriages.

When detailing the statistics of the country, we stated that the public debt of the colony was about seven millions. This debt has been mainly incurred in the construction of the railways, the whole of which belong to the government. There are three trunk railways, of two of which Sydney is the maritime terminus. You go from Sydney to Parramatta junction on a common line, then you branch off to the west, climbing the Blue Mountains till you get to an elevation of between 2,000 and 3,000 feet. This is an unpromising country for the most part; but afterwards the rich west opens to your view. Bathurst will be the terminus of this line, while the southern line reaches to Goulbourn, 150 miles from Sydney, and the seat of a bishop's see. The northern railway has its maritime terminus at Newcastle, and proceeding westward to Singleton it crosses the river and turns northward to Murrumundi. The return obtained as yet has been far from satisfactory, not more than two per cent. on the capital;

SUMMIT OF THE CASCADE BOUGAINVILLE, BLUE MOUNTAINS.—*page 86.*

but when once completed and in full working order, a much better result is confidently anticipated.

But it is time that we refer to what is the "vexed" question in New South Wales, as well as in all the colonies—the *land*. In the early days there were free grants of land. The upset price was afterwards five shillings an acre; that was raised to twelve shillings, and subsequently to a pound. With such an extensive territory as that which New South Wales possesses, there were those who thought that it would have been wiser not to have raised it to a pound. There is a good deal of land of very inferior quality, only fit for pasturage, and it was considered that it would have been wiser to have attached to the soil a proportion of that shifting population who might have been settled permanently down if they could have obtained the fee simple at a remunerative rate. Before the year 1861, all the land which had been previously surveyed was sold by auction. But by "the Crown Land Act" of that year sale by auction and previous survey were both dispensed with. A man can now go and make his free selection before survey of any quantity of land, not less than 40 nor more than 320 acres, at twenty shillings an acre. But the intending settler cannot at once obtain the freehold by paying the purchase money. He makes a deposit of five shillings an acre, resides on his land for three years and makes specified improvements. He can then pay the balance and get his title, or, should he prefer it, he can leave the unpaid balance as a kind of mortgage at five per cent. This plan is generally pursued. There is a kind of vague hope that ultimately the government will forego the payment of the balances. When the conditional purchaser, as he is called, selects his 320 acres, he has a grazing right over an area of three times the land selected. After all, the grand point is to get an increased population identified with the country and permanently settled therein, and whichever colony can put forth the most liberal land bill, soil and climate being equal, will draw to it the largest population of immigrants. Of course when this bill was first introduced the large body of squatters were violently opposed to it, and have since suffered much from it. They could not view with a favourable eye a class of men who went prowling about, looking anywhere and everywhere for a bit of good land, and disturbing the cattle and sheep upon the runs; and frequently this was the greatest grievance and did serious injury to the settler. And since the passing of the Act, the settlers complain that the conditional purchasers have in a great number of cases evaded the law as to residence and improvement. The squatter's homestead is secured to him as a pre-emptive right to the extent of 640 acres, at the price of twenty shillings an acre. A great impetus has been given to the occupation of land under the new Act, and it is said that there is very little available land

anywhere in the colony which is not now under lease. The country east of the Darling River is all mapped out in runs, and to the north-west of that country, as far as Cooper's Creek, at which place the explorers Burke and Wills died, has been taken up. This inland salt-bush country suits the settler's purpose well. Although the squatters may not make the large fortunes they once did, yet I think they will be protected from the sudden fluctuations in the value of their stock, to which they were formerly subjected. The system of curing meat for the English and continental markets appears to be a great success. If the smallness of the local population presents no demand for the meat, an opening to any extent is to be found in the English markets, which will prove of great benefit to the Australian settler and a boon to the English labourer. The meats which have been sent to our markets from Mr. Mort's establishment, and from some other places, are exceedingly good. The other day a clergyman procured three tins of Australian mutton, and with the addition of vegetables and rice or barley, made an excellent dinner for 120 people. The cost of the meat was 3s. 6d. a tin; a meat dinner for rather more than a penny. A short time ago a cask of sheep's tongues was sent to me from a relative in Victoria; there were 900 of them, and they are as sweet as though they had been cured last week in my own kitchen. The essence of beef prepared at Mr. Mort's establishment is so good, that it is of the greatest service in the sick room, where you want a nourishing beef-tea made without any trouble and at a trifling cost. So good is it, and so much better than any kinds that I know of, that I went a long journey the other day in order to secure some. As long as this demand lasts—and as far as I can see there is no limit to it—there is no fear for the squatter. I remember however the day when his position was a sad one. I was dining once in Sydney with a very rich man. The night's post brought my host a letter which seemed to disconcert him. He told me that he had a mortgage on a run, and that his debtor had written to say that he was quite unable to pay the amount due, and that he had better take the run over. On calculating, it turned out that the sheep would cost tenpence a head and the run be obtained for nothing. And this *disconcerted* my friend who was anything but pleased at having this run thus forced on him.

When the last mail left the colony a bill was before the Legislature on behalf of assisted immigration, and if it be carried and be a judicious measure, we believe that it will add materially to the population. It contemplates the emigration of mechanics of every description, agriculturists, labourers, and female domestic servants. The terms are very liberal, and will we do not doubt be highly appreciated, if the bill becomes law in its present shape, as it is expected that it will. We give a copy of the bill below for the benefit of the general reader:—

"ASSISTED IMMIGRATION.

"The following is a copy of the bill introduced into the Legislative Assembly, and read a first time on the motion of the Hon. the Colonial Treasurer (Mr. Samuel), to authorise and regulate Assisted Immigration:—

"*Preamble.*

"Whereas it is expedient to promote and assist immigration to this colony by the issue upon condition of certain payments being made of Immigration Land Receipts available in the purchase of Crown lands in manner hereinafter provided Be it therefore enacted by the Queen's Most Excellent Majesty by and with the advice and consent of the Legislative Council and Legislative Assembly of New South Wales in Parliament assembled and by the authority of the same as follows:—

"*General provision as to immigrants nominated in colony and others not so nominated.*

"1. Upon certain payments being made as hereinafter provided by persons already resident in the colony passage certificates shall be given for the introduction of immigrants to be nominated by them as hereinafter mentioned and Immigration Land Receipts available as hereinafter provided in that behalf shall be given to the resident persons so nominating immigrants for introduction And upon condition of certain other payments as hereinafter mentioned passage certificates and land orders or scrip certificates as hereinafter in that behalf mentioned shall be given to or for persons not so resident who shall be desirous of emigrating to this colony from ports in the United Kingdom Provided always that such immigrants and persons emigrating shall be of a suitable class and description as hereinafter required.

"*Residents in colony may nominate immigrants on certain payments.*

"2. Persons already resident in the colony who may be desirous of introducing other persons as immigrants shall be entitled upon payment of eight pounds for each adult and four pounds for each child under twelve years of age to nominate any number of such persons being suitable and thereupon to receive passage certificates for their introduction at the cost of the Government of the colony and also to receive Immigration Land Receipts for the amounts which they shall have so paid Provided that the persons to be introduced shall be named or sufficiently designated and that such particulars shall be furnished concerning them as shall be required by the regulations to be made under this Act.

"*Passage certificates to be given and Immigration Land Receipts. Certificates to be used within twelve months.*"

"3. The persons so nominated shall be provided with passages by her Majesty's Emigration Commissioners in London or such officer as shall be appointed by the Governor in Council for that purpose unless they shall be found by such Commissioners or officer to be ineligible under the provisions of this Act in which case the passage certificates will be cancelled but nevertheless the Immigration Land Receipts for the amount paid as aforesaid will remain in full force Such passage certificates must in all cases be presented to such Commissioners or officer as aforesaid within twelve months of the date thereof and the proposed immigrants named therein must within that period also present themselves for emigration otherwise the certificate will lapse unless such Commissioners or officer shall in any case think fit to enlarge the time for any period not exceeding three months.

"*Such Immigration Land Receipts how available.*"

"4. The Immigration Land Receipts to be given to residents in the colony upon such nomination and payments as aforesaid shall be transferable by the holders thereof and shall be available for the amount therein mentioned (together with interest thereon at the rate of one shilling in the pound for every complete year from the date thereof) in payment for Crown Lands in the manner following that is to say—During the first three years from the date thereof in payment for Lands purchased under the thirteenth section of the Crown Lands Alienation Act of 1861 and thereafter during a further period of twelve years and no more in payment by the holders thereof for any lands purchased by them from the Crown under any of the provisions of the same Act or of any other law then in force for regulating the sale of Crown lands.

"*Persons not nominated by residents may receive passage and Immigration Land Receipts upon certain payments.*

"5. Persons in the United Kingdom being of a suitable character and description as hereinafter provided who may desire to emigrate therefrom to the colony or who may desire to assist others in so emigrating shall upon payment to her Majesty's Emigration Commissioners or such officer aforesaid of the sum of fifteen pounds for each adult and ten pounds ten shillings for each child under twelve years of age be entitled to receive passage certificates for their passage to this colony and also certificates from the same Commissioners or officer on the payments made by them as aforesaid And the persons emigrating in virtue of such payments shall if duly approved of on arrival become entitled to Immigration Land Receipts available in the purchase of Crown Lands as hereinafter next mentioned.

"*Immigration Land Receipts to such immigrants as last mentioned. How available.*

"6. On the arrival in this colony of immigrants under the last preceding clause and upon their being approved and passed as eligible under this Act by the Immigration Board of Sydney the immigrants holding the certificates of payment mentioned in that clause shall be entitled to receive in substitution therefor Immigration Land Receipts bearing the date of such arrival and available in the purchase of Crown Lands in the colony in manner and subject to the conditions herein mentioned that is to say—During the first three years after the date of such Immigration Land Receipts as herein mentioned they shall be available for the amount therein mentioned (with interest at the rate of one shilling in the pound for each complete year) in payment for land selected under the thirteenth section of the Crown Lands Alienation Act by the persons originally receiving the same or by members of their families who shall have immigated with them and thereafter during a further period of twelve years and therefore such Immigration Land Receipts shall be available on payment of the amount therein mentioned without interest by the holders thereof for lands purchased by them of the Crown under any of the provisions of the said Act or of any other law then in force for regulating the sale of Crown lands And after such period of three years the Immigration Land Receipts shall be transferable by the original holders thereof then being resident in the colony or by their representatives if they shall have died in the colony.

"*All persons eligible as immigrants. Immigrants under s. 6 to be subject to approval on arrival.*

"7. The persons eligible for immigration under this Act will be mechanics of every description agriculturists domestic servants and all persons of the labouring class being of sound bodily and mental health and ability and fitness for industrial employment and of a moral character And in the case of persons arriving as immigrants under clause six of this Act they shall be subject to approval by the Immigration Board at Sydney and no Immigration Land Receipts as aforesaid shall be given in respect of the payment made for any person who shall be found ineligible under this Act.

"*Immigrants how forwarded. Ten days for hiring after arrival in port.*

"8. Immigrants introduced under this Act shall be forwarded to the colony in ships chartered by and subject to regulation by her Majesty's Emigration Commissioners in London or such officer who shall have been appointed as aforesaid or otherwise in such ships and subject to such arrangements as the said Commissioners or officer may make on behalf of such immigrants Provided that in all cases such immigrants (unless they be single females and be removed as hereinafter mentioned) shall be entitled to be maintained on board of the ships in which they shall arrive and to be accessible and have access from and to the shore so as to give full opportunity for engagement in service for ten days after their arrival at the port of destination but after the expiration of that time they will be discharged and will be required to provide for themselves.

"*Single females to be at Depôt under due protection.*

"9. All single females not being members of families immigrating with them and desirous of continuing with them shall so soon as conveniently may be after arrival at the port of destination be conveyed to the Female Immigration Depôt to be provided at the public expense to be there properly cared for and maintained until they shall be removed by their relations or persons who shall have nominated them or shall have engaged in service with the approval of such persons as shall be appointed by the Board in that behalf And no engagement shall be made by any such single female immigrant unless such persons as last mentioned shall be satisfied of the respectability and suitableness of the intending hirer and shall sanction such engagement Provided nevertheless that the right of any such female to such protection and maintenance shall cease and determine so soon as employment approved by any such person or persons so appointed shall be offered to her.

"*Lunatics, Criminals, &c., may be returned to port of embarkation.*

"10. If any person shall arrive in the colony as an immigrant under this Act who shall be a lunatic or idiot an habitual pauper drunkard or prostitute or who shall have been convicted of any serious crime it shall be competent to the Governor in Council to direct that such person be returned to the port at which he shall have been shipped and thereupon he may be returned accordingly at the public cost and shall be detained in safe custody until a convenient opportunity shall be found for his removal.

"*Power to make Regulations.*

"11. It shall be lawful for the Governor in Council to make such regulations as may be necessary for carrying this Act into effect in respect of all matters to be done in this colony and in the United Kingdom and elsewhere in furtherance of the objects hereof and for enforcing cleanliness order and good conduct on board of the ships chartered for immigration under this Act and all such regulations shall so far as they shall not be inconsistent with this Act have the same force and effect as if enacted therein.

" *Commencement and Short Title of Act.*

" 12. This Act shall take effect on the first day of January now next and shall be styled ' The Immigration Act of New South Wales passed in 1869.' "

The progress of the colony has been very marked up to the present time, and there is ground for believing that its onward progress will even be accelerated. What would Collins think if he could stand in the streets of Sydney and see to what it has grown? Besides the steam communication by the P. and O. boats, *viâ* Melbourne, the government are entertaining a new route, *viâ* Torres Straits, so as to have a fortnightly mail. And ere long the electric telegraph will be in direct communication with Europe.

Although the area of New South Wales is so vast, and the room for selection so great, not five millions of land have as yet been sold; whilst the Crown tenants hold on lease about 120,000,000 of acres.

It only needs an increase of population and capital to develop the mineral resources of the country. Iron, copper, lead and tin are scattered all over the land. Arts and manufactures in like manner are but in their infancy. But still enough is being done to give a happy omen of the future.

There was a great clamour made for powers of self-government, and concession was made to the full extent of what was demanded, but strange to say the mass of the people do not exercise the franchise. At the last election 44,000 persons only voted out of a roll of 120,000, that is not much more than one person in three exercised a privilege which we should have thought would have been highly prized. Life and property are quite safe in all the towns. The remote parts have been disturbed by bushrangers, it being extremely difficult to protect a country of such an enormous area.

Great excitement prevailed lately in the neighbourhood of Mudgee at the supposed finding of an enormous diamond, which would have made the far-famed Koh-i-noor hide its diminished head. But it proved to be a mistake—perhaps worse. There is however no doubt that diamonds are being found, and they will be discovered now in far greater numbers, as special attention is being paid to the subject by the formation of "Diamond Companies."

There is no State Church in the colonies; all are on a perfect equality. In 1862 an Act was passed by the Legislature whereby government aid is for the future to be discontinued, protecting however the interests of all the present incumbents. There are about 400 registered clergymen of all denominations. The Bishop of Sydney and Metropolitan is the Right Rev. Dr. Barker, who is provided with an income of £2,000 a year, and who is much beloved. The amount of good which he has done since his appointment is very great indeed. Mrs. Barker is also a great helper, and she takes a special and lively interest in the " Clergy Daughters' School," which is a great boon to the clergy having large families, and who are so often situated at such remote places as to be quite unable to procure suitable education for their children in their own localities, and whose incomes are such as to shut them out from the advantages of the best class of boarding schools. There are now five bishoprics in the colony, viz: Sydney, Newcastle, Goulbourn, Grafton and Armidale, and Bathurst. Each diocese is governed by a synod, the powers of which in 1866 were agreed upon, and an Act of the Legislature made any of its rules and ordinances binding for all purposes of Church property on its members. The synod meets annually, each incumbent is summoned to attend, and each district according to its size sends two or three lay representatives, who sign a declaration that they are members of the Church *in full communion*. The bishop presides; he has no vote, but each ordinance must have his assent, and as the members can insist on voting by orders, it follows that each act must have the assent of bishop, clergy, and laity. It is provided also that a tribunal may be established for the trial of offences by clergymen; the punishment, if found guilty, being deprivation of licence. The constitutions also provide for the holding of a "Provincial Synod of all the New South Wales Dioceses" once in three years. In this the bishops are to sit in one house and the diocesan synods or representatives in a separate one. The object of the new Church Constitution is gradually to supersede the provisions of the "Church Temporalities Act" of 1837 by others better adapted to the wants of the Church; and although the Church has many difficulties to contend with we look hopefully to the future.

The poor aborigines. This is a sad subject. Here, as elsewhere, they are disappearing before the march of civilization and its attendant vices. The last man of the Sydney tribe died in 1846. It has been the fashion to deride the poor creatures, to regard them as little better than the beasts. But this they did not merit. Many years ago, a gentleman settler picked up in the bush a deserted infant, a boy, and instead of leaving the little one to perish as so many would have done, especially in those early days, he took him to his station and had him properly cared for. As he grew up he had him educated, and I was once asked to examine him; he not only could read and write and cast accounts, but he knew the elements of geometry, algebra, and Latin.

The physical aspect of the Australian continent

is devoid of any of those striking features which, from its great superficial extent, it might have been expected to present. The great dividing range, extending throughout the whole length of eastern Australia—a distance of upwards of thirty degrees,—attains in many points an altitude of not less than from seven to eight thousand feet. The summits of some of the mountains in Gipps' Land would appear to be within the limits of perpetual snow. The proximity of the dividing range to the coast necessarily circumscribes the course of the rivers flowing to the eastward. Those best known are the Hawkesbury, the Clarence, and the Brisbane, which collect the waters of the eastern slope of the Blue Mountain Range. The general character of these streams is, that in the upper part of their course they consist of mere mountain torrents, dry, or forming water holes during the summer, and becoming converted into rapid streams in the rainy season.

So far as climate may be considered as influencing the organization of man, its effects in New South Wales appear to be analogous to those observed in countries elsewhere of a tropical or semi-tropical character. Rapid growth, with early development of the physical as well as the intellectual powers, characterises each sex, but more particularly the female. But this remarkable precocity appears to be compensated for by early and premature decay. The girl of fifteen, possessing all the charms and

RIVER NEPEAN.—*page* 100.

many of the graces of womanhood, must at the age of thirty yield the palm to her who, realizing the triumphs of her sex at a later, preserves them to a more advanced period of life. These remarks apply to those born in the colony. The climate would seem to have an opposite effect on such as come into the country in middle or advanced life. A hundred years has been the age attained by many even of those whose past lives had been fraught with hardship and severe penance—the fruits of irregular and vicious living.

Catarrhal affections often prevail epidemically. Rheumatism, especially in the early days when men were exposed to great privations, was prevalent. Remittent fevers are seldom met with, from the absence of marsh miasmata. Measles and scarlet fever have been productive of great mortality. The last named disease carried off large numbers of the native-born population who were attacked by it, and for the time it lasted, its influence was scarcely less fatal than that of the Asiatic cholera on the first introduction of that disease into Britain. It seems to be a law with epidemics of this class, that they should prove much more devastating on their first appearance in any country than subsequently, after having expended their morbid energy, and when they become as it were acclimatized. The course of disease is much more rapid than is the case in England. There are none of those bed-ridden years which it is the sad lot of many to spend there; you either recover rapidly or you are carried off. On the sea-coast, or on the coast side of the great dividing range, the climate is moist and warm, but tempered by a cool sea breeze during the summer months. Snow and ice are very rare, but the westerly winds are keen in winter and are felt by invalids. To those who are however in robust health, the bright clear days of winter are most enjoyable. The hot winds in summer are trying, and the nights also are hot then. I think that if a person were to spend the three summer months in Hobart Town and the remaining nine months in Sydney, he would have the perfection of climate. As you get farther away from the coast and ascend the hills the climate is much cooler, for though the summer days are hot the nights are cool. In the winter it is really cold.

In speaking of this colony and referring to its past history it is necessary to say a word on the subject of *transportation*. The last convict ship arrived in 1840; and the different colonies have arrived at that stage when it would be most injudicious to attempt a revival of transportation to them. I had an opportunity of watching the whole system both in Van Diemen's Land and in New South Wales. I have no hesitation in saying that it is an admirable mode of punishment. I consider that England must go back to the old system. I believe that she will not long be able to endure the letting loose of her prisoners at home when their sentences have expired. They too often go back to their old associates; they find extreme difficulty in turning over a new leaf in their native land; many refuse to employ them, and so they become confirmed in their evil habits. But send a man to a far off country where all is new, let him see the prospect of regaining the position he had lost and of becoming a respectable member of society, and vast numbers will avail themselves of the opening; nay, under the old and most imperfect system in the Australian colonies great numbers became respectable members of society. If only a suitable country could be obtained, I am sure that economy and philanthropy would alike commend a return to the transportation system. I know full well all the evils of the assignment system as it was administered, but a "knowledge of a disease is half the remedy" and a *judicious* system of assignment is an admirable system. It separates the prisoners from their partners in crime, and it brings them or ought to bring them under domestic influence. It will be found that it was too often the bad master who made the bad man. And the system of ticket-of-leave is an excellent one; not, I grant you, in England, but away from that country. I do not shrink from saying that I know intimately and respect highly many men, and many women, who originally left their country for their country's good. All honour to them that they raised themselves by their industry to independence, and won the respect of their neighbours by the goodness of their character. I repeat it, that I should deeply regret seeing Australia become a receptacle for criminals again. That is not to be thought of; at the same time I never could quite agree with the old settlers in their denunciation of the transportation system, nor did I ever feel that they had a right to be aggrieved thereat. When I went out to the colonies I knew that they were the receptacles for England's criminals, and so did others. And I cannot consider that the Home Government were wrong in continuing that system. At all events we, as colonists, had no right to complain; it was our own act and deed. We went there knowing all about it, and what we should have done without the prisoners I cannot tell. In one word then, I consider that transportation with *judicious* assignment is the perfection of prison discipline, and the sooner England can remove the plague spot from her own shores the better will it be for herself and for her criminals.

The local journals on the Macleay report favourably of the sugar growing enterprise in that locality. The climate and the soil will both suit. The fear we have is about the cost of production, both in this colony and in Queensland.

A movement is on foot, we learn from the *Bathurst Times,* for the establishment of a meat preserving company in that locality, an enterprise that will surely prove remunerative in a district where all the essentials to success are close at hand.

His Excellency the Governor, just prior to the sailing of the last mail had opened Parliament in person, and as the " speech " contains much valuable information we give it below :—

"Honourable Gentlemen of the Legislative Council, and Gentlemen of the Legislative Assembly—

"1. I have not considered it advisable to call you together at an earlier date. It appeared to me preferable to meet Parliament with the measures of the Government and other arrangements in such a state of forwardness as to enable honourable members to proceed at once with their Parliamentary duties, rather than to incur any risk of inconvenient or unnecessary delay by a premature commencement of the session.

" 2. During the recess Ministers have been occupied in the preparation of important measures of administrative and legislative reform, some of which it may be unnecessary to complete before the close of this session, but all of which will be found worthy of attention.

" 3. Progress has been made in effecting such moderate reductions in the Public Expenditure as have been found compatible with efficiency, and with due recognition of the just claims of Public Servants. Efforts in this direction will be continued.

" 4. Among the documents which will be laid before you, will be a Despatch from her Majesty's Principal Secretary of State for the Colonies, announcing an important change in the policy of the Imperial Government with regard to the employment in this colony of Imperial Troops.

"5. Negotiations have been entered into with the Government of Queensland, with a view to the establishment of Telegraphic Communication with Europe, and of additional Postal Communication by way of Torres Straits, with the particulars of which you will be made acquainted. Attempts have been also made to bring about, upon various subjects of common interest, a conference of the neighbouring Colonies, which is only delayed in consequence of their Governments not having as yet agreed as to time and place.

"6. The controversy between Victoria and this Colony, as to the ownership of Pental Island, has been the subject of further correspondence; and a proposition has been submitted, by the Government of this Colony, which is likely to lead to an early and satisfactory settlement of this vexed question.

"7. New arrangements for the conduct of the Colonial Agency in London have been adopted, which, it is hoped, will place our interests there upon an improved footing.

"8. Provision has been made for the commencement of a Free Library in Sydney. The premises of "The Australian Library" have been rented, and the books of that Institution purchased. Steps will be taken without delay for the erection of suitable buildings.

"9. The area of land sold, particularly by conditional sales, has increased this year to an unprecedented extent, as compared with previous years, not excepting even that which followed the passing of the existing Crown Lands Acts. This increase has, during the first six months of the present year, reached a rate of 50 per cent. over that of any like period since 1862. Every effort has been made to render more effective the collection of revenue from this source, by holding out larger inducements to Land Agents and by the issue of additional Land Regulations calculated to facilitate and encourage the payment of interest and of outstanding balances by conditional purchasers.

"10. Changes have been made in the Gold-Fields Regulations; but this subject will be brought under your special consideration by a Bill which will be immediately introduced.

"11. Railway Lines have been completed to Musclebrook and Goulburn. Those to Bathurst and Murrurundi are progressing. A proposition for further Railway Extension will be submitted. Other important Public Works are rapidly approaching completion.

"12. The Telegraph Lines of this Colony have now reached

an extent of about 5,500 miles, and nearly 500 miles more are in course of construction.

"Gentlemen of the Legislative Assembly—

"13. I have directed the Estimates for the ensuing year to be laid before you forthwith. They have been prepared with a due regard to economy and to the requirements of the Public Service.

"Honourable Gentlemen of the Legislative Council, and Gentlemen of the Legislative Assembly—

"14. The Debentures of this Colony continue to command the confidence of English capitalists, the rates last reported being higher than they had been for some years past. The Treasury Bills issued under the Act 32 Victoria, No. 14, have been all negotiated in the Colony, at prices which were never before realized for securities of this nature.

"15. Bills will be submitted to you for the following and other purposes :—

"Correcting anomalies in the Electoral System of the Colony as regards particular districts, and shortening the duration of Parliaments ; Amending the Law relating to Gold-Fields ; Reduction of the Salaries of future Governors and of other high functionaries ; Amending the Law relating to Marriage ; Amending the Law relating to Municipal Institutions ; Providing for Immigration ; Amending the Law relating to Railways ; Aiding and facilitating the Artificial Supply of Water ; Defining the Grazing Rights of Conditional and other Purchasers ; Amending the Superannuation Act ; Regulating Minor Roads ; Amending the Impounding Law ; Regulating Commons ; Amending the Law relating to Distillation ; the more effectual Audit of Public Accounts ; Consolidation and Amendment of Customs Laws ; Amendment of the Law relating to the Mercantile Marine ; Amendment of the Law relating to Lunacy ; Preventing the spread of Contagious Diseases ; Abolition of Ad Valorem Duties and Newspaper Postage Rate ; to Amend the Laws relating to Friendly Societies.

"16. Notwithstanding the depression consequent upon the low price of wool and the effects of the severe drought of last year, the Revenue up to this time considerably exceeds that of the corresponding period of last year. There is reason confidently to expect that the Revenue of 1869 will not fall short of the amount estimated.

"17. The prospects of Agricultural and Mining Industry are highly encouraging.

"18. I now invite you to proceed to your arduous and responsible duties, in fervent trust that, under Divine Providence, your deliberations may tend to a happy issue."

The *Sydney Morning Herald* gives the following "leader" on the matters contained in the speech :—

" Our Parliament has been once more assembled for dispatch of business, but whether business will be dispatched remains to be seen. There are scarcely three months available for its transaction, and before the end of January Parliament will expire by effluxion of time. When we take out the Christmas holidays, the days on which the House does not sit, the days devoted to private business, and the time invariably and apparently inevitably devoted to surplus talk, there is not much time left for hard work. The apology given by the Government for having postponed the session so long is, that they have thereby really saved time, inasmuch as they have been fully occupied in preparing measures to submit to Parliament. They have, however, rather overdone this sort of preparation, for they have presented a list of twenty-one bills, all said to be in a state of forwardness, if not absolutely ready to be produced. And, in a short session, which will not probably have thirty real working days, it is not at all likely that the whole, or even a half, of the bills will be got through. Certain it is, however, that the work is in a greater state of forwardness than usual for Parliament to deal with. It has been too much the custom for Governments to dawdle over the first weeks of the session, and to sound the feeling of honourable members before they introduce their measures. The present Administration, however, is ready to go on with some of its bills at once, and provide work for both Houses. At the same time several of these bills relate to matters which have already been pretty fully discussed, and on which the opinions of the present Assembly have been already taken.

" The propriety of doing any business at all, except what is absolutely necessary for the purposes of Government, has been disputed on the ground that a Parliament so close to dissolution can hardly legislate with the requisite independence, inasmuch as any serious opposition that would put the Government in a minority would immediately send honourable members to the hustings. But the threat of dissolution now is a very different thing to what it would be at an earlier period of the Parliament's life. That threat is scarcely a threat, and its execution could at the most only anticipate by a few weeks what must inevitably take place. The House generally has not accepted the theory that it is not fit to work in its last hours, and is going into the discussion of the measures prepared for it. In fact, it suits the political purposes of both parties to get the programme developed. The Government is proud of, and confident in, the goodness of its policy, and is anxious to have the whole of it thoroughly displayed prior to the appeal to the constituencies. The Vice-regal Speech on the opening of the session has been stigmatised as an electioneering placard, and, as the soft indictment was not resented, but rather admitted, it is clear that the Administration rests its claims to the support on its ability and willingness to carry on important reforms.

" On the other side, the Opposition also wish the programme to be unfolded, being confident in the destructive power of hostile criticism. It is never very difficult to discover something that can be found fault with in any measure, and, out of twenty-one bills, some weapons of attack are sure to be forged. But though both sides thus have reasons for wishing the principal measures of the session to be produced, it does not follow that there will be the same unanimity in carrying them through all their stages, and we cannot therefore assume that this session, which has opened so exuberant in bills, will close fruitful in Acts.

"The Budget is to be produced on Thursday next. The chief anxiety in respect to the Treasurer's statement relates to possible changes in taxation. We already know pretty well how the revenue stands for this year, but the Government has distinctly promised the abolition of the ad valorem duties, and as they are now producing not very much less than £200,000 a year, we are curious to know how the deficiency is to be made good. The projects of retrenchment hitherto disclosed, even if they are all as effective as anticipated by the Ministry, will not make good so large a loss in revenue. It is probable that some additions may be made to the Stamp Act, which, in its present form, is not so comprehensive as it might be—or, indeed, as it was intended to be; but whether anything further is designed in the shape of direct taxation—whether there is to be anything like a beginning made in the way of an income and property tax—is a point on which much natural curiosity exists. The mercantile community are very anxious to get rid of the ad valorem duties, which have proved themselves to be a great nuisance, and have immensely interfered with the intercolonial and re-export trade; and therefore they would put up with a good deal to see them finally abolished. But whether the country at large is prepared for even an instalment of direct taxation is very doubtful, seeing that even municipal institutions are taking root very slowly.

"The Estimates laid on the table disclose the fact that somewhat over two millions sterling will be required for the purposes of Government. This, no doubt, seems a large sum for taking care of 400,000 people, especially as we have no army or navy to support other than the cost of our Volunteers and our contribution to the troops stationed in the colony. But then, it must be remembered by English critics that our population is scattered over a territory six hundred miles square, that we have to pay the interest on a considerable debt incurred for public works, inasmuch as our railways at present do little more than pay their working expenses, and that we have to provide out of the public revenue for nearly all the local works and local wants which in a more settled country press on local revenues.

"Although the railway policy of the Government has not yet been expounded, it is clear from the Estimates that that policy is not finality. They propose to add two millions to the public debt, and of this amount about one million and three-quarters is required for railway purposes. The demand for improved communication is so great that no Government can resist it, and unpopular as taxation is, the general feeling of the country is in favour of railway extension, even at the risk of increased taxation. There is an instinctive feeling that the country cannot get on without railways, and that they are essential to our progress even though they may press inconveniently on our incomes."

"Quartz mining is exciting more and more attention in the colony every day, and reefs are being discovered and opened up in every direction—south, west, and north. Even since our last summary some rich reefs have been opened upon and adjoining to the old Major's Creek Gold-field. From these the accounts are so good that the Bungonia reefs have been well nigh deserted for the new land of promise. Reports from that quarter mention that the stone shows well, as, though the gold is very small, it is well diffused through the stone. No crushings have yet been had there, but steps are being taken to test the quality of the stone prior to the erection of crushing machinery. On the Little River, also in the Braidwood district, there has been a very rich find of gold in the Homeward Bound claim on the Mosquito Reef. A leader was struck, which at one part contained nearly more gold than stone, and the parties netted some £3,000 only by hand crushing. Since then the country round has been regularly rushed, and several new reefs, some of them showing excellent prospects, have been opened. From the experience gained by prospectors it is now evident that the whole of the first fall of the land, or rather the first plateau from the table land on the east coast of Australia, from Bungonia southward to the boundary of the colony, is auriferous, and more or less thickly intersected by gold-bearing quartz reefs.

"Kiandra is once more looking up, owing to the plentiful supply of water furnished by the winter's rains. This has enabled sluicers to go to work, though it has stopped proceedings in some of the deep claims. The reefs in the Gundagai district have also been turning out well, and rather more than the usual quantity of gold has lately been received there. One parcel of stone crushed at Kimo gave $27\frac{1}{2}$ oz. for $6\frac{1}{2}$ tons quartz, whilst the Adelong crushings have averaged over an ounce.

"In the South bordering on the Riverine country, reefs are being opened and worked with good success. Melbourne speculators, in this as in other cases, have set the ball going, and the New South Wales men have not been slow to follow the lead given to them.

"New alluvial workings have just been opened on the Emu Creek Gold-field, at a place called the Quondong, some seven miles from Grenfell. The wash dirt has not yet been tested, for there is no available store of water on the ground, but three shafts put down at intervals over a line of some two miles have each bottomed on auriferous drift with wash dirt from two to three feet deep, and calculated by the test of the dish, to go about 12 dwts. to the load. The alluvial workings on this field have been altogether very successful lately; a great portion of the gold sent thence by escort being due to this source. The stone has not gone so well lately, and the average of the crushings shows something less than an ounce to the ton.

"Of the Western Gold-fields, Tambaroora and its reefs certainly keeps the lead which it has so long held. From 40 tons of stone from James Brown's claim, no less than 650 oz. were obtained; whilst 247 tons of stone crushed during seven weeks at the Victorian machine gave 1,120 oz. Trunkey Creek promises to become an established reefing country. Three companies are now actively engaged there, two being Sydney, and one Melbourne, companies. The first established of these Sydney companies is now well on in its preparation, its dam being nearly finished, and the machinery rapidly arriving, and being fitted up as quickly as received. The Melbourne company have the One Eye property on lease where there is a store of permanent water. Here their machinery will be erected as it arrives. New reefs are being discovered in this district in all directions.

"From the Northern Gold-fields we learn that a rich auriferous vein has been struck in a reef at Bowling Alley Point, in Williams' and Co.'s claim, from this by hand picking and crushing. The party have been making for some time past from £15 to £17 per week per man. The Denison reefs, on a tributary of the Hunter, near Scone, have lately been exciting more than usual notice; the last crushing reported being 29 tons of Landrigan's stone which gave 51 oz. The crushing from January to August, eight months, 415 tons had been crushed, the product being 750 oz. gold. There is only one quartz-crushing machine on the ground, and it is worked by a water wheel."

The *Sydney Empire* gives the following description of gold from the neighbourhood of Braidwood:—

"According to the official telegram just received by the Colonial Secretary from Braidwood—and it would be difficult to conceive any more authentic intelligence—the New South Wales gold-fields are now 'looking up' in the inventory of our local assets. At a time when the strong tendency of opinion—not in the colonies but in the mother country—seems to be in favour of the proposal to turn us adrift at the very first favourable opportunity, it is as well that we should keep stock of our resources as they are developed. The telegram to the Colonial Secretary stated that three hundred and fifty pounds weight of gold was awaiting conveyance by escort to Sydney, *viâ* Goulburn, and the Braidwood papers received this morning report the particulars. It seems that a quantity of quartz, of most surpassing richness, had been taken from the 'Homeward Bound' claim, the whole weighing about three hundred and fifty pounds. But, instead of being like quartz mixed with gold, it is described as 'gold mixed with quartz.' The net weight of gold was supposed to be about a hundred and twenty pounds, valued at £6,000 sterling. This prize was found at a depth of only about twenty-four feet from the surface. 'The stone,' says the report, ' clings together with the precious metal, and many of the thinner pieces bend like so many pieces of lead.' The same report adds, 'there is no saying how much more of it there may yet be to take out;' and as it is only a few weeks since seventy-five pounds weight of gold quartz was taken from the same claim, it is certainly not unreasonable to anticipate the unearthing of many a 'find' as rich, or richer. Such incidents give life and energy to the digger, by reviving hopes which had perhaps declined through long periods of weary disappointment, and proving that, while millions upon millions in value of the precious metal had continued to be exported, and long after the desponding had pronounced the New South Wales gold-fields to be worked out, mines of wealth, literally speaking, continued to remain as they had done for ages, though enterprising men and experienced diggers may have passed over them unheeding. So it will long continue to be; and the experience of every month and every week serves to show that the auriferous resources of this country are only yet in the infancy of their development. Further to the westward, also, the prospects of the steady miner, who goes to work with a will at quartz reefing, are highly encouraging; and the magnificent specimens of auriferous quartz from Trunkey Creek, as exhibited in the lobby of the Assembly in Sydney the other day, reminded old miners of the palmy days of Ballarat. The remarkable success of gold mining in Victoria at the first, attracting, as it did, a vast population, not only from Europe and other parts beyond seas, but also from our own mines, which were held in disparaging comparison, caused our Southern neighbours to outstrip us to an extent not warranted by the natural capabilities of one colony as compared with the other. People are now, to use a nautical expression, 'trying back;' and with the inestimable benefit of experience, they are likely to discover much that they had before overlooked. The Braidwood paper compares the quartz reefs at the Little River to those of the Thames district, in New Zealand; and, judging from results already obtained, we see no reason why the comparison should not hold good. From Burrangong, also, we learn by this morning's post that the Junee reefs are making a profitable yield."

Much dissatisfaction has been expressed at the infrequency of the wool sales held in London, and the heavy taxation which was levied on the Colonial producer. Influential meetings have been held on this important subject both at home and abroad. At the last meeting on the subject in Sydney, the following resolutions were agreed to:—

"1st. They are of opinion that all enquiries into the matters alluded to, from the absence of the proper channels of information in the colony, may be best made in London.

"2nd. That to enable these enquiries to be made as searching and as independent as possible, a committee of gentlemen, representing all the Australian colonies, be appointed in London, and that the following gentlemen be invited to represent New South Wales there, viz.:—Donald Larnach, Esq., W. F. De Salis, Esq., William Mort, Esq., Edward Hamilton, Esq., Sir D. Cooper, Bart., John Peters, Esq., F. H. Dangar, Esq.

"3rd. That the gentlemen above named be requested to confer with the committee which now regulates the sale of wool by public auction in London, and from that and other sources of information ascertain the reasons, if any, which uphold quarterly sales of the wools of these colonies in preference to bi-monthly or even monthly sales; to enquire into the mode of warehousing, with a view of affording greater facilities for exhibiting the wools of the different colonies separately; to ascertain whether any reduction can be obtained in the existing charges; and generally, in the interests of the colonists, to investigate the question whether any and what improvements can be made in the mode of selling Australian wools in London.

"4th. That the said Committee be also requested to consider the propriety of the formation of a permanent committee in London to represent the interests of the colonies in regard to the sale of wool generally, and to prevent such misrepresentation as is exposed in the letter of John L. Bowes and Brother, published in the *Home News* of 13th August, 1869.

"5th. That a copy of these resolutions be forwarded to the chairmen of the various Chambers of Commerce of the Australian colonies, requesting them to appoint such parties as they may deem desirable to act with the committee appointed to represent this colony in London."

To those interested in "station" property, the extracts from the late papers given below will impart some useful information:—

"There is still a fair demand for really good stations, and these have been disposed of advantageously during the past month. We have sold by private contract the Tooloom Station, in the Clarence district, with 1,100 head of cattle, at £2 15s. per head, stores, horses, &c., to be taken at a valuation. Terms, as usual. Fattening cattle-stations, well situated for this or the Victorian markets, have changed hands at higher rates, according to their quality and position, and in one instance reached £5 per head for a run on the Lachlan River. For Northern Queensland cattle-stations there has not been the enquiry we anticipated. In sheep-stations we do not expect any business until after the shearing is over, when we hope to see more confidence in these properties, as the result of the cheering news per last English mail. Store Cattle:—There has been but little done in these, but as there have been fine rains in Victoria and Riverina, we shortly expect numerous demands for bullocks of suitable ages for fattening. In consequence of the fall in the price of fat cattle in Melbourne, Southern buyers are offering rather lower rates; and we quote superior bullocks, delivered South, £3 15s. to £4; superior bullocks on Northern stations, £2 10s. to £2 15s.; store cattle (equal sexes) two to seven years, on Northern stations, £2 to £2 5s.; mixed cattle, six months and upwards, on Northern stations, £1 10s. to £1 15s. Store Sheep:—There is only a limited demand for large framed wethers, at about 3s. 6d. to 4s. for shorn sheep. We have sold 7,300 from the Barcoo, deliverable on Liverpool Plains in January next, with nine months' fleece, at 5s. 3d. per head."

"Fat Sheep:—Although stocks are abundantly supplied, the supply of the present week falls very short of that of former weeks, and competition at auction sales is decidedly greater for every description. An advance of 6d. to 1s. 6d. per head may be noted. The carcase price remains at $\frac{3}{4}$d. to 1d. per lb. Goldsborough, Burt, and Co. sold Hunt and Crawford wedders, from 8s. 8d. to 8s. 9d.; ewes, 7s. 10d. They also sold of another flock 1,000 wedders, at 8s. The market for fat lambs has been better supplied, and prices have ranged from 4s. to 12s. 6d. Three lots were sold as follow: Christian's at 10s.; Dine's at 12s. 6d.; and M'Innes at 7s.

"Store Stock:—In this description of cattle there is little doing. Good lots of mixed sexes have realised £3 10s. to £4. But a glut reported at Melbourne will doubtless keep prices down.

"Farm and Dairy Produce is very plentiful and cheap. Fowls, 2s. 9d. to 3s. 3d. per pair; ducks, 3s. 6d. to 4s.; geese, 6s. to 6s. 6d.; turkeys, 6s. to 12s.; eggs 7d. per dozen; bacon, $3\frac{1}{4}$d. to $5\frac{1}{4}$d. per lb.; store pigs, $2\frac{1}{4}$d. to 3d. per lb.; calves, 10s. to 25s. each.

"Breadstuffs and Cereals.—The market in breadstuffs is very dull, vendors holding on with confidence for an advance in prices, and buyers being little disposed to pay current rates.

Quotations are quite nominal. For best Adelaide silk dressed flour £15 to £16 is asked; for flour manufactured in Sydney, £14 10s. to £15. Californian rules also at these latter rates, but very little has been quitted. For wheat 7s. per bushel is asked, and we have heard of no sales of Adelaide at a lesser rate. Maize is easy at 4s.; barleys, Cape, 2s. 9d. to 3s.; English, 3s. 9d. to 4s.; bran, 15d.; lucerne hay is quitted at £2 to £2 10s. per ton: oaten, £2 to £3; straw, £1 10s. to £2 10s."

From the above it will be seen that the expense of all the necessaries and many of the comforts of life is small, while the rates of wages for mechanics, for labourers, and for domestic servants are very high.

Although New South Wales is the parent of the Australian colonies, and a good deal of her strength and vigour have been transferred to her offspring, yet when we consider her fine climate, her commanding position, her noble harbour, her vast area, and her exhaustless resources, we feel assured that she is herself as yet only in her infancy, and that a great future is in store for her.

Chapter III.

TASMANIA.

IT is but of late years that the island has officially borne this name. It was formerly called "Van Diemen's Land." In 1642, Abel Jansen Tasman discovered and named it after Anthony Van Diemen, the Governor-General of the Dutch East Indies. That it was an island, and not a part of the mainland, was unknown till 1798, when Bass (whose name was subsequently given to the Straits which separate the mainland from the island) discovered a passage through. It was in the year 1802 that the Home Government, jealously watching the movements of France, sent out instructions to the Governor of New South Wales to form a penal settlement on this island. In consequence of this Captain Bowen, R.N., was sent down with a gang of convicts, guarded by a body of marines. They passed through d'Entrecasteaux Channel, and entered the beautiful river Derwent, in the month of June, 1803. They met with many difficulties and suffered no little from the cold. Bowen went up the river for a good many miles, and then fixed upon a spot for the infant settlement, which, wearied as he was with his undertaking, he called "Rest down," which name remains to this day, but it has been corrupted to "Risdon." Things were going on favourably in the infant settlement when Bowen was somewhat unexpectedly superseded by Governor Phillip's secretary, Colonel Collins. Perhaps one of the most interesting works which we have on the colony of New South Wales is from his pen. This book brought him under the notice of the government, who subsequently (1804) employed him to go to Port Phillip (now the colony of Victoria) for the purpose of forming a settlement there. He was accompanied by a fleet of convict ships, and all things necessary for the formation of an extensive settlement. After entering the heads he went to the eastward, and subsequently went some distance in the direction of Western Port. But he was disappointed. He saw no good land, and found no good water. Somewhat hastily, therefore, but we presume under instructions furnished to him, in the event of his inability to establish a settlement at Port Phillip, he left the country and steered for the Derwent.

Somewhat strangely, it is said that Collins knew nothing of Bowen having been previously dispatched to this locality. As two settlements were not needed, Bowen retired, leaving Collins as the first lieutenant-governor of the island. This island, from Cape Grim to the north-west to the South Cape, extends about 230 miles, and its greatest width is about 190 miles. It contains 24,000 square miles, and has an area of nearly seventeen millions of acres. Collins very wisely removed the infant settlement to the opposite side of the Derwent, and here he laid the foundation of Hobart Town, at the foot of a mountain more than 4,000 feet high, and which was afterwards called "Mount Wellington." The town was called "Hobart," from Lord Hobart, who was at this time one of the Secretaries of State in England. Collins was accompanied by the Rev. R. Knopwood, government chaplain, a surgeon-superintendent, three assistant surgeons, a mineralogist, commissary-general, surveyor, and two superintendents of convicts. There was a small body of marines, commanded by Lieutenants Sladen, Johnson, and Edward Lord. The convicts amounted to 367. From the "Official Record of the Intercolonial Exhibition," to which we are much indebted for some interesting particulars, we learn that the first Tasmanian house was built by Edward Lord, on land adjoining the Macquarie Hotel. It was a rude concern, just like the huts in the bush, with port-holes instead of windows. The first government house was a little cottage, hardly fit for the residence of a mechanic.

The land in the immediate neighbourhood of Hobart Town was found to be very inferior; but, to a certain extent, this was compensated for by the beauty of the scenery. Ascending to the top of

Mount Wellington, by a route which is at least ten miles long, through forests of gigantic growth and fern-tree valleys of extreme beauty, you get from its summit a most magnificent view of the town, the shipping, and the river. The whole island is more or less mountainous. Many of the early settlers were Scotchmen; and hence we meet with Ben Lomond and other names, marking our fondness for carrying our home associations and names with us wherever we may go.

Tasmania rises towards its centre to about 1,500 feet, and so all the rivers run from the centre towards the sea on every side. The two chief rivers are the Derwent, running south, and the Tamar, north. As we remarked with reference to New South Wales, the convicts' labour was at once employed in road making. They constructed at an early period a beautiful road right through the island, from south to north, a distance of 120 miles. It continues to this day in admirable order; and, especially considering the mountainous character of the country, it was a gigantic undertaking. In the interior of this country there are some most fertile valleys and plains, the alluvial soil reaching to a depth of from three to twenty feet. As the work of exploration went on, these charming localities were soon taken up. As Van Diemen's Land at this time formed part of New South Wales, the same land regulations prevailed, which were these: On your arrival you stated what means you had;

the government then gave you a tract of land in proportion to those means. The maximum grant was fixed at 2,560 acres, and the minimum at 320. You had 640 acres given to you for every £500 sterling that you possessed, up to the maximum named above. Stock and implements of husbandry, and half-pay, were all taken into account as so much money. It was not therefore to be wondered at that as soon as it became at all known, many men of good family, and retired naval and military officers, made this their home. And this accounts for the allowed fact, that from the earliest days there was to be found a small but most select and exclusive body of gentlemen, into whose society it was not easy to get. In fact there were but two classes in the early days, the gentry and the prisoner population. Lieutenant Jeffreys, one of these early settlers, gives us the following account of his own experience in Tasmanian farming. He says, "Having fixed upon a spot, I was supplied by the governor with three or four convict labourers, to whom were added a ploughman and overseer, both free men. The site of the intended farm was previously well known to the overseer. These men were provided with three weeks' provisions, and such tools and implements as were necessary to their labour. Having a cart to carry their tools, they arrived at the spot about four o'clock in the afternoon. It was out of my power to accompany them, but as they themselves relate the story, the ploughman was appointed cook, and whilst he was making the necessary arrangements for refreshment, the rest, with their axes, cut down such timber as was requisite to erect a temporary hut. This they completed and rendered perfectly water-tight before sunset, when they all sat down to such a repast as the cook had provided for them. Their meal consisted of the hind-quarters of a kangaroo cut into mincemeat, stewed in its own gravy, with a few rashers of salt pork. This dish is called a 'steamer.' They added to that a sufficient quantity of potatoes, and a large cake ('damper'), baked in the wood-ashes of the fire. Afterwards the grog went merrily round, and the plains and valleys rang with three times three, and 'Success to the Captain's farm.' In a few days the plan and foundation of a garden were laid out, after which they all set to work to build a more commodious house for themselves and their master. This house consisted of two rooms, occupied by the overseer when I was not there, and a large kitchen and sleeping place for themselves. In a very short time I had the satisfaction to see 20 acres of land broken up, and about 200 acres fit for the plough. In doing this it was not necessary to cut down more than 500 trees. In this manner it is possible for hundreds of settlers, at a very moderate expense, to establish themselves in this delightful part of the globe, the abode of peace, plenty, and rural happiness."

It is a curious fact that as sailors generally took to farming, soldiers took to sheep and cattle stations. On one occasion I had an opportunity of going carefully over the farms in a celebrated agricultural district, and on enquiry I found that not one of the farmers had had any previous knowledge of his work. There were tinkers, tailors, soldiers, sailors, apothecaries, and thieves in abundance, but there was not a ploughboy amongst them. And yet these people, scratching the surface of the virgin soil, produced from it, year after year, 30 or 40 bushels of wheat to the acre, without change of crop, rest, or manure.

We have hitherto been speaking of the southern portion of the island—of the land in the vicinity of Hobart Town. But at or about the same time a settlement was formed in the north. A vessel was sent round to Port Dalrymple to survey the entrance of the river Tamar. The report was a favourable one; and it was followed by a detachment of prisoners being sent to it from Sydney, under the command of Colonel Paterson. This was towards the close of 1804. After staying for a time at York Town they removed to the land above the North and South Esk, where they discovered beautiful plains, free from timber, ready for the plough. At this time Captain King was the governor of all the Australian settlements. He came from Cornwall, and so in honour of him Paterson called the new town "Launceston," and the river the

"Tamar." The two establishments, at the north and south of the island, were quite distinct. It was not until 1807 that Lieutenant Laycock made his way to Hobart Town—a distance of 120 miles—and he appears to have excited great astonishment in the minds of the inhabitants of the southern town. A cart was shortly afterwards driven through the bush the whole distance, without having to cut down a single tree. In 1812 the whole island was placed under one governor.

Collins was governor for six years. His time was employed in settling things at head-quarters, and but little progress was made in agricultural or pastoral pursuits. So little was done that they had to get their supplies from New South Wales. And when, owing to floods, this supply failed, wheat and maize rose to from £5 to £6 a bushel. And in the year 1810, in which year Collins died, the population were on the verge of starvation. The first governor just before his death established a newspaper called the *Derwent Star*. A temporary church had been erected in Hobart Town, called "St. David's," and in its churchyard the remains of Colonel Collins were deposited. He appears to have been much respected, for 600 persons followed him to the grave. In 1838 Sir John Franklin erected a monument over his burial-place.

It was not until 1813 that Colonel Davey was appointed as the second lieutenant-governor. In the interval good progress had been made in agricultural pursuits, and the stock in the country had greatly increased. At this time General Macquarie was the governor-in-chief; and before the second permanent appointment he visited the island. He seems, both in New South Wales and in Van Diemen's Land, to have thrown himself much into the improvement of towns and the erection of buildings. The number of places that bear the name of "Macquarie" is very great indeed. The inhabitants of the infant town were delighted to welcome him. He found the people building their little cottages any how; every one doing what was right in his own eyes. He got the town properly laid out, and the streets named. They were, of course, Macquarie Street, after himself; Elizabeth Street, after his wife; Liverpool Street, after Lord Liverpool, the prime minister, and so on. The new governor (Collins) did not pay very much attention to etiquette, for report says that if the day were warm, he forgot his dignity, in a regard to his personal comfort, and was to be seen walking about the town with his coat hanging on his arm.

Until the year 1813 the ports had been closed; but now they were opened. Expeditions were formed for exploring the country, both by sea and by land. In 1816 Mr. Birch fitted out a vessel to explore the western coast of the island, and a monopoly for one year of the trade he thus opened was granted to him. The first large houses of business were kept by persons whose names "old hands" will not fail to recognise, such as Edward Lord, Kemp, Gatehouse, and Reiby. Port Davey and Macquarie Harbours were discovered at this time. Another colonist, whose name is not yet forgotten, Andrew Bent, started a newspaper called the *Hobart Town Gazette*. This was in 1816, about which time the first flour-mill was erected, thus showing the gradual extension of agricultural pursuits. From early days a good deal of attention had been paid to the whale fishery, for which this island has continued to be so noted. A deputy-judge-advocate (Abbott) was appointed; a local court, for the recovery of debts under £50, was established; and the new church of St. David's was built in 1817. After his term of office had expired, Colonel Davey went and settled himself on a grant of 3,000 acres of land which had been made to him, but subsequently went home, and died in 1823.

The country was steadily if not rapidly progressing. But it received a great check about this time from the terror caused in the country by armed and desperate gangs of "bushrangers." A system of assignment had been commenced, whereby the settlers got the services of the prisoners in their houses and on their farms. This was a great benefit to the settler or farmer where labour was so scarce, and it was encouraged by the government, because it saved them the expense of feeding and clothing the prisoners. As we remarked before, a great many of the early settlers were naval or military men. From their previous habits these men were great disciplinarians, and the punishment of the "lash" was very common indeed. Too common by far. It cannot be doubted that many men were by means of it driven to desperation, and quitting their masters' employ had no alternative but to take to the "bush," where, partly from revenge and partly from necessity, they became desperate characters, turning their hand against every man. We shall see more of their sad doings as we proceed with our history.

The next lieutenant-governor of the island was Colonel Sorell, whose administration extended over seven years, that is from 1817 to 1824. He was a cautious man, and just the man who was wanted for the colony at the time. Free immigration received a great impetus now. Several interesting books appeared in England treating on the advantages of a settlement in the island. The goodness of the climate, the excellence of the soil, the free grants of land, the loan of seed and stock, rations for the emigrants, and too the convicts who were assigned to them as labourers, for six months, and the high prices which the produce fetched in the Sydney market, were all inducements of no ordinary character to men whose circumstances or whose love of novelty led them to think of seeking their fortunes in a new land. An addition of at least 10,000 was made to the free population during his administration. In 1820 the large sum of £20,000 was obtained for wheat exported. The live stock also had increased very fast. In 1821 there were 170,000 sheep, 35,000 head of cattle, 5,000 swine, and 550 horses. Attention was also attracted to wool as an export. In the early days it was considered valueless, and the skins with the fleeces on them were thrown to the pigs. But one enterprising settler, Mr. Henry Hopkins—a man who rose to great wealth in the colony and was most highly respected—bought up wool at fourpence a pound and sent it to England, where it was sold at sevenpence. When the duty and all expenses had been paid, the margin was very small, if it did not actually entail a loss. But it had the effect of turning men's attention to their wool, and it was more carefully prepared for market. The returns from wool in 1821 were only £88, but within two years of that time they had reached the comparatively large sum of £4,399. As trade increased, the want of a suitable currency was much felt. Hence most of the transactions were by barter. Even the government frequently paid their debts in rum at £1 a bottle, and this rum passed as currently as sovereigns or bank notes do in more civilized communities. Every man who was considered a "good mark," that is a solvent man, issued his own notes, at sums varying from sixpence upwards. During the time of the French war, when specie was very scarce, the Spanish dollar was much used. A circular piece was struck out of the centre about the size of a shilling, and it was called a "dump," and the rest of the dollar, called from the circular piece taken out a "ring-dollar," was valued at four shillings. At one time six sheep had to be given for a gallon of rum, and two or three hundred acres of freehold land, valued at half-a-crown an acre, were given for a horse. The first bank was established in 1823. In the year 1822 the Rev. W. Bedford was appointed as senior chaplain. This gentleman for a great many years took a prominent part in all that took place in the colony. He enjoyed the confidence of the Bishop of Australia; and before his death, His Grace the Archbishop of Canterbury marked his sense of his lengthened services by granting him the honorary degree of a doctor of divinity. The Wesleyans and the Presbyterians established themselves in the island during Colonel Sorell's term of office. The first Roman Catholic priest was the Rev. P. Connolly. The British and Foreign Bible Society established a branch at a very early period, which has continually remitted from that day to the present most liberal contributions to the Parent Society. I shall never forget my own association with this Society. Approaching my new home in 1835, I felt sadly cast down. I was in a strange country, where I knew not a single individual. One of the first things that happened was a request that I would attend a meeting of this body which was about to take place; and when I saw its work, and met its friends, "I thanked God, and took courage." The Rev. J. Youl (a name still well known in England and in Victoria) was the first Church of England chaplain in Launceston. His little wooden church was in those days also used as a court-house, as a bed-room for gangs of prisoners, and, report says, also as a stable!

Whilst Colonel Sorell was governor, coal was discovered at Tasman's peninsula, and a penal settlement was formed there for the purpose of working it. Another settlement of a similar character was formed at Macquarie Harbour, where the prisoners were employed in cutting timber for building purposes. On one occasion fourteen prisoners effected an escape from Macquarie Harbour in a boat, and landing within a few miles of Hobart Town formed a hiding-place, whence they used to issue out on the defenceless settlers, and rob and not unfrequently murder them. There were two desperate fellows amongst them, named Brady and McCabe, each of whom became the head of a powerful gang. Lieutenant Gunn with a small body of soldiers was sent against Brady. Many a man who reads these pages will remember Mr. Gunn, a fine man, standing six feet seven inches high. Failing to find the miscreants, he had gone to a friend's house, when he was asked to go out to speak to some one. This turned out to be Brady himself, who came thus to beard the lion in his den. The lieutenant, suspecting treachery, came out with a loaded pistol in his hand, on seeing which the ruffian discharged the contents of his rifle at him and shattered his arm. Colonel Davey had tried the effect of martial law. Sorell mustered the inhabitants of Hobart Town, and urged them to take the matter into their own hands, and help to put a stop to these atrocities. From eighty to a hundred guineas were subscribed, and rewards offered for their apprehension. An engagement took place, and Geary, the leader of one of the gangs, was slain. Still three desperate characters were known to be at large, named Howe, Watts, and Brown. But they were all taken. At the penal station of Port Arthur the discipline was very severe. The men loathed the place so much, that it came out in evidence in the supreme court in Hobart Town that murder was committed, simply that the prisoner might be taken to the capital for trial, although he knew that death was sure to follow. The number of persons who were hanged was sometimes frightful. On one occasion it is said that the kind-hearted chaplain to the gaol went in a great hurry to the governor, and complained that they were going to hang thirteen together, whereas he was sure there was only room to hang twelve " comfortably."

The inhabitants parted from Governor Sorell with great regret in 1824. He died in 1848, having enjoyed the whole time a pension from the colonial government.

Colonel Arthur was the next governor—a man of fixed purpose and stern resolve. His character seemed to have reached the colony before him, for he met with but a cool reception. He seems to have regarded the colony simply as a receptacle for prisoners; whereas there was becoming a strong feeling against this idea being entertained, by a large and wealthy body of free settlers. A Scotch company, with a capital of £100,000, was formed for the purpose of exchanging the products of the country for home manufactures; and a large body of intelligent Scotchmen came out under these auspices, and did a great amount of good. By means of this company the old "monopolies" in trade were done away with for ever.

Just before Colonel Arthur's arrival, a supreme court was opened, and Mr. Pedder, afterwards Sir J. L. Pedder, appointed as the first judge. The names of Gellibrand, the first attorney-general, and Mr. Joseph Hone, who was so greatly respected for a lengthened period, and who was the first master of the supreme court, are familiar to all old residents.

When Mr. Bent started his newspaper, to which reference has already been made, the government had helped him, so as to enable him to buy his material. The paper had always been under official supervision. This Mr. Bent now threw off, and Mr. Thomas commenced his duties as the editor. Mr. R. L. Murray became a correspondent, and wrote so strongly as to startle the governor. A long and angry altercation took place. Mr. Howe and Dr. Ross became printers of the *Government Gazette.* The colonists protested against Colonel Arthur's attempt to interfere with the freedom of the press, but he replied that the press in a convict colony could not be free. But the press could not be "gagged." A little later, and two papers were started in Launceston, by Mr. Fawkner and Mr. Dowsell.

"His Excellency," as the governor was henceforth called, instead of "His Honour," had to submit to the controlling powers exercised by a legislative and an executive council, which were the shadows in the distance of those great legislative privileges which were in a few years to be conferred on all the colonies of the Australian group.

A great company was formed at this time, named the "Van Diemen's Land Company," professedly for the purpose of improving the stock in the colony, and of making England independent of foreign supplies of wool. Mr. Edward Curr was the local agent. They ultimately got 350,000 acres of land in different parts, which, including the cost of survey, did not exceed half-a-crown an acre for the purchase of the freehold.

So rapidly was the country advancing, that the single bank we mentioned just now, enlarged its capital to £50,000. The "Tasmanian" and the "Derwent" were then established. The "Cornwall" was started in Launceston. Then came the great Bank of Australasia, and the Tamar in the northern capital. It is said that the manager of the former went to the latter every morning with a wheelbarrow, and carried away, to the disgust of the Tamar, dollars in exchange for notes. The "Union of Australia," at a later period, was added to the number. But the colony did not progress only in its commercial transactions. A Mechanic's Institute was opened, and has continued from that time forward to be well supported. The King's Orphan School, now called the Queen's Asylum, one of the very finest buildings in the colony, was established for the reception of destitute or neglected children. The nucleus of the present "Royal Society of Tasmania" was projected.

It was during Governor Arthur's time that the settlements of Port Phillip (now Victoria) and of South Australia took place; and the demand for stock and colonial produce of all kinds was enormous. From the statistics of 1836 it appears that the population had increased from 12,000 to 40,000; the revenue from £16,866 to £106,639; the imports from £62,000 to £583,646; the exports from £14,500 to £320,679; the colonial vessels from 1 to 71; the churches from 4 to 18.

As yet we have said nothing of the poor aborigines of the island. A sad war had long been going on between the settlers, the convicts, and the natives. For some years after Colonel Arthur's arrival things only got from bad to worse. We wish it were possible to pass this subject over without any allusion to it. We have just risen from the perusal of that most interesting but very sad book "Bonwick's Last of the Tasmanians," and our sympathies are deeply stirred on behalf of the poor sons of the soil. It would appear that at first the natives were quite disposed to be friendly, and that we have ourselves to blame for the frightful atrocities which were subsequently committed. It was in 1830 that the "line," a very important feature in the "black war," was formed. The idea suggested by Colonel Arthur was, that they should try and drive all the natives from the interior to Tasman's Peninsula, by forming a "line" right across the country. There were 119 leaders of parties, with a guide to each; 738 prisoners also were allowed to take part in it. The whole force amounted to 4,850 men in arms. They formed a complete military *cordon*, extending sometimes for 60 miles. It was supposed that they were thus driving before them the whole of the natives, whose number was estimated at nearly 2,000. After six weeks of hard work they deemed their work nearly over, for the *cordon* narrowed to East Bay Neck, which is not more than half a mile wide. Instead of the 2,000, the prey consisted of *one old woman and a sick man!* The rest had, of course, with that cunning which is so prominent a feature in the wild savage, escaped, if they had ever been enclosed at all. This expedition cost about £30,000 of govern-

K

ment money. But it had its effect on the natives, and helped in a very great measure the steps which were taken at a subsequent period.

The government knew not what to do in this dilemma, for the depredations of the blacks still continued. At this juncture a builder named Robinson came forward and proposed a scheme of conciliation, believing that by promises of clothing and of food he could lure them into the town. He proposed to take with him two native men who had been partially civilized. The government were only too glad to accept his proposals and to give him supplies. Mr. Robinson had been favourably known amongst the Wesleyans, to which body he belonged, for a long time. He had been engaged as a tract distributor, Sunday school teacher, and secretary to the Bethel Mission. He had long taken an interest in the poor creatures, and was much liked by those who knew him. The terms which were made with him were not very liberal—a pound a week and certain rations. But I suppose the government were suffering under the loss of the £30,000. This allowance was shortly afterwards raised to £100, and afterwards to £250 a year. In 1831 Mr. Robinson reported that 123 of the natives had yielded. He went on with his good work, overcoming great difficulties by his indomitable perseverance, until, on the 22nd January, 1835, he was enabled to report to the government that his work was accomplished—that the island was swept of its aboriginal inhabitants. They were removed to Flinders' Island, in the Straits, and Mr. Robinson was appointed as commandant. In 1838 he left that port and was appointed protector of the aborigines of Port Phillip, with a salary of £500 a year. He ultimately returned to England, and died at Bath in 1866.

Flinders' Island is about 40 miles long and from 12 to 18 miles broad. The natives never liked their place of residence; great mortality took place amongst them; and at last it was resolved to remove the miserable remnant that was left to Oyster Cove. Their number was then reduced to forty-four, and there were no infants amongst them. And so it went on, until in October, 1864, one man alone remained, named William Lanné. The *Hobart Town Mercury* of that date says: "At the last ball at Government House, Hobart Town, there appeared the last male aboriginal inhabitant of Tasmania. He was accompanied by three aboriginal females, the sole living representatives of the race beside himself, but not of such an age or such an appearance as to justify the expectation of any future addition to their numbers." Lanné became a whaler. When the Duke of Edinburgh was in Tasmania, in January, 1868, he warmly greeted the aboriginal king, who, clad in a blue suit, with a gold-lace band round his hat, walked proudly with the prince, conscious (says Mr. Bonwick) that they alone were in possession of royal blood. But on the 5th of March, 1869, we find this sad record in one of the local papers: "Launé had an unfortunate propensity for beer and rum, and was seldom sober when on shore. He was paid off on Saturday last, when he received a balance of wages and lay amounting to £12 13s. 5d. He took up his residence at the "Dog and Partridge" public-house, at the corner of Goulbourn and Barrack Streets, and died of a severe attack of English cholera. His body was removed to the Colonial Hospital, where it awaits burial, and to-morrow the grave will close over the last male aboriginal of Tasmania." Mr. Bonwick closes his "Last of the Tasmanians" with these words: "The 'last man' has gone. The woolly-haired Tasmanian no longer sings blithely on the stringy-bark tiers, or twines the snowy clematis blossom for his bride's garland. The concern awakened for his condition comes too late. The bell but tolls his knell, and the Æolian music of the she-oak is his hymn and requiem. We cover our faces while the deep and solemn voice of our common Father echoes through the soul 'Where is thy brother!' Oh, if he were here how kindly would we speak to him! Would we not smile upon that dark sister of the forest, and joy in the prattle of that piccaninny boy? And would not the Christian cheek, once pale with reproaches and tearful with penitence, glow with delight to tell of a found Saviour to the lost savage? But now the burden of each saddened spirit is,

'*Would I had loved him more.*'"

Colonel Arthur's administration extended over the long period of twelve years, and he left the colony in October, 1836. He was succeeded by a man of a character totally different to his own—the mild and benevolent Sir John Franklin. He continued in office for seven years, and during that time, or rather for the greater part of it, the colony went on steadily progressing. Shortly after his arrival he made a tour through the island, and was much struck with all that he saw. The people of Launceston were specially pleased with his visit, for they had a grievance. They found that "Hobart Town was the island," and that Launceston, with its very great advantages of soil and position, was all but ignored. Sad altercations were carried on at this time between the government officials and the free settlers, which all the kindly efforts of Sir John and Lady Franklin could not allay.

Up to this time the day schools for the working classes were entirely under the control of the Church of England, subject to the government regulations; but in 1838 the British and Foreign system was introduced. The archdeacon at this time was an old college friend of Bishop Broughton's, named Hutchins, and he protested against any change in the plan, as did also the first bishop (Nixon) on his arrival; but no alteration was made during Sir John Franklin's term of office.

Shortly before Colonel Arthur left his government he was anxious to establish a grammar school on liberal principles, and the head mastership was offered to and accepted by the Rev. Mr. Rusden. But it did not get on. Shortly after my own arrival in the colony the governor kindly laid a proposition before me, offering the head mastership of a somewhat similar institution to me, with a large salary annexed to it; but I did not feel myself at liberty to accede to His Excellency's wishes, and so the matter was left in abeyance. When Sir John arrived the question was re-opened, and in 1839 he put himself in communication with the late Dr. Arnold, of Rugby, on the subject. An old and favourite pupil of Dr. Arnold's—the Rev. J. P. Gell, now incumbent of St. John's, Notting Hill—was appointed to the mastership, but after existing for a brief time it was closed. A proprietary school on a more liberal basis was afterwards suggested, and after some time was established.

Lady Franklin was a great benefactress to the colony. She spent nearly £1,000 in endeavouring to extirpate the venomous black snake, giving a bonus of a shilling for every one which was brought in to her.

Poor Sir John Franklin! His subsequent career and his martyr's death are known but too well. I hold him, and with reason, in affectionate remembrance. On one occasion I was voyaging in company with Lady Franklin from Sydney to Hobart Town; the owner of the ship had just sold it, but having a few days' provisions on board, he asked the purchaser to allow him to utilize them by taking the party down. On the third day we were signalized at Hobart Town as entering the channel; but then a fearful hurricane arose and blew us off the coast, drove us past New Zealand, where we were under bare poles for more than a month. Nearly all our provisions were gone, we had barely enough to keep life in us. The crew were disabled and were unable to work the ship, and all hope that we should be saved appeared to be gone. We were meanwhile mourned as lost. I was residing at this time at Boa Vista, which is situated at some distance from town, but Sir John Franklin regularly every morning sent his orderly out to my house with the news from the telegraph station to my family. And at last the good old sailor-governor ordered out the government schooner, went on board himself, and cruised about for a long period, and at last providentially picked us up, had us removed on board, fed us little by little as we were able to bear it, with great judgment; and thus, after a *seven weeks'* cruise—a longer time than it now takes to make the voyage out from England—brought us to the haven where we would be.

This voyage I remember was full of mishaps. When I first went on board in Sydney Harbour to select my cabin, the steward drew back in order to open the door, I was behind him, and stepped away to give him space, not seeing that the hatch was off leading into the main hold, and I fell backwards to the bottom of the ship among a number of oil casks. I was completely stunned. On coming to myself I heard them say, "Poor fellow, he's done for!" But when they drew me up by ropes it was found, thank God, that I was *not* done for; no limb was broken. A little brandy and water was given to me and it revived me, and though I was lame for a long time, I completely recovered. I remarked just now that we had privations to endure during this voyage. One thing however appeared to be plentiful. Did you ever hear of Holloway's Pills? There was a sick woman on board. The captain had great faith in these pills; he administered them in oft-increasing doses, till at last she took so many, that they were mashed up in a saucer and eaten something like pease-pudding. The poor creature died, and I consigned her body to the deep, till that day when, at the sound of the Archangel's trumpet, the sea shall give up its dead. One day I was sauntering through the empty hold of the ship, and amongst the ballast I kicked against something, which turned out to be a keg of tripe. O, what a luxury did we deem it. It served us by careful management for dinner for many days. I never see tripe now, after a lapse of nearly thirty years, without thinking well of it, and my mind reverts with satisfaction to the boon we then considered it. Lady Franklin had on board a favourite Arab mare. Unknown to her ladyship, we sat in solemn council on the life of this beast more than once, and nothing but a strong desire to please her saved its life. Had we been out much longer it would undoubtedly have proved our only food.

Sir John Franklin was with Captain Flinders on his voyage of discovery, and held his memory in great veneration. Accordingly Lady Franklin went to Port Lincoln, *viâ* Adelaide, for the purpose of erecting a monument to his memory. An obelisk was put up entirely at Sir John's expense, and bearing a suitable inscription. It cost £250.

The sum of £60,000 was voted about this time for the introduction of free immigrants. But the plan adopted did not succeed, and great dissatisfaction existed in the minds of the immigrants when they found they had to compete with prison labour. After a period of unusually high prices and of mad speculation, a great crash came, which seemed to threaten universal ruin. Wheat was down to half-a-crown a bushel, and sheep to half-a-crown a head. But somehow there is such elasticity in a new country that, phœnix-like, she seems to rise from her ashes with new vigour. And such after a time was the case here. Sir John's recall was very hasty and unexpected. Although many persons might differ with him as to some of his public acts, all were agreed in this, that he was a man of deep and unaffected piety, and of a most philanthropic disposition.

Sir Eardley Wilmot, formerly M.P. for Warwickshire, assumed the reins of government in 1843.

The same struggles between the two great classes agitated his term of office. A formidable petition was got up against him by many of the leading colonists, praying for his recall. The Secretary of State for the colonies saw reasons for acceding to their request, and he was superseded. At this time, however, he was in a very delicate state of health, and he only survived his recall a period of about three months, and died at Hobart Town. He was buried in St. David's burial-ground, near to the tomb of Governor Collins.

After a brief interval, during which the government was administered by Mr. La Trobe, who was afterwards first the superintendent and then the governor of Victoria, Sir W. T. Denison arrived as governor of the colony, to assume the reins of office. For some time past the Home Government had been pouring in convicts in increased numbers, greatly to the annoyance of the free population. Petitions were got up against Lord Stanley's probation system. It was found that 5,500 prisoners were scattered over the country in twenty gangs. The petitioners prayed that by degrees a total abolition of transportation should take place. The Cape colonists refused to let convicts land; Victoria did the same; and Sir Charles Fitzroy was desired to send away the cargo by the *Harkaway*, even at the cost of the colony. Tasmania could not go thus far, but a feeling so strong was excited, that it hastened on the time for the total cessation of transportation.

The great Australian League was formed in 1851. It was "The League and Solemn Engagement of the Australian Colonies, declared by the Delegates in the Conference held at Melbourne." The different delegates took this pledge:—

"1st. That they engage not to employ any person hereafter arriving under sentence of transportation for crime committed in Europe.

"2nd. That they will use all the powers they possess—official, electoral, and legislative, to prevent the establishment of English prisons or penal settlements within their bounds, &c.

"3rd. That they solemnly engage with each other to support by their advice, their money, and their countenance, all who may suffer in the lawful promotion of this cause."

These bold and united steps on behalf of the colonies had due effect. But whilst the agitation was at its height, the discovery of *gold* took place, first in Sydney and then in Victoria; and statesmen in England at once saw that England's penal settlements could not be in such close proximity to the rich gold-fields of the mainland. On the 10th August, 1853, the despatch announcing the discontinuance of transportation reached the colony. The greatest joy prevailed. It was just fifty years since the formation of the settlement, and the jubilee was right merrily kept.

When Sir W. Denison left Tasmania for New South Wales, a purse of 2,000 guineas was presented to him by the colonists.

Hitherto the officer at the head of the government

had been only a lieutenant-governor, but from this time he became "Governor-in-Chief of Tasmania." Sir Henry Young was the first who held this rank. He had been governor of South Australia before his removal. He was the first civilian who had held the office of governor. Sir W. Denison before leaving had predicted that the cessation of transportation would convert Hobart Town into a fishing village. But the time for its decay had not come yet. The gold-fields in the neighbouring colonies raised the price of all colonial produce to so high a rate, that trade was brisk and money plentiful. In 1865 the colonists subscribed no less a sum than £26,294 for the relief of the widows and children of those who had fallen in the Crimea. It was very tantalizing to the Tasmanians to see gold so abundant in the neighbouring colonies, while they themselves were without a gold-field. Fingal had been suggested as a likely place for gold. The government devoted £2,000 towards a fair trial of the ground, and that there *was* gold was evident from the fact that about 120 ounces were obtained. As yet no paying field has been opened, but strong hopes are still entertained, and by those too whose geological knowledge is very considerable, that it is but a question of time, and Tasmania will be found to be auriferous. Sir Henry Young left the colony in 1861, and then came Colonel Gore Brown. He had to contend with many difficulties. Responsible government, when but recently established, and an empty treasury, are great trials. The capital is now lighted with gas; an International Exhibition was held in Hobart Town; a handsome Town Hall has been erected there, near the new monument to the memory of Sir John Franklin, and not far from the site of the old Government House in Macquarie Street.

The present governor is Mr. Du Cane. This gentleman was formerly M.P. for Maldon, in Essex. He married the only daughter of the late Lord Lyndhurst. The family residence is Baxter Park, Essex. When in parliament he was an unflinching advocate of the agricultural interest, and great hopes are entertained of the benefits likely to arise to the colony from his administration.

Tasmania has up to this time had a great many serious drawbacks to its prosperity. First, its being overcrowded with prisoners, so that at length free immigration was diverted from its shores, and many of its wealthy and most respectable colonists left it; then, the settlements of South Australia and of Port Phillip drew away merchants and settlers, as well as a large proportion of the free labourers; and before it had time to rally from these drawbacks there came the discovery of gold in New South Wales, Victoria, and New Zealand. The southern part of the island suffered most severely, because Launceston had still a good deal of trade with the gold colony. House property became a drug in the market, so that many landlords who had previously been considered in prosperous circumstances, had to begin life afresh. But notwithstanding the present depression, we feel confident that ere long things will take a turn, and this island will become a favourite residence. Many of the old inhabitants, whose estates are in the hands of the banks, may probably have to succumb; but it cannot but be that a country for which nature has done so much, will rise superior to her present difficulties, and become a prosperous home for large numbers of people. The government are doing all in their power to attract population. Strange to say, little or nothing is known of great part of the island to the present day. When the exploring spirit which has up to this time been diverted to discovery on the mainland turns its attention thitherward, we may hear of much that will help to develop its undoubtedly great resources, and cover the land with the homesteads of the industrious. An Act has lately passed proposing liberal terms to those who are disposed to become residents in the island. The following epitome of the land regulations will be read with interest :—

"Any person desirous of proceeding from Europe to Tasmania to settle there, on paying his own passage out shall be entitled to a grant of land of the value of £18 for himself, with a like grant for every person of the age of 15 years and upwards whose passage money he pays, and to a grant of the value of £9 for every immigrant child between the age of twelve months and 15 years he so brings out with him. Again, any person arriving in the colony from Europe or India, with a view of settling in it, whose passage money has been paid by himself as a cabin or intermediate passenger, and who has not previously received or accepted any order for a grant of land as above referred to, shall be entitled to demand thirty acres of land for himself, and, supposing him to be a married man with a family, he shall also be entitled to demand twenty acres of land for his wife and ten acres for each child, provided that be done within twelve months of the date of arrival. In neither case, however, is the grant of such land to be issued until the person claiming it has resided five years in the colony, although the person claiming the grant may reside on the land and cultivate it."

Small as this island is there are great parts of it up to this moment quite unknown, and although much of it may prove unfit for cultivation, it cannot be doubted that there is a large area which will eventually be thickly populated. The whole island has so greatly the advantage of the mainland in the number of its rivers and the abundance of its supplies of fine fresh water. In point of climate, too, it has to my mind the advantage over all the other colonies for persons coming from Europe.

Beyond the remarks on this subject which I made in the introductory chapter, I would refer to some valuable information on this subject, contained in the "Official Record of the Intercolonial Exhibition of 1866-7," to which I have already been so much indebted. The great salubrity of the climate is universally admitted. In that respect it has the advantage not only of the Australian mainland, but of most parts of the world. It is neither too hot in summer nor too cold in winter to be agreeable. At all seasons of the year, but especially in summer, it is the resort of visitors from the other colonies. An old resident in Tasmania, Dr. Hall, bears his testimony on this point to the following effect. He says that the island has an undulating surface throughout; that its highest mountains only attain a height of 5,000 feet in two instances; that the country rises from all its shores gradually to its central watershed, along which is arrayed a chain of lakes that give origin to the principal rivers of the island; that these rivers generally have a rapid fall, and marshes are certainly exceptional; that the northern side of the colony has a warmer and moister climate than the southern; that there are no volcanoes and no earthquakes. Again, during the summer months a cool south-east breeze may be expected to set in about 11 a.m. and is very bracing and refreshing. The climate is decidedly breezy and invigorating, for after the hottest day one may calculate on having a cool night. With reference to the effects of the climate on health, Dr. Hall says: " Invalids from China, India, and the hotter colonies of Australia, if not past recovery, mend speedily in Tasmania, and the increased appetite for food is the first and most surprising change. With such clear skies, abundance of ozone, and bracing sea breezes, the lamp of life burns quickly as well as brightly, and demands a much more abundant and nutritious supply of food than suffices elsewhere.

Food of the best and most varied kind is plentiful, and the actual consumption per individual greatly exceeds the highest European calculations. Tasmanians spend much of their time in the open air, and many of the diseases which afflict European communities are unknown, others have a minimum of intensity. Even eruptive fevers, scarlatina and measles, though frequently imported, and at times severe, have speedily worn themselves out, only re-appearing at long intervals and in mild type."

Tasmania has always been a favourite resort of officers from India when on furlough. This was more frequently the case formerly than it is now, because of the facility of reaching Europe speedily by means of the P. and O. steamers. In 1858 a commission, presided over by Colonel Hamilton, reported in substance as follows, on the subject of the probable effects which would result from the establishment of a Military Medical Sanitarium in Tasmania. That the salubrity of the climate is equal, if not superior, to that of the healthiest part of Europe; and for the restoration of health to those who suffer from the diseases incidental to exposure in a tropical climate, better than that of any other in the world. That the voyage from Calcutta or Bombay to Hobart Town, in the steam vessels which carry Her Majesty's mails, would be performed in less than a month; the accommodation would be good, and an immediate change to a better climate. That Tasmania could be reached more readily than the Hill Sanatoria, in the Himalayas; the prospect of restoration to health greater, and the house accommodation better; and that 2,000 men could be received and housed and attended at small expense. It came out in evidence before the Commission that the mortality amongst the troops during fifteen years had not been quite 8 in 1,000, whilst in England it was 33, in India 50, in China 103.

The Parliamentary Librarian of Victoria, Mr. James Smith, visited the island in 1865, and delivered a lecture on the subject of his impressions, which was received enthusiastically by the audience, and was afterwards published. He was greatly struck with the thoroughly English character of all he saw. He travelled from Launceston to Hobart Town, which charmed him greatly. He says, "The coach was English, the pace was English, and even the very inns and wayside villages were English. I almost expected to see the village green, the worm-eaten stocks, and the waggon-headed tents of the wandering gypsies; to hear the caw of the rooks wheeling homeward from the upland fallows, and to catch a glimpse of an ivy-mantled tower peeping from its leafy covert in some sequestered nook. I don't think I should have been very much astonished if I had come upon an old English pound, with Mr. Pickwick seated on a wheelbarrow in the middle of it, looking the picture of perplexity, and amazed at the pertinacious curiosity of the bystanders. The rosy faces of the children, too, smacked of the old country. Many of the houses I passed had a square, solid, substantial look about them, suggestive of permanence and comfort. They seemed to say, 'Look at us! We were not run up by a speculative contractor the week before last; and we have no intention of tumbling down the week after next.'" In very felicitous language he describes the glorious view from the top of Mount Wellington, whence "The city itself sloping to the water's edge looks like a collection of the tiniest of toy houses, dropped by a child in careless play; and the altitude at which you stand, coupled with the amazing extent of country comprehended in the view, enables you to realise the prospect visible from a balloon." One more extract we must just find room for: "There is a green lane at New Norfolk, than which I know of nothing more thoroughly English in the pages of Mary Russell Mitford, or on the canvas of Gainsborough, Constable, or Creswick; or in the beautiful county of Kent itself. All the elements of the picturesque are there—the lofty hedgerows, white with blossom in the spring and crimson with berries in the autumn, the luxuriant foliage, the winding lane, the sweet breath of the new-mown hay, the sweep of the scythe through the long bush grass, and the rustic bridge spanning a brawling brook; the hop-gardens, with their long drawn aisles of vivid green, the delicate curves and spiral movements of the graceful vine, the sunshine dropping in golden rifts, and the shadows falling in dark brown lines—all hint of good old Saxon Kent; so do the gurgling rivulets that wind away in the secrecy and darkness among the pollard willows, until they empty their waters into a stream, cool, shadowy, transparent and impetuous—such as Sir Humphrey Davy or Christopher North would have delighted to angle in, and old Izaak Walton have loved to have written about."

Some years ago a Committee of the Assembly was appointed to consider and report on the introduction of salmon into Tasmania. Messrs. Youl and Edward Wilson, who were residing in England, entered heartily into the matter. After several failures Messrs. Money, Wigram and Sons, the great Australian ship owners, offered, in 1864, to send the ova out in one of their fine clipper ships, and it has now proved a complete success.

The Church of England in the colony has now for its head the Right Rev. Dr. Bromby, who was formerly principal of the Cheltenham Training College. He is the son of the late venerable vicar of Hull, and the brother of the popular head master of the Melbourne Church of England Grammar School (Rev. Dr. Bromby). The Church in Tasmania has lately suffered a severe loss in the death of Sir Richard Dry. His remains are interred under the communion table of Hagley Church, which was built at his expense and to which he gave an endowment of £400 a year.

The editor of the *Melbourne Argus*, having received the latest statistics of the island, devotes a leading article to the subject, which is so important, that we offer no apology for transferring it to our pages entire. He says :—

"Tasmania is bound to progress some day, having, in certain natural circumstances, so much the advantage of the mainland colonies, which are progressive now. She has a finer climate, a more picturesque and better watered surface, and the special facilities for trade offered by an insular position. She has superior forests and fisheries, orchards and gardens; and though the search for gold appears to be a delusion, there are a variety of minerals, including coal. And, as will bye-and-bye prove the not least important fact, her shores are within easy reach of the principal city and busiest port in the hemisphere, the headquarters of Australasian enterprise and capital. These things are sure to tell in time, but the time has not come round yet, as we see by the report furnished for the year 1868 by the Government statistician, Mr. Nowell. There is some improvement, but, in the main, the figures repeat the same story as in previous years. The tide has not yet turned. Progress has not yet begun. Other colonies, with their gold-fields, their more commercial towns, their more energetic life, induce a yearly emigration from Tasmania; and population, industry, and trade do not advance. The change must be effected, the impetus must come from without. But the leading colonies are still too much occupied with the development of their own resources to spare attention to those of Tasmania. And when their activity does overflow, it is attracted just now to other quarters. The rapid spread of gold-discovery in New Zealand, with its attendant mercantile openings, the growing of high-priced tropical produce in Fiji and Queensland, and the unlocking of a vast expanse of grazing land in the centre and north of the continent, all combine to delay the investment of Australian capital beyond Bass's Straits.

"The population of the island at the end of last year was 100,706, of which fifty-six per cent. were males. The increase during the year was 2,251, to which immigration contributed 723 persons. The year before, the number of arrivals was 3,559, and of departures 4,025; in 1868 the arrivals were 5,043, and the departures 4,320. And we see that an emigration agent was despatched to Germany, for Germans being less ambitious and restless than the British emigrant, are more likely to settle down on the soil and not be attracted away to the gold countries. As for the increase of births over deaths, ' so low a rate has not occurred since 1858, the furthest date to which the investigation was carried.' And there appears to have been for years a constant decrease in the ratio of births to deaths—so much so, that if it continue, 'all accession to the population from that source would in little more than seven years entirely cease.' The circumstance is not accounted for. The climate is favourable to health, and the emigration, though composed almost entirely of the grown youth, should be more considerable to cause it. The births in 1867 were 2,971, and the deaths 1,418; the births in 1868 were 2,990, and the deaths 1,464.

"Imports decreased last year by the value of £11,196. In 1867 they amounted to £856,348 sterling; in 1868 to £845,152. But exports, £920,820 in 1868, showed an increase of £130,326 on the previous year—being the largest increase in any two consecutive years since 1857. The imports are principally from and through Victoria. About half as much comes directly from the United Kingdom. The Mauritius, with a long interval, ranks next, and New South Wales is close behind. Nearly half the exports go to the United Kingdom, more than a fourth to Victoria, and New South Wales comes next, followed by New Zealand. There is only a trifling trade with the other colonies, and none with foreign countries, except now and then a cargo from China, Valparaiso, or Calcutta. It is only in Launceston, as the northern port, that the enlargement of exports is exhibited. The shipments of wool, we are told, exceeded any year since 1858, and were thirty per cent. more than last year. Of barley, also, there was a great increase, and, in minor degree, of bran and pollard, flour, oats, hops, sperm oil, sawn and hewn timber, and vegetables; and a diminution in bark, butter, cheese, fruit, wheat, hides, leather, horses, and sheep.

"As regards the consumption of various necessaries and luxuries some interesting statistics are given. There is a remarkable and beneficial change in the drinking habits of the population. In 1838, the consumption of spirits per head was 2 gal.; in 1851, it was 1·1 gal.; in 1857, 1·7.; in 1861, 1·2 gal.; and in 1868, only 0·66 gal. In the United Kingdom in 1867 the consumption was 0·98 gal. The report remarks:—'It is not easy to say with any certainty what are the causes of this decrease in the consumption of spirits. Some have supposed that it is brought about by the substitution of malt liquors of home produce; but here we are met by the significant fact that the number of breweries was returned as 38 in 1858, and only 31 in 1868. The emigration of large numbers of working men, the increase of 2s. per gallon in the duty on rum in 1863, and the general decline in the consuming power of the people, must certainly have had a large share in causing the decline.' Such causes, however, cannot fully explain the fact. For our part, we feel no hesitation in ascribing it to the naturalisation of the inhabitants. The taste for intoxicating drinks is not among the faults of the native-born in these colonies. It is a taste which weakens with each successive generation, and the Tasmanian settlement is now several generations old. Moreover, as the period of the convict system becomes more distant, the habits of the populace naturally improve. As for other articles, the consumption per head in the five years 1859-1863 was of tea, 7·40 lb.; sugar, 91·41 lb., and tobacco, 1·93 lb. In the five succeeding years, namely, 1864-1868, the rate was, of tea 6·08 lb.; sugar, 70·29 lb., and tobacco, 1·58 lb. But though Tasmania is just now the least prosperous of these colonies, the consumption of articles which are necessaries is nearly double that in the United Kingdom. There in 1867 the proportion was, of tea only 3·68 lb., and sugar 40·58 lb.; of tobacco it was 1·35 lb. We agree with the report that nothing can more clearly prove how much better is the condition of the people than it is in old countries.

"An Australian Customs union is strongly urged. To illustrate the want, 'we need only point to the injury which Tasmania suffers in her trade from the duty imposed in Victoria on her grain, timber, and fruit.' A keen public sense of this requirement has now grown up in all the colonies as well as Tasmania.

"The shipping returns are favourable. The tonnage inwards for the three years 1866-7-8, is set down respectively at 107,903, 93,390, and 110,553. Outwards the figures are 106,065, 102,754, and 111,491. There were six more whaling ships than in 1867, with 150 additional men, and the increased value of the produce was £29,000, or 130 per cent. Of coal 9,054 tons were raised against 8,341 in the previous year. As to debt, 'the actual indebtedness' of the public treasury is £727,400. The general revenue amounted to £333,069, being an increase of £60,116 on 1867. The insolvencies were 63 against 107 in 1867, and the number of persons tried in the Supreme Court was 87 against 127. The returns of crops and live stock having arrived late, are added in an appendix to the report without a comparison with 1867, but we are told that there is 'an absence of agricultural improvement.' Two lines of railway—the Launceston and Western, and the Mersey and Deloraine—are in construction, and a survey has been made for one between Hobart Town and Launceston. As a whole, these statistics for last year exhibit some improvement, though still very far short of the required change."

His Excellency the Governor, in proroguing the Parliament, read the speech which we give below:—

"HONOURABLE GENTLEMEN OF THE LEGISLATIVE COUNCIL, AND GENTLEMEN OF THE HOUSE OF ASSEMBLY.

"1. In relieving you from further attendance in Parliament,

I desire to thank you for the earnest devotion which you have manifested in discharging the responsible duties that devolved upon you.

"2. I announce to you with pleasure that the official accounts of the progress of gold discoveries, in various parts of the island, continue to sustain the expectation of improved material prosperity as the result of the successful development of the mineral wealth of the colony.

"3. I acknowledge with satisfaction the patience and assiduity with which you have prosecuted your Parliamentary duties; and congratulate you upon the large amount of useful legislation that has resulted from the labours of the session, and upon the enactment of several measures for amending and consolidating the laws affecting the interests of the trading and commercial classes.

"4. In the Acts to authorise the construction of a Main Line of Railway, and the completion of other large and useful public works, you have consulted the general anxiety and growing demand for extended and improved means of internal communication, with a due regard to the financial capabilities of the colony. I anticipate the happiest results from this recognition of the first and principal requirements of a new and mainly agricultural country.

"5. I trust that the appointment of a Minister of Lands and Works will ensure the efficient control and more economical working of the important branches of the public service intended to be combined under the new department.

"6. The provision which you have made for taking a census of the population early in the ensuing year will supply a valuable groundwork for revising the existing system of the representation of the people in Parliament.

"7. It may be reasonably hoped that the measures which you have passed to permit distillation, and to encourage manufactures from colonial products, will prove beneficial both to the agricultural and the industrial interests of the country.

"8. I thank you for the Supplies you have granted for the service of the year: and desire to express my gratification that you have been enabled to make suitable provision for the public requirements without imposing any additional burdens on the people.

"9. I entertain an earnest hope that the various measures to which I have referred, and the general effect of your legislation, may be found to conduce, under the Divine blessing, to the happiness and well-being of the community.

"I now declare this Parliament prorogued to the 2nd day of June next."

There appears some hope that the anxious wish of the inhabitants as to the discovery of gold will be promptly gratified :—

"Some half dozen gentlemen from Ballarat arrived in Launceston, and sent two of their number to Waterhouse to examine and report. The report was most favourable; and the result was the formation of a company, whose office was to be in Ballarat, but with some of the directory in Tasmania. The shares were launched at £5, and subsequently increased to £7 10s. It is understood that all that were meant to be disposed of in Tasmania were taken up, and now we await the result. Some disappointment has been felt that operations have not been gone about more speedily. The principal claim, the Pioneers', has been in the possession of the company for some weeks, but no men have as yet been set to work. Meantime a partial reef-seeking mania has set in; scores are now at Waterhouse prospecting, and claims innumerable have been taken up. A small steamer has made her first trip, and is again advertised for a second; and the prospects of a veritable gold-field in this colony are discussed with greater eagerness than the probable results of the Australasian harvest. Nor is Fingal behind with her claims, which Ballarat is to take advantage of also. There, at the Break-o'-Day, have the good folks from the mining capital taken interests, and are again arranging to float another company. The country the inspectors saw there surprised them, being rich beyond their anticipations. Although all is not gold that glitters, a spirit seems to be now abroad which in the end may set at rest that question which, although before us for years, has so pertinaciously remained in doubt."

The last mail has brought an encouraging account from the new gold-field :—

"The Waterhouse diggings are now assuming such proportions that the opening up a proper means of communication with that gold-field has become a necessity so well recognised by Government that the Director of Public Works accompanied by Mr. Gunn, Assistant Commissioner of Crown Lands, is on the 16th inst. to commence an inspection of the country, and the best routes for a road. These gentlemen will generally make themselves acquainted with whatever may be necessary for the convenience of persons travelling to or from the diggings, or the accommodation of those located there, and report thereon to Government, who will acting on that report do whatever is necessary for the development of the diggings and opening up of the country. Without full information not only as to the work required, but also the probable permanency of the diggings, the hon. the Treasurer could not under his pledge to Parliament expend any of the money placed at his disposal for roads in the Waterhouse district, but fortified by such a report, the necessary roads will be at once proceeded with, the condition attached by Parliament to the vote having been fulfilled."

The commercial article of the *Hobart Town Mercury* gives a cheering account of things in the island :—

"Although we cannot report any considerable improvement in business since our last summary of news for the home mails on the 9th October, yet a busier month has been passed by our commercial classes. The arrival of two London vessels, the *Ethel* and *Sea Wave*, with general cargoes, and in the case of the *Ethel* a large one, and the unprecedented arrival of a vessel direct from the Mauritius with a cargo of sugars, has naturally given a spurt to business. The approach of the wool season and the preparations of the jam makers, with the brightening prospects of the agricultural classes, have also tended to throw a spirit of hopefulness and an appearance of bustle amongst our community which has not of late pervaded it. The drapery trade still seems the most depressed, and wholesale houses are heavily stocked both by direct shipments, and by imports *viâ* Melbourne. With the retail branch of this trade, the same complaints of dealers prevail that was reported last month. The grocery and ironmongery trades are in a better state, though we have to report the failure of one small house in the latter trade, for a small amount, principally affecting Victorian houses. In our last we noticed the splendid rains that the country had been favoured with, and the favourable appearance of the crops in consequence; after the lapse of a month it is gratifying to again be able to record that the hopes of the farmers have every prospect of being fulfilled. The weather has been most seasonable, fine warm days have alternated with refreshing showers, and the growth of all descriptions of vegetation has been marvellous. A large breadth of land has been placed in crop, and all hands will be busy in another month or two in securing the fruits of their winter and spring labours. The hop-gardens are said to be in fine bearing this year, and we shall have a considerably increased yield on last year's produce of the rapidly extending export. Shearing has commenced in several districts, and we yesterday noticed the arrival of the first lot of country packed wool, for shipment per *Ethel*. The wools this year, from the fine feed that has prevailed, and the abundance of water for washing, will be in good condition, and notwithstanding the ravages of the scab in some quarters, it is anticipated that from the increased care observed in the preparation of the wools for market, that the character of the Tasmanian flocks will be fully maintained by this year's exports. It is not expected that there will be any falling off in quantity. The first wool ship that will leave this port for London will be the *Ethel*, Captain Harmsworth, who expects to sail somewhere between Christmas Day and the New Year. The *Ethel* will be followed by the new ship the *Runnymede*, Captain Hay. It is not possible at present to say when she will get away. The cargo of sugars ex *Tasso*, imported direct from the Mauritius by Messrs. Crosby and Pearce, was disposed of by public auction and privately, and realised fair prices, fully sustaining previous rates. Another cargo of sugars is expected daily, per *Argo*, from the same port, to the order of Askin Morrison, Esq.

"At the time of the departure of the last mail, the Houses of Parliament were in session. They have since been prorogued, and the several measures we then noticed as under consideration, which have a direct bearing on the commercial prospects of the community, have become law, having received the royal assent at the hands of the Governor, Charles Du Cane, Esq. The principal item of these, and as more directly having reference to the London Money Market, is the authority granted to the Governor-in-Council to issue, as a bonus, the sum of £300,000, in six per cent. debentures, to any company that will undertake to construct and work a Main Line Railway from Hobart Town to Launceston. The Government have the power of offering any such company the option of having £25,000 paid them annually for a period of 20 years, in lieu of the total sum of £300,000. We refer to another column for fuller details of the measure, merely remarking that the grounds on which hopes are placed of this railway, if constructed, giving an increased prosperity to the colony, are the effect railways have always produced where constructed between great centres of population. The other measures which affect our commercial or pastoral interests, are the Bill for the production of colonial industries, such as the establishment of woollen factories, salt factories, and the growth of sugar from beet-root, by the offer of bonuses. The only one at present started of these factories, is one on a small scale for the manufacture of salt, by evaporating the salt water of the sea. It is calculated to turn out about 20 tons per week, and if successfully conducted will stop shipments from home to the other colonies to some extent.

The Scab Bill has become law, and its effects will be apparent in the course of a season or two, but for the first eighteen months its provisions are only precautionary, and admonitory, to the sheepowners, but if at the expiration of that period the flocks are still found to be scabby, the penal clauses of the Bill will begin to take effect, so that virtually the sheepowner is allowed 18 months to clean his sheep, and if after that period he has not got rid of the scab from his flock, he comes under the supervision of the Inspector.

"Our money market presents few features to notice. Money is plentiful for all discount purposes, and the banks report that trade bills are well met. There have been a few share sales during the month, the largest of them to-day, when 85 shares in the Tasmanian Steam Navigation Company were offered at auction, by Messrs. Guesdon and Westbrook, and all sold at £11 per share, being an advance of 7s. per share since the last reported sales, when £10 13s. was realised. Some Tasmanian Debentures, 6 per cent., were also disposed of by auction on the 29th October, and realised £107 to £108.

". Consequent on the fine season, and the news that the other colonies had received abundant rains, and so saved their crops, the breadstuffs market has been depressed ever since last mail. Shortly after the departure of the mail, wheat receded from 7s. to 6s. 6d., and it now hangs at from 6s. 3d. to 6s. 6d. Flour also receded to £15, and these prices still prevail, with great heaviness in the market, the demand being entirely confined to local wants. We shall, however, be dependent on the northern side of the island for some month or two, before our harvest comes in, but the price continues on the decline there, and wheat is quoted in Launceston at 6s. Flour, £13 10s. Potatoes, which were in large demand for export at our last mail at £5 5s., have continued in fair demand during the early part of the month, but have recently declined in value to £3 10s., and the export demand has slackened. With the exception of butter, all other colonial products remain as at last. Butter has fallen to about 10d. to 1s. per lb., the large quantity of fresh now coming into the market preventing the sale of the potted.

"A considerable quantity of bark will be shipped home this year, both by vessels direct and *via* Melbourne. The present price for green bark is £2 per ton; for dry long, £3 to £3 10s. is the quotation.

"We may mention that the first lot of washed fleece wool loose, arrived in town this morning. It was scarcely of sufficient quantity to test the local market for loose lots. The same party obtained 8½d. last year for his clip. This year he sold at the same price. Generally growers look to obtaining last year's rates, but the feeling of buyers tends to a decline of a 1d. to 2d. per lb. The sale to-day would tend to show that growers will obtain their prices.

"There have been no meetings of our public companies since our last. The prices of shares are well maintained, showing that money for investment is abundant. There has been another company formed on the northern side of the island for working one of the reefs discovered at Waterhouse, making two companies now in existence. The certainty of the commercial value of the reefs at Fingal is now established without a doubt, the government having deputed a gentleman named Hurst to inspect the locality, and act as gold commissioner. Mr. Hurst has returned to town after a sojourn on the spot of some time, and the government have decided on his report to erect buildings for a Commissioner's residence, and to accommodate a necessary Police Force. As the prospects of the colony as regards her gold reefs are fully reported on in another column, we refrain from repeating it here.

"Our whaling fleet continues successful, and there have been several arrivals of oil since our last, but we refer to our shipping columns for full information on this head. With respect to the quantity of sperm oil at present known to be afloat in colonial ships, it will be seen by reference to the reports of the whalers in our shipping columns, that there are 186 tuns of sperm oil in 9 vessels. In addition to this quantity, there are the takes of three vessels now in port, the *Emily Downing*, 68 tuns; the *Runnymede*, 62 tuns: together 130 tuns, 100 of which will be shipped by next Monday in the *Ethel*, leaving

30 for the *Windward*, in addition to the 9 tuns ex *Offley*. The 130 tuns of oil above mentioned, have been disposed of in this market to one firm, at about £76."

The rates of wages are not so high as in some of the other colonies. Still they are not to be despised. Coachmen get from £35 to £50 a year; grooms, £30 to £35; gardeners the same; female cooks, £25 to £30; laundresses, £25; housemaids, £20 to £22; nursemaids, £16 to £20; general servants, £20.

From all that we have said, it will be gathered that we think highly of this island as a place of residence. And we may safely recommend it to those for whom a mild but decidedly healthy climate and a charmingly picturesque country have attractions. Those who are in haste to be rich, and who love an exciting life, may probably do better elsewhere; but if you are content to "plod on," and are satisfied with making a comfortable living, Tasmania should present ample scope for any reasonable man.

Chapter IV.

WESTERN AUSTRALIA.

ALTHOUGH we have become well acquainted with the eastern and the southern coasts of New Holland, we have up to the present day but little knowledge of the western half of the continent. It is only now that the settlers, feeling that the land is taken up in the older or the more favourite localities, are turning their attention to new fields for the pasturage of their flocks and herds.

When, after the war with France, that country began to look about for new territories abroad, the English government, fearing lest she should carry out an intended project of settling on the west coast of Australia, sent out instructions to the governor of New South Wales to be beforehand with her, and to take formal possession of it in the name of England's king. This was done in 1826. Vancouver had, in 1792, discovered one of the finest roadsteads on the Australian coasts, King George's Sound, which is an inlet from the Indian Ocean. This was the place fixed on for a settlement. The town of Albany stands now on its site. All the country in the neighbourhood is a vast tract of sand; but the climate was found to be exceedingly good. The military occupation of this post was during the term of three years, during which the soldiers had to depend on the elder colonies for all such supplies as could not be obtained from the whaling ships which put in there.

About this time public attention in England was being directed to these far-off colonies. Some attractive books had been written, speaking in glowing terms of the climate and of the rapid progress which was being made on the sheep and cattle stations, the owners of which, aided by convict labour, were reaping a rich harvest. Still there was the great drawback—they were convict colonies. And though many men of good family and with some capital would like to follow in the prosperous career of which they read such satisfactory accounts, they could not make up their minds to go to "Botany Bay." After the agitation of the question for some time, it was suggested that Australia was a vast island continent, and there was ample room to found a *free* colony on its shores, so remote from the penal settlements as to run no risk of contamination from association. This was taken up at length by some of our aristocracy and by some members of Parliament. Sir Francis Vincent, Colonel Latour, and the Peel family took an active interest in the proposed colony. Large capitalists remembered the fortunes that had been made in the

American colonies, by obtaining vast tracts of freehold land on low terms, and so they looked forward to the probability of pursuing the same plan on the coasts of Australia. The plan being favourably received by the government, a commission was appointed for drawing up a kind of constitution for the new colony, and arranging the terms on which land should be acquired, and emigration carried out. The exact spot was settled by Captain Stirling, R.N., who had surveyed part of the western coast, and he was fixed upon as the first superintendent of the infant settlement. It is a vast colony, including all that portion of New Holland situated to the west of 129° east longitude. It is 1,280 miles from north to south and 800 miles from east to west. The area is 1,000,000 square miles, or eight times the size of Great Britain and Ireland. It was far enough off from the dreaded convict settlements, for Sydney was more than 3,000 miles away, and Van Diemen's Land 2,300. The commissioners fixed on Melville Harbour as the exact spot for the first settlement, into which "Swan River" flows. And so the colony was commonly known as the "Swan River Settlement." Persons taking out emigrants at their own cost, or introducing live stock, &c., had grants of land made to them on nominal terms, viz., one shilling and sixpence an acre. In fact *land* was the mode of paying salaries. All the government officers, surveyors and others, received part of their incomes in land. This all seemed so attractive that there was a perfect rush as to who should get on to the spot first so as to secure a priority in the selection. Endless confusion followed. Before the governor arrived several ships had got there, crowded with passengers, who knew not what to do or where to go. And we can very readily believe that they were sadly disheartened at all they saw on the shore. It was mid-winter, June, 1829, when they got there, and before the year was out twenty-five ships had landed their immigrants on the inhospitable shore. During the next year thirty more ships came in. Great delay took place in surveying the land. In the meanwhile the poor immigrants, many of whom were persons belonging to the upper classes, and knew nothing of "roughing" it in a new land, went just where they liked and settled themselves on the shore. All the eagerness to take possession of what they had considered in imagination as an "El Dorado" gave place to gloomy forebodings. Meanwhile provisions ran short; the settled colonies, whence supplies could have been drawn, were far off, and money was not very plentiful. Live stock had been introduced, both sheep and cattle, but there was some plant upon which they fed which killed them. And yet it was as a pastoral country which the greater part of the settlers had been looking forward to the occupancy of. The first settlement was named Perth. But it was found inconvenient to take the cargoes from the ships as they arrived to it, and so a seaport was established at the entrance to the harbour, fourteen miles distant by water, and which was called Freemantle. There was also a town-site called Clarence. Before two years had elapsed the most wretched accounts had reached England, and emigration thence was abandoned. An address was presented to Governor Stirling complaining most bitterly of their losses and of the wreck of all their fondly-cherished hopes. Amongst other grievances they found fault with the regulation which required that an amount equal to the value of the freehold had to be spent in permanent improvements, which in the great majority of cases proved to be useless; and that the preferential claims of officers in the army and the navy, and even of absentees, shut out the *bonâ fide* farmer from obtaining land so situated as to be of benefit to him. And so it went on struggling against the greatest difficulties till the year 1849. In the interior, many of the settlers who were in a position to do so, had gathered together the wreck of their substance, and left for those very colonies which they had originally so much despised—New South Wales and Tasmania. And it is a curious fact that the very colony which was fixed at so remote a point, in order to avoid any connection with convicts, should at this very time be *the* convict colony of Australia, and that too at the urgent solicitation of the colonists themselves. Governor Stirling left in 1838. His successor, Governor Hutt, was at the head of the colony for seven years. Colonel Clarke succeeded him; but he died in the following year. He was succeeded by Captain Fitzgerald in 1849. The colony recovered from its sadly depressed state, but by very slow degrees. The establishment of a settlement at Leschenhault Bay, named "Australind," was commenced in 1835, but proved a failure.

In 1849 it was found that the colony had a population of nearly 5,000; that 7,000 acres of land were under cultivation; the live stock numbered 157,855; the imports were £45,411; the exports £29,598; the shipping inwards 15,494 tons. This was the position of the colony just twenty years after its establishment. It seemed to have failed as a *free* colony, and so at this time the inhabitants prayed that it might be taken up as a receptacle for convicts. Up to this period the colony had borne a high character for morality, which, however, was very soon lost after the prayer of the petition from the people had been granted, and the colony became a large gaol.

At this time the members of the Church of England numbered three-fourths of the whole population. The other fourth was made up of Roman Catholics, 337; Wesleyans, 276; other Protestants, 311; Protestant Dissenters, 188. Archdeacon Hale was the local head of the Church of England; but since that time the colony has been erected into a bishopric, and the late archdeacon is now the Bishop of Perth. There were seven clergymen of the English Church, partly supported out of the proceeds of 8,000 acres of land; ten churches; several chapels, which were served by three ministers; and a Roman Catholic bishop, who had three priests under him.

The manner in which the aborigines were treated by the settlers at the Swan River stands out in favourable contrast with what we have seen in the other colonies. There was a kindness and consideration shown to them from the very commencement, which the natives themselves were not slow to appreciate; and it only shows us how different might have been the state of things in the other colonies if the same course had been pursued in them. The natives in Western Australia became the servants of the settlers; regular wages were given to them, and they proved invaluable, especially during that part of the colony's history when immigration all but ceased. The most pleasing accounts have reached us from time to time of the great progress in education made by the natives, both in the Church of England and Wesleyan institutions. In this colony the government gave the aborigines the same right as British subjects, and their disputes with the settlers are willingly referred to the English courts of law.

The English government, smarting under the increase of crime arising from the system of keeping their prisoners at home, gladly availed themselves of the opportunity of sending them out to this colony. Wishing to avoid the evils of the old system, it was arranged that they should not be assigned to the settlers, but should be employed in the construction of roads, bridges, and jetties, at the expense of the Home Government. After they had received their tickets-of-leave, they could enter into the service of the free inhabitants. At first all seemed to go well. There was a large expenditure of money, and great works were carried out to completion. But by-and-bye, when the lock was no longer turned on them in the gaols, but they began to mix in numbers among the colonists, then discontent arose. The settlers were alarmed at the great increase of crime, and the free labourer did not like the prisoner coming into competition with him, and thus lowering the rate of wages. In ten years 5,465 were sent out, and they cost the British government £180 a head!

And then in 1851 came the discovery of gold in New South Wales and in Victoria. As soon as this was known, the great body of free labourers—all those at least who could manage to do so—rushed away; and the prisoner population were eagerly on the look out for opportunities to escape to lands where honestly by labour, or dishonestly by depredation, they could get gold.

The colonies on the eastern shore had purged themselves of the convict element, and were not likely to bear quietly this wholesale introduction of the old leaven. Victoria and South Australia passed an Act, which was afterwards annulled by the Queen in Council as beyond their powers, forbidding any convict to set foot on their shores. Petitions were got up to the Queen to do away with transportation to Western Australia. A commission of enquiry was appointed, who recommended not the discontinuance of transportation but an *increase* of it. This was met with extreme indignation by the colonies, who showed their earnestness by actually sending a ship-load home to England at their own charges. This was in 1865, and it had its effect, for the Queen was advised to discontinue transportation by degrees, so that in three years it should cease.

Still, in the midst of all, Western Australia was making considerable progress. Fitzgerald was succeeded in office by Governor Kennedy, in 1856. And his successor was Mr. Hampton, the well-known superintendent of convicts. And now the colony began to suffer from another cause. Although many of the gentlemen who had been amongst the original settlers had left it in disgust, some had remained, and they had met with success. But having become possessed of considerable property, they left the colonies with their gains, and went to enjoy the fruits of their labour in their native land.

When New South Wales was first settled, for a considerable time the people were disheartened from the sandy nature of the soil; when they went to

Port Phillip it was the same, and the original immigrants at the Swan appear to have lost all energy, and gave up the whole country as worthless, because the sand prevailed so much on the coast. This sand does prevail for fifty miles or so; then come the ranges, like the Blue Mountains in New South Wales, and beyond these ranges there are fine grassy plains and valleys.

Gregory, Roe, and Lefroy discovered well-grassed and arable land, and going northwards, at 1,000 feet or more above the sea level, fine grassy downs were found sufficient to depasture millions of sheep and cattle. And from this period we may consider that the prosperous days of Western Australia commenced. In the other and more thickly peopled colonies, the land was being very quickly taken up, or the new land bills had so raised the rent of runs or encroached upon them, that the attention of squatters was directed to this vast country. The government did all they could to give an impetus to this movement. They offered 100,000 acres of land rent free for twelve years to the first settler who should come westward with stock, and companies were formed in Melbourne and in Sydney, managed by skilful old colonists. It is but a question of time, and we shall hear of this becoming a great and prosperous colony. It is just the place for young men to go to who wish to turn their attention to pastoral pursuits. The area is so vast that there is plenty of elbow room, and this is always a thing to be specially looked out for. *The younger and the larger the country, the better the chance for the enterprising settler.*

The prevailing winds are from the west, and there are abundant rains, so that this colony does not suffer from drought. Fish is abundant. The heat of summer is moderated by alternate sea and land breezes. All sorts of vegetables and fruits (especially the vine) flourish luxuriantly. The Darling and Roe Ranges, rising to about 1,500 feet, are at a distance of from ten to twenty-five miles from the western coast, and parallel to it, and they are dotted about with thriving farms. These ranges are from twenty to fifty miles across, and on their eastern side are the chief stations.

The Colonial Secretary in his report for 1868, says, "The colony possesses one of the most healthy climates in the world. The mortality since its occupation *has not averaged one per cent.* I doubt if any portion of the world is better suited to the European constitution. It is subject to no extremes of heat or cold. Snow is never seen." Maize, potatoes, the apple, pear, orange, banana, fig, peach, and apricot, with the melon and the vine, grow most luxuriantly. Attention is being paid to drying fruits, and excellent specimens of figs and raisins have been exhibited. The cultivation of the vine promises to be highly remunerative, but though the soil is of very varied character, it appears to flourish in them all. The wine made is as yet very limited in quantity, and is consumed in the colony itself. On one occasion some was sent to Queensland, to a gentleman holding a prominent position there, and he reported most favourably of it, estimating its marketable value at 12s. a gallon.

In the year 1861, Lord Grey spoke of Western Australia in the following terms: "The development of the resources of Western Australia is a matter of the highest moment. Coal is to be found there, and, in steam communication with India, I need scarcely remind you of the vast value of such a product. Further, I may state that Western Australia abounds with forests of the finest timber, while it possesses a climate and soil capable of producing anything which a tropical region of the earth may be expected to yield." The coal referred to above is found on the Irwin River, in the Victoria district, and also on the southern coast, near the Fitzgerald River. Its character is that of the Welsh coal, well adapted for engine purposes. The mines have not yet been worked, but the attention of capitalists will be turned ere long in this direction. The forests of timber are very extensive and valuable. There is the jarrah (*eucalyptus marginata*), a wood very similar to the Honduras mahogany. Its grain is fine, and highly effective in point of ornament. It has the advantage of being extremely durable, and the property of resisting the attacks of the *white ant*. Some of the seeds of the jarrah tree were recently forwarded to Dr. Müeller, the superintendent of the Botanical Gardens in Melbourne, who reports that they are worth from 15s. to 25s. a pound, and perhaps more, when once the value of this important tree is properly and generally understood. The wood of this tree, if cut at the proper season, *when the sap is down*, will be found the most enduring of all woods. Time, weather, water, the white ant, and the sea-worm have no effect upon it; and it is so abundant, that Admiral Sir James Stirling stated before a committee of the House of Commons, that there is sufficient of it to build twenty British navies. It is of the greatest value for railway sleepers, and is likely to be much used for this purpose both in India and in the other Australian colonies.

Another valuable tree is the tooart, a kind of white gum. It is very close-grained, and is used for keels, naves of wheels, capstans, windlasses, &c. The sandal-wood has long proved a valuable export.

If the price of freight could be reduced, there is a fine field for the employment of capital in the woods of this country. The government are holding out all encouragement to those willing to embark in the enterprise, by issuing licenses to cut timber at merely nominal rates.

The *Perth Inquirer* is recommending the cultivation of the castor-oil tree, since the oil prepared by the newly-discovered process is worth £40 a tun in the English market.

It would seem that there is an inexhaustible

quantity of *iron ore*. Gold has not been discovered as yet, but copper is found in abundance, and the ore is exceedingly rich in quality. Lead is also found. It would be impossible in such a book as this to enter fully into this subject, but those who seek for more exact information can readily obtain it from a paper by Frank Gregory, Esq., F.G.S., to be found in the "Official Record of the Intercolonial Exhibition." The Geraldine lead mines turn out ore having from 70 to 86 per cent. of pure lead.

The pearl fisheries are yearly advancing in value. By a vessel which lately arrived in Melbourne twenty-five very handsome pearls were received, which were exhibited at a jeweller's shop in Collins Street. Some of them were declared by good judges to be perfect in shape, and of very fine colour. It is said that one of the finest would fetch £25 in the London market, and there are several others worth from £8 up to £15.

This colony has room for many thousands of enterprising settlers. As was formerly the case in the older colonies, so now here, the squatters are pushing out farther and farther every year. It is expected that there will before long be a rush in the direction of Nichol and Roebuck Bays. Between these two bays the government surveyor recently reports having passed over *millions of acres of first-class pastoral land.* The grasses have a peculiarly succulent character, and are found to remain nutritious even after a drought of eighteen months.

The land regulations offer great inducements to squatters and others. Country lands are sold to the first applicant, without auction, at ten shillings an acre, in blocks of forty acres and upwards.

Town lands in small allotments, by auction, at an upset price of from £1 to £6.

The pastoral lands are divided into three classes, and are let on the following terms:—

Lands in class A, which comprises all the land *nearest* to the settled districts, are let on an annual tenure at the rate of £1 for 1,000 acres. These lands are open to purchase to the first applicant.

Class B includes all lands in the settled districts *not* in class A. They are let on lease for eight years in blocks not exceeding 10,000 acres, the rent for each lease being £5 a year and ten shillings for every thousand acres comprised in it. The lessee has a preferable claim for a renewal of his lease. He has also the pre-emptive right over the whole lease during the first year, and over such portion as he may choose for his homestead during the two succeeding years, after which all the land is open to general purchase.

Class C includes all the newly discovered districts to the north and east. Permission for *free* pasturage for one year is granted to applicants, during which year they are entitled to select 100,000 acres of land in one block, of which a free run is granted for three years, after which period leases are issued in blocks not exceeding 20,000 acres for eight years on the annual payment of £5 for each lease, and five shillings per 1,000 acres during the first four years of its currency, and ten shillings per 1,000 acres during the last four years. And lessees are entitled to a preferential claim for a *renewal* of such leases.

Tillage leases are also granted, in blocks not exceeding 320 acres for eight years, on an annual payment of £5 for the lease, and one shilling an acre for each acre comprised in it, the lessee having a pre-emptive right over any portion of the land during the currency of his lease.

Every facility is afforded to test mineral lands, by annual license, on payment of two shillings an acre for the first and four shillings for the second year. And when such lands have been satisfactorily tested, leases of ten years' duration are issued at eight shillings per acre per annum, with a preemptive right during the currency of the lease.

Mineral lands are sold at a fixed price of £3 an acre; £1 payable on application for the land and £1 in each of the two succeeding years.

We have copied out these regulations at length because of their importance to the intending settler. To the squatter, the farmer, and the miner they offer great inducements. And if a man does not get on under such a land law the land must be very poor indeed, far poorer than we have reason now to believe that it is.

From its proximity to India, this colony has been

looked to for a supply of horses for that country. A cargo of 130 were sold to the Madras government at £58 a head.

Some time ago Dr. Rennie, a staff-surgeon who had been stationed for several years in the colony, gave the following testimony, in a letter to the Editor of the *News Letter*, on the important points of (1) the climate, (2) the physical effects of the climate on European constitutions, (3) the effects of the climate on children, and (4) the effects of the climate on longevity :—

"SIR,—In reply to your letter requesting me to furnish you with some remarks for publication respecting the capabilities of Western Australia as a sanitarium for the invalids of the Indian Army, I have to state that I have no hesitation in doing so—a residence of upwards of six years in the colony, during which I had a very large professional charge, consisting of soldiers, women, children, foreign officers, and convicts, having afforded me extensive opportunities for forming definite conclusions on the subject. The following embrace the chief facts upon which an opinion very favourable to the formation of an Invalid Establishment in Western Australia, for the sick of the Indian Army, has been based by me :—

" 1. *Climate.*—It would be difficult to imagine a more delightful temperature and climate generally than that of Western Australia, more especially the winter, which, though invigorating, is never very cold. The summer is warm, but the average heat does not very materially exceed that of the warmer portion of the winter months; and, as a general rule, it is free from any depressing effects, readily admitting of active occupation and ordinary labour being carried on in the sun by the European settlers, military, emigrants, and convicts, without detriment to health. At Freemantle the temperature of the winter months, extending from May to October, is 60°, and that of the remainder of the year about 73°, which figures may be taken as giving a fair average of the temperature over the colony generally, and certainly neither of them in excess, being, if anything, rather over than under the average ranges of the thermometer in other parts of Western Australia. The climate of this portion of Australia is also materially modified by its geographical position, the whole of the inhabited parts of the colony being within the influences of the sea-breeze, which, as a general rule, sets in every afternoon, and is distinctly perceptible seventy and eighty miles inland.

"2. *The Physical Effects of the Climate on European Constitutions.*—It is almost impossible, by any description I can give, to do justice to the Western Australia atmosphere. To be appreciated, it must be experienced. Many a time, on leaving my house in the morning, have I been struck with the wonderful elasticity of body and mind which the cloudless sky and refreshing atmosphere seemed to develop: and often has the thought occurred to me, 'What a splendid climate for a sanitarium!' My impressions in this respect are by no means singular, and I believe them to be those of residents there generally—except, perhaps, a few whose vicious habits tend to counteract the blessings of climate they enjoy; sensations of debility arising from sensuality and vice being attributed by them to their residence in a temperature warmer than England —climate being too frequently made the scapegoat for the evil effects of gluttony, narcotism, and intemperance. I have been assured by old settlers, that at a time when the affairs of the colony presented the gloomiest aspect, and everything connected with it was calculated to depress them, still that their minds seemed to refuse to yield to the pressure from without; and their spirits kept up in a manner so remarkable, that they could account for it in no other way than by referring it to the clear and exhilarating atmosphere in which it was at that time their misfortune, in a financial point of view, to be residing.

"3. *Effects of the Climate on Children.*—They enjoy a remarkable immunity from the infantile diseases which are so fatal elsewhere. The Registrar-General of the Colony, in his report accompanying the last census returns, drew attention to the fact that one-fourth of the population of Western Australia consisted of children, as a proof of the comparative exemption which the colony enjoyed from infantile disease of a serious nature; and I may here mention, as a farther illustration of the general salubrity of the climate, that small-pox, measles, scarlet-fever, &c., are as yet unknown in Western Australia. I may add, also, that the same remark almost applies to acute pulmonary affections, their occurrence being rare in the extreme.

"4. *Effects of the Climate on Longevity.*—The settlers, as a general rule, retain their mental and physical faculties to a very considerable age in Western Australia. The per centage of deaths in the whole colony by the last census returns was only 0·55, or 5½ in the thousand. Frequently, on taking into consideration the habits of many of the residents, I have been astonished at the apparent immunity from disease they enjoyed, and accounted for it only from the fact that they were living in a primitive atmosphere, and in a settlement free from any of the ordinary external exciting causes of disease; also that their occupations were active, and their circumstances of life were generally such as to counteract the injurious tendencies of their special habits—the sun in Western Australia being, as a general rule, free from those debilitating effects which usually characterise solar heat elsewhere. The climate of Western Australia is vastly superior to that of any other of the Australian colonies, including Tasmania, and the period of the year best adapted for the arrival of invalids from India will be the end of March to the middle of July; through which, as a general rule, they will be able to enjoy six months uninterrupted cool weather, and, if sufficiently recovered, return to India as the cool season is setting in there."

With this testimony in its favour we may well bring our remarks to a close. This colony has been as it were under a cloud for a long time, from the disappointments experienced by its first settlers;

from the apparently barren and sandy nature of its soil, until the recent explorations had taken place, and afterwards from its penal character. But we predict that it will be a great and rich colony yet; and we advise young men of energy who want to push their way in the world, and are not afraid of those difficulties and that isolation which naturally fall to the lot of the pioneers in a new land, to have a look at Western Australia before they settle down.

ST. KILDA, NEAR MELBOURNE.—*page* 180.

Chapter V.

VICTORIA (FORMERLY PORT PHILLIP).

WE now come to Victoria, the smallest almost, but in extent the richest, of all the Australasian colonies. Its boundaries, as settled by statute 13 and 14 Vict. c. 59, and passed in the year 1850, when it was separated from New South Wales, are as follows: It is bounded on the north and north-east by a straight line drawn from Cape Howe to the nearest source of the River Murray, and thence by the course of that river to the eastern boundary of the colony of South Australia. The whole southern boundary is formed by the waters of Bass's Straits. Its extreme length from east to west is 420 miles, and its greatest breadth 260. It is estimated to contain 86,831 square miles, or 55,571,840 acres. If we bear in mind that it is only 35 years since the foundation of this colony, and then look at its present state of prosperity, it must strike us as presenting a marvellous instance of rapid growth, almost if not quite unexampled in the history of colonisation.

In 1770 Captain Cook sighted Cape Howe, the extreme south-eastern point of the continent, but thence bent his course northwards. In 1797 Bass went on a voyage of discovery from Sydney in a whale boat, and passed through the strait which bears his name; but he went westward only as far as Western Port. Port Phillip, the splendid harbour of the colony, was not discovered until 1802, by Lieutenant Murray, who commanded the *Lady Nelson*. Fancying that a hill at the south-east of the harbour was like "Arthur's Seat" in Edinburgh, he gave it that name. Somewhat strangely, within a few weeks of his discovery, Baudin, the French explorer, and Flinders, both entered this bay. It was the latter of these who named Indented Head and Station Peak, and whose own name is presented in the busy Flinders Street, of Melbourne, and in that fine river in the north which Burke and Landsborough have made so well known to us. Murray's account of his discovery induced the Home Government to form a second convict settlement there. It was in 1803 that Collins was sent with a detachment of prisoners. Owing to the want of fresh water, and to the unfitness of the spot they selected, this settlement was abandoned, and Collins went to the Derwent, in Van Diemen's Land. We hear little or nothing of this part of the coast until 1824, when Hamilton Hume and Hovell projected an overland journey from Sydney to the Southern Ocean. The governor of New South Wales was anxious to ascertain if any large rivers passed towards the east coast through the country that lay to the south. He was liberal in promises if they succeeded, but he gave them but little present help. They started from Hume's out-station, and reached the Murrumbidgee, which they found to be a broad river and full of water, and which they crossed on a raft. Going on towards the south, they discovered the Upper Murray, which was eighty yards wide. They also came upon the Ovens and the Goulbourn. Hence they proceeded as far south as 37° 8', but were so impeded by the thick scrub and sharp grass, that at a hill, which they called "Mount Disappointment," they altered their course to the south-west, and shortly afterwards sighted a well-known hill, which is now called "Mount Macedon." Shortly afterwards they saw the waters of an inlet of the Southern Ocean, and were told by a native that it was called Geelong, a name which at a later period was given to a large town, ranking as the third, if not the second in the colony.

Ten years roll on. The little island of Van Diemen's Land, or rather all that was known of it, was getting covered with flocks and herds, and the settlers were eagerly on the look out for fresh pastures. A native-born colonist, named John Batman, sailed from Hobart Town, and arrived in the harbour of Port Phillip in May, 1835. John Pascoe Fawkner followed him, but did not arrive himself until November in the same year. The question has been keenly agitated as to which of the two was really the father of the colony. It would appear that without doubt Batman was the first settler on the land; but Fawkner selected, as a good site for a village, that spot on which the capital now stands, and he may therefore well be styled the "Father of Melbourne." Batman obtained a grant from the natives of a thousand square miles of land for a few blankets and gewgaws, which were to be given them yearly. This bargain was very properly annulled by the government. It has been calculated by Westgarth (the well-known writer on Victoria, to whom we are greatly indebted for much valuable information) that within twenty years this so-called purchase might have been valued at £40,000,000 sterling. As soon as Batman got his "title deeds" he returned to Hobart Town and formed a company, who were the fathers of Port Phillip colonisation; the names of the partners were Charles Swanston, Thomas Bannister, James Simpson, J. T. Gellibrand, J. and W. Robertson, J. H. Wedge, John Sinclair, Henry Arthur, J. T. Collicott, G. Mercer, W. G. Sams, A. Cotterell, and M. Connolly. When the government disallowed their bargain with the natives, it was arranged that if they purchased lands at auction they should have a remission of purchase money to the extent of £7,000. And in 1838 they bought lands in fee simple, to the west of Geelong, at the rate of five shillings an acre. Batman had entertained the idea of emigrating to Port Phillip eight years before he went. He had detailed his plans to Mr. Gellibrand, who had agreed to assist him, but the government declined to listen to his request. Messrs. Gellibrand and Hesse, in 1836, were lured on further and further to the westward, by the beauty of the country and the fineness of the grasses, and never returned. It is presumed that they were both killed by the natives; in fact, many years afterwards, the remains of one of the murdered gentlemen were found, and were brought into the town of Belfast, where I then resided, and were identified. It is reported that one of the natives got Mr. Hesse's watch, and took it for a god, but hearing it "tick," he got so frightened that he threw it away and rushed from the spot. In November, 1835, Batman came and settled himself permanently on the slopes of the green hill in Melbourne, which was called "Batman's Hill," but which has lately been cut down for railway purposes. He opened a "general store," and Fawkner commenced a public-house. The former died about four years afterwards; the latter lived to a good old age. He saw the colony rise to its present state of great prosperity; he witnessed the rise of Melbourne from a wilderness to a beautiful city; he took an active part in the politics of the day, and became a member of the Upper House, and died in September, 1869. His funeral was one of the largest ever seen in Melbourne. Persons of all political creeds, and of every religious denomination, laid aside for the day their private feelings, and combined in order to do honour to the brave old man who had been identified with the colony from its birthday. He was 77 years of age. 228 carriages followed his remains to the grave. He always had a regard to the intellectual improvement of the people amongst whom he was cast. When he kept his inn he always provided a large supply of periodicals and of books for the use of his customers. He published the first newspaper in the infant settlement. Some day, if not now, it will be regarded as a curiosity, and so we give a copy of the first number of it. It was brought out at first in manuscript. We make the extract from the *Australasian*, that enormous and most ably-conducted Melbourne paper, which is indeed a giant by the side of Fawkner's tiny dwarf:—

THE
MELBOURNE ADVERTISER.
PORT PHILIP AUSTRALIA.
No. 1. Written for and published by John P. Fawkner.
January the 1st Monday 1838 Melbourne.
Vol. 1st.

We do opine that Melbourne cannot reasonably remain longer marked on the chart of advancing civilisation without its Advertiser.

Such being our imperial Fiat We do intend therefore by means of this our Advertiser to throw the resplendant light of publicity upon all the affairs of this new Colony, Whether of Commerce or Agriculture or of the arts and Mysteries of the Grazier. All these patent roads to wealth are thrown open to the adventurous Port Phillipians. All these sources of riches are about to (or already are) become accessible to each adventurous Colonist of N. O. U. S. The future fortunes of the rising Melburnians will be much accelerated by the dissemination of intelligence consequent upon the Press being thrown open here. But until the arrival of the printing Materials we will by means of the Humble pen diffuse such intelligence as may be found expedient or may arise.

The energies of the present population of this rapidly rising district have never been exceeded in any of the colonies of Britain.

Its giant-like strides have filled with astonishment the minds of all the neighbouring states. The Sons of Britain languish when debarred the use of that mighty Engine the Press. A very small degree of support timely afforded will establish a newspaper here, but until some further arrangements are made it will merely be an advertising sheet and will be given away to Householders.

"After the issue of nine weekly manuscript numbers, Mr. Fawkner obtained a small parcel of refuse type from Launceston, and secured the services of a 'Vandemonian youth of eighteen,' who, when about ten years old, had worked for a few months as a compositor. Thereupon a printed *Advertiser*, about twelve inches long, containing four pages of two columns each, was issued. The *Advertiser* was not destined to run a long career. Captain Lonsdale, government superintendent, discovered that money had been received for advertisements, and this circumstance bringing it under the existing Newspaper Act, he forthwith suppressed it until the heavy sureties required by law could be entered into at Sydney. In the beginning of 1839, however, Mr. Fawkner was once more in the field with the legal *Port Phillip Patriot*. About the same time, he purchased a block of 800 acres of land at Pascoevale, and engaged extensively in farming operations. The year 1845 was a period of commercial depression, and Mr. Fawkner, who had become interested in many mercantile adventures, was forced by the misfortunes of others, to succumb and seek the protection of the Insolvent Court. He was soon at work again, however, with his accustomed energy, converted the *Patriot* into a daily paper, formed a sheep-station, and finally devoted himself to gardening and wine-making. During the period of his own private troubles he still found time to render the state good service. In 1842 he served as one of the market commissioners, and in 1843, 1844, and 1845 he was elected a member of the City Council. The large blocks in which land was sold preventing the poorer colonists obtaining sites for houses, he projected a freehold land society, which was a great success. Many persons now owning valuable properties in the suburban districts owe their position entirely to Mr. Fawkner's disinterested efforts. In the anti-transportation movement, also, he played a prominent part; and he was one of the leading actors in the struggle which led to the separation of the Port Phillip district from New South Wales. It was upon his proposition that the electors determined not to send any more members to the Sydney Legislature. Instead, Earl Grey was returned—a proceeding which attracted attention to the movement, and gave point to the remonstrances of the Port Phillip settlers.

"In 1850, when the colony of Victoria was proclaimed, a Legislative Council—partly elective and partly nominee—was called into existence, and Mr. Fawkner, now one of the acknowledged champions of popular rights, was returned as member for the counties of Dalhousie, Anglesea, and Talbot. The discovery of gold, and the consequent rise in the value of property, fortunately placed him in circumstances of moderate independence, in which he afterwards remained. Though his name is not connected with the introduction of any important measure, he took an active part in the proceedings of the Council. He was one of the warmest opposers of the extravagant claims put forward by the squatters under the Orders in Council, and the new Constitution Act received his support, though he opposed both the ballot and state-aid-to-religion clauses. When the Constitution Act came into operation, and two Houses of Parliament were established, Mr. Fawkner, upon whom age was now creeping, and whose health was far from firm, felt unequal to the turmoil, work, and strife attendant both on an election and on a seat in the Lower House. He sought, however, the suffrages of the electors of the Central Province, and was returned second on the poll as member for that district in the Legislative Council. He speedily became a necessary part of the Council; the House would have been well nigh as complete without the President as without him. The absence of the President would not have been more strange than that of the velvet skull-cap and the old-fashioned blue cloak in which Mr. Fawkner was wont to sit, and the interjectory remarks he was prone to indulge in. He watched narrowly all questions which came before the House ; he spoke also distinctly and decidedly upon nearly all, and his natural shrewdness and large colonial experience caused his advice to be of great value.

"Mr. Fawkner's health had been failing for some time, and his death, which took place shortly after eleven o'clock on Saturday morning, at his residence, Smith Street, Collingwood, did not, therefore take any one by surprise. He had been suffering for a very long period from chronic asthma, in addition to one or two other ailments incident to old age, but his death was the result more of a general breaking up of the constitution than of any specific malady. He had just completed his seventy-seventh year, and his system seemed to have completely worn itself out. He, however, retained his faculties to the last, and only two days before his death, he rode into town in his carriage for the purpose of seeing his medical attendant, Mr. James."

But, willing as we have always been to give due honour to Batman and to Fawkner, it would appear that not sufficient credit has been awarded to the Henty family, who, in 1833, that is two years *before* the other two, had gone over to Portland Bay and established a whaling station there in connection with their extensive mercantile firm at Launceston. True, Portland has not become so great a place as Melbourne, and that may make a difference; but the fact remains the same.

When the first settlers landed on the shores of Port Phillip, the natives showed a disposition to meet them in a kindly spirit. This may, perhaps, be partly accounted for from the fact that a white man was not quite a novelty to them, for they had one with them who had been enrolled amongst, and been as it were one of themselves for a period of 32 years. This was an English prisoner named Buckley, who escaped from Collins' fleet in 1803. Three others escaped with him, but they perished. The natives behaved well to him; he became one of them, and had a black wife or wives. His great stature (for he is variously stated to have been six feet nine inches, and six feet five inches in height) had probably great influence on the aborigines. It would not appear that he raised them at all in the social scale, but he himself adopted their savage habits, till his very face in time looked like that of one of the aborigines. This was his appearance when I knew him in Van Diemen's Land, after his recovery. The Australian natives have a superstition that white men are of their own race, who after death have come to life again. This may have had a good deal to do with the way in which they treated Buckley. Many years ago a near and dear relative of my own was living on the banks of the Campaspe River, and a black woman came begging for a gown. It was not convenient to give one (for I dare say gowns were gowns in those days), when the poor woman said, "Some day me go dead, and jump up again white woman; and then me give *you* plenty gown." The promised reward had, I believe, the desired effect, and the poor lubra got the coveted garment. When the first settlers came over, in 1835, Buckley resolved on going to them; but as he approached them strange emotions seized him. He could not remember a word of English; but when he went up, one of them gave him a piece of bread, and repeated the word "bread." This seemed to have a wonderful effect upon him, and by degrees other words came back to his recollection. A free pardon was obtained for him. He was for a time very useful as a mediator between the two races; but afterwards he began to feel himself placed in an awkward position between his old and his new friends. Strange to say, Captain Lonsdale was sent down from Sydney in 1836 to take charge of the new settlement, and Buckley discovered in him an officer of his own regiment, for he had been a soldier at the time of his transportation. Buckley ultimately went to Hobart Town, where he was a constable. He married a white woman, was allowed a pension of £12 a year from Tasmania, and afterwards of £40 from the Port Phillip government. He died at Hobart Town in 1856, at the age of 76. His name will ever be remembered in connection with the colonisation of Port Phillip.

Batman and Fawkner had settled in their new home, and Buckley had retired from the scene. But what was it that gave such an impetus to the infant settlement, and caused it to rise into importance so quickly? In 1836 the late Sir Thomas Mitchell, the surveyor-general of New South Wales, had been despatched on his overland journey. His object was to complete the survey of the River Darling, which had been previously discovered by Captain Sturt. Having executed his commission he turned to the south—to the country explored by Hume and Hovell, and in which Batman and Fawkner had recently settled. He passed the Yarraine, and afterwards the Loddon; he sighted the

Pyrenees, and the great range of the Grampians. Proceeding westward, he came upon the river Glenelg, 120 feet wide. He sailed down it till he came to its junction with the Southern Ocean. To the eastward of the Glenelg he came to Portland Bay, and to his extreme surprise found the farming settlements of the Messrs. Henty. Mr. Thomas Henty had seven sons, several of whom had been sent over with flocks, which were at this time depasturing over this beautiful country. The Hentys applied for a grant of land, but their claim was but partially allowed. It seems very hard that little or no encouragement is thus held out as a reward to those brave men who are the first to discover and then to convert a lonely wilderness into a fruitful field. Mitchell turned his face homewards. From the top of Mount Macedon he got a bird's-eye view of the beautiful country to the south, with the waters of Port Phillip Bay in the distance. Charmed with all he had seen, he called the land "Australia Felix," and his glowing description of the new country had great influence with those at home and in the other colonies, whose attention was at that very moment strongly attracted to this the most promising of the Australian colonies.

Mr. Stewart, a magistrate from New South Wales, was sent down by the governor to report upon the infant settlement. He caused a census to be taken in 1836. There were then 177 persons —142 men; 35 women. Mr. James Simpson was the first magistrate. By all the old colonists he was well known and highly respected, and filled no mean place in the new colony for many years afterwards. Towards the end of 1836, Captain Lonsdale was appointed from Sydney as a kind of superintendent. It was in the same year that Lieutenant Hobson, R.N., surveyed the harbour. Hobson's Bay was named after him.

In June, 1837, the first sale of allotments of land in Melbourne took place. The average price was £35 for half an acre. Mr. Westgarth tells a story of a cautious buyer, who thought he had given too much when he had purchased at £80, and so forfeited his deposit of ten per cent. It was afterwards resold, first for £72, then for £5,000, and afterwards for £40,000. The three original towns in the settlement were Melbourne, Corio, or Geelong, and Portland. The river Yarra Yarra, on which Melbourne stands, was so called in the first place by Mr. J. H. Wedge. It is a native word, and was supposed to mean "ever flowing." But he understood afterwards that the term "yarra yarra" meant the falls, inasmuch as the natives used the same word for the falls of the Werribee. A runaway convict of Collins' party discovered this stream of water. In two years from the arrival of Batman and Fawkner, it was found that nearly all the land available for runs, within 60 miles of the capital, had been taken up, and that there were 140,000 sheep, 2,500 cattle, and 150 horses, and that the population had increased to 450. The new comers at first settled down just where they liked, and gave themselves the names of "squatters" and their homesteads "stations"—terms which came from the backwoods of America. At a later period the runs were defined, and the occupants received licenses, by which they could depasture 4,000 sheep or 400 head of cattle by paying to the government £10 a year. In such a climate as that of Port Phillip, little practical knowledge of cattle seemed to be necessary. The sheep grazed in the open plains in flocks of 1,000 or 1,500. Gentlemen with means, or who had been educated for the learned professions, came out and became squatters. The "new comers" found already settled in the country a class of gentlemen like themselves; and the society of very many of them is a great privilege to enjoy, and to partake of their unbounded hospitality.

In 1843, Sir George Gipps, the governor of New South Wales, came down to inspect Melbourne, and to see how things were progressing in Port Phillip. Mad speculation in land, both in town and country, had been going on for a lengthened period. Buying and selling allotments was the only occupation pursued by many of the people, giving very lucrative employment to a set of land-jobbers, auctioneers, and attorneys. The conveyance of land was very loosely managed in those days; and it is to be feared that there will eventually be found many a

" hitch " in the title to properties which have passed through so many hands. The governor expressed his surprise at finding the neighbourhood of Melbourne strewed with empty champagne bottles ! Every land sale was preceded by a "lunch," the prefix to which was generally " champagne ;" and the auctioneers used to find that it told upon the liberality of the bids afterwards, so as to be remunerative at all events to the auctioneer and to the seller, though very probably not always so to the liberal purchaser.

After Melbourne was laid out, the traffic was at first inconsiderable, and the gum-trees stood boldly up in the chief thoroughfares for a long time. But as population increased and years rolled on, the Melbourne corporation, which had been called into existence, stood aghast at the work before them. Where that noble street (Elizabeth Street) now displays a broad flagged pavement, handsome shops, and one of the finest post-offices in the world, there was formerly a little wooden post-office, and all about it gardens with palings in front. And in wet weather the whole street was flooded. If I wanted to get to the post-office, and stood clinging to a rail for support, some stalwart Irishman would come and offer, for a consideration, to take me across on his back; and drays used to ply backwards and forwards for passengers. A story is told of a man seeing a black hat swimming in the deep water at the side of this street, and he went to seize upon it, thinking that perhaps it might cover the head of some drowning man, when a voice from beneath roared out, "Get out of the way man, there is a bullock team behind me!" Indeed the navigation was very difficult. I was once going to a vice-regal or episcopal dinner late in the evening, and could get no carriage; I set out to walk in full evening dress, but I had not proceeded far before I lost my shoe and sank up to my knee in mud, and after limping in one shoe to a cottage, I saw one leg covered with a black silk stocking, and the other brown with mud. To present oneself in that trim was impossible, and an apology the next morning was all the amends I could make. One Sunday morning, when I was unfortunately staying on the wrong side of Elizabeth Street, I had an engagement to take the service in the cathedral. Timing myself so as to have five or ten minutes to spare, I started and got to this unfortunate street, and found it in a flood. What could I do? The bells were ringing, and the precious minutes were flying fast. I rushed back to my host and stated my difficulty. He said, "I have a pair of long jack-boots, which will reach above your knees. This is all I can do for you." Hastily I drew them on, and set off again. I dashed into the stream and got across, and reached the vestry just in time; my boots were wet to the very top, and soaking inside with water. I covered all defects by my robes, and went through the service. I do not know what the feelings of the congregation were, but I was heartily glad when, the service being over, I was enabled to hasten back and pull off my seven-leagued boots. I remember distinctly how uncomfortable I felt when I had to mount the long flight of steps which lead to the pulpit. I did all I could to draw my gown over my boots to conceal their grotesque appearance. I fancy I succeeded, but I fear that some one's gown suffered not a little. The streets now are admirable. "When things get to the worst they mend." And so at length the government came to the relief of the corporation, and a loan was negotiated to the amount of £500,000 for Melbourne, and £200,000 for Geelong, for the purpose of forming and metalling the streets.

But this has led us on too fast. To retrace our steps, we would remark that Captain Lonsdale was relieved of his duties by the arrival of Mr. C. J. La Trobe, as the superintendent of the district of Port Phillip. This was in 1838. His income was £800 a year, raised afterwards, first to £1,500, and in 1851 to £2,500. In the height of the gold-field time it was raised to £15,000, but subsequently reduced to £10,000 a year and a house. When, in 1854, it was desired to rent a suitable house for the governor, the only one at all coming up to the wants of an officer in his position was a place called "Toorak," which had been the residence of a merchant. But it was let on lease at £300 a year, two years of which were unexpired. For these two years the government gave the tenant a bonus of £10,000!

Mr. La Trobe had been formerly known as a writer, and as belonging to an active Christian body, before his arrival in the district. His post was a very difficult one. He held it for fifteen years, and during that period the changes which the district went through were great and strange indeed. Of course, politically, he made many enemies, and was regarded by some as being too quiet in disposition, and deficient in decision of character. But yet, on his quitting the colony, a most elegant and substantial testimonial, manufactured from the gold of the country, testified to the high appreciation in which he was held. In fact his opponents were only *political* ones. In all other respects no man commanded more respect than Mr. La Trobe.

In the year 1841 there was great depression throughout the country—the consequence of the reckless speculation of bye-gone days. And in the midst of all, the very richness of the country proved a drawback. So great was the increase in the sheep and cattle, that the squatters' runs became overstocked and they knew not what to do. Sheep were down to half-a-crown a head, or less, and cattle to twelve shillings. In this dilemma a settler thought of "boiling down" the surplus stock, and by this means a minimum value was found, for sheep six shillings, and for cattle thirty shillings. At this time you could get a good leg of mutton for sixpence, and beefsteaks at a penny a pound. And though prices are not quite so low now, yet are they very low indeed. And I heartily wish that thousands of strong men and women could be conveyed to a land where, *three times a day*, they could enjoy a substantial meal of beef or of mutton.

Before the year 1847 the members of the Church of England had been under the episcopal charge of the Bishop of Australia, who lived in Sydney. But in that year the Right Rev. Charles Perry was appointed as first Bishop of Melbourne. He came out bringing with him the highest character as a scholar and as a parish priest. He was senior wrangler of his year, was in the first class of the classical tripos, and was senior Smith's prizeman. He had afterwards been a Fellow of Trinity College, Cambridge. To Cambridge itself he had proved a great blessing, and all his pious exertions for the spiritual improvement of that place will not soon pass away from the memory of the residents therein. He has held his all-important office for twenty-two years, and he has seen under his mild but fatherly control a wonderful growth in the church. He is, like the good Dr. Wilson, late Bishop of Calcutta, another of those remarkable men whom God in his providence raises up from time to time for special work in his church. His views are strongly those of the Evangelical party, and he is therefore greatly opposed to all Tractarian and Ritualistic doctrines and practices. We shall have an opportunity of speaking of the state of the church as he found it, and as it is now, on another occasion, and we have only alluded to him here as it came naturally before us to do so in the order of events. Being removed now from his episcopal control, I may without impropriety say, what I long have felt, that I esteem his friendship as one of the greatest privileges of my life, and value his counsel and advice most highly.

In the midst of those ups and downs which are so characteristic of the fortunes of colonies, as well as of the individual members of them, Port Phillip winced continually under the heavy yoke of bondage to New South Wales, and her struggles were incessant to obtain *separation*. She sent up six members to be added to the thirty who formed the Sydney Council, and no one had a chance of being returned unless he were a decided friend to the popular clamour. A little later the Rev. Dr. Lang, a well known and very clever Presbyterian clergyman in Sydney, became one of the members for the distant province. He suggested the idea of all the Port Phillip members sending in a petition to the Imperial authorities, praying for separation. And in this they were supported by Mr. Robert Lowe (now Chancellor of the Exchequer), who was then living in Sydney and was a member of the Legislature. This was in 1844. Considerable delay took place. It was not until 1849 that the people heard that their great constitutional struggle was crowned with success. Still there was some delay, arising from the difficulty in preparing the necessary Bill.

On the 1st July, 1851 the electoral Act and other necessary arrangements having been passed, the district of Port Phillip was henceforth to be known as the free and independent colony of Victoria, being so named by the express wish of Her Most Gracious Majesty the Queen. This day, called "separation day," is still observed as a holiday by all classes of the people. At the time of separation the population had risen to 77,000, of whom 23,000 lived in Melbourne. On the 1st January, 1851, there were 21,219 horses; 378,806 cattle; 9,260 pigs; and 6,032,783 sheep. The wool exported in the preceding year weighed 18,091,207 lbs.; tallow, 4,489 tons; and salted beef 975 tons. Look back, please, at our previous statistical statements, and see what a marvellous increase had taken place in a few years. And all this, bear in mind, was *before* the discovery of gold. At this period the imports for the year amounted to £1,056,437, and the exports to £1,422,909, showing a balance in favour of the colony of £366,472. The shipping inwards numbered 669 vessels, with a tonnage of 126,411 tons. The total revenue was £379,824. The three banks had a circulation of £180,058; specie, £310,724, and deposits £822,254. This may appear as nothing compared with what we shall say presently; but for a district so recently peopled to have reached this point, without any extraordinary impetus, is to me far more astonishing than all the vast results which we shall see arise from the discovery of *gold*.

After the proclamation of "separation" and of the new "constitution," there came the exciting time of the first elections. When the bustle and excitement had partially subsided, the first Council assembled in November, ·1851, and proceeded in the distribution of the revenue named above. It was just before this that the whole colony was startled by the news of the discovery of gold at Bathurst, in New South Wales. A great number of the labouring population of the new colony of Victoria had already started for the gold-fields. Poor Victoria stood aghast! Landholders and householders in Melbourne and Geelong, and in fact in every petty town throughout the land, anticipated nothing but ruin. Those who went were full of glee; those who were compelled to stay behind were filled with gloomy fears. When lo! some shrewd colonists calculated that it was just possible that gold might be found in Victoria as well as in New South Wales, since the geological formation of the country was in some parts precisely the same. It may be remarked that some three years before, a sailor lad who had been a shepherd near Buninyong, about seventy miles to the west of Melbourne, brought thirty ounces of gold to Melbourne and sold it. Whilst the newly-elected members were sitting in their council chamber, doling out £600 a year to the chief public officers of the colony, they were startled to hear that a *ton* weight of gold had been brought into Melbourne

MOUNT ALEXANDER.—*page* 211.

from Mount Alexander. Nearly ten thousand diggers quickly rushed to the famous "golden point," which was the nucleus of the great Ballarat gold-field. Thence the mass moved off to Mount Alexander, and then to Bendigo. In 1852 it was reported that there were 50,000 diggers along the Bendigo creek. Provisions rose wonderfully. Any one who had a team of horses or bullocks then made a fortune. £100 a ton was given for the mere carriage of flour to Bendigo; and flour, worth £25 in Melbourne, was sold on the gold-field for £200. Ballarat had been nothing but a sheep station; and the shepherds had in their ignorance been kicking against blocks of gold.

It was quickly found that Victoria beat Bathurst hollow in the richness of its gold-fields; and then the intoxication became complete. Gold to the value of twelve millions sterling was exported in twelve months; and since the year 1851, this little colony alone has exported gold to the amount of £160,000,000. South Australia soon sent her hordes; Tasmania, her old hands, determined on getting gold "somehow;" Sydneyites and New Zealanders all flocked to the El Dorado. Ere long Chinese came in multitudes; in vain did the government impose a poll-tax of £10 on every Chinese entering Victoria. But the climax was complete as soon as there had been time for the news to reach England; then, in three months, upwards of 60,000 people arrived from home. There were no houses in Melbourne for them; a canvas town was erected, and laid out in regular streets—there was Regent Street, Holborn, the Strand, and so on. When the poor passengers got to Williams Town, nine miles only from Melbourne, they had to get their baggage to the city as well as they could; £2 a ton was the price charged, so the nine miles cost nearly as much as the 12,000 miles from England. A condescending blacksmith did, I know, once at least, to *oblige* a travelling clergyman, put a single shoe on a horse for which he charged £1. In my own parish, nearly every able-bodied man without exception left; and before going they came up to me in crowds, praying that I would take charge of their wives and little ones, promising to send me money as soon as they got any. I had thus forced upon me a very numerous family to provide for. Week after week passed away, and no money came. I supplied a great many with meat and flour and tea and sugar, and other necessaries, until at last I was seriously alarmed as to how it was all to be paid for. I became so nervous and anxious that I could not sleep at night. But after a long interval, in the dusk of the evening, a regular string of bearded, yellow-looking men came round to my library, bringing with them (for they had been afraid to send it) bags of gold, or unloosing a shot-belt poured out its glittering contents. In a great many cases the men could neither read nor write; they left their hordes with me to take care of, and to dispose of them in Melbourne for them, as there was no bank in the place. Frequently I have had thousands of pounds worth of gold kept for a lengthened period in my room, waiting for an opportunity of sending it away. It speaks well for human nature, when I tell you that they all paid me back what I had advanced; I lost not one farthing. And in every case they had made a point of keeping out one of their finest "nuggets" for the doctor to buy himself a ring with; so that *I* too had my bag of gold, and had I been fond of rings I might, like her of whom we read in ancient story, have been overwhelmed by the accumulation.

The state of the colony at this time was really frightful. "Conditional pardon" men from New South Wales and from Tasmania rushed over; men free by servitude and escaped convicts managed to get to the golden harvest, helped not a little by the government of the latter colony. The Victorian legislature was forced to pass, in 1852, the "Convicts' Prevention Act," the purport of which was that no man, unless he held a perfectly free pardon, would be allowed to land in the colony. Mr. La Trobe gave his assent to it; but it was disapproved at home, as it interfered with the royal prerogative of pardon. But virtually the colonists carried their point, and the law has been acted on ever since. All this time the diggers, and those who ministered to their wants, were getting on swimmingly and making money fast. But those depending on fixed and small incomes suffered extremely. Comfort there was none. Every necessary of life, and rent, went up to ten times their former rates. Imagine a cabbage being worth five shillings at the gold-fields, and half-a-crown even in Melbourne. The scenes in the streets were amusing beyond description. When the diggers had made their "piles," they came down to Melbourne for a holiday. They would hire the cabs and carriages and drive about with them, having their legs over the sides, and their pipes in their mouths, and their companions by their sides. If they wanted to get married (which was a very common thing) they would go to a surrogate and get a license. On being told the fee, they would throw a bank note, frequently of no small amount, on the table, and prepare to be off. On being told of the amount, and reminded that a large amount of change was due to them, they would say, "Oh, bother the change!" or make use of some such expression, leaving no unwelcome balance in favour of the hard-up surrogate. A man would go into a fine shop in Melbourne, and ask for a shawl for his "missus"—not one of your common things, but a real good one. He would be shown at first something of really good quality, but he would throw them aside one after another as not grand enough; and when at last the shopman, beginning to know his customer, brought out some flaring yellow thing, and said, "That's the kind the governor's lady wears, but then its price is thirty guineas," he would be charmed at once, and buy it.

And probably within half an hour you would see it gracing the person of some lady who took an airing with him in his free-and-easy carriage. So great was the desire in some cases to get a bit of land, on any terms, in a good situation, that a shrewd old colonist gave 700 guineas a foot for a frontage to one of the main streets. The fortunes that were made by public-house keeping were enormous. From £1,000 to £5,000 a year was the rental of a public-house. In a couple of years a fortune was made by keeping a tap; and a country publican is reported to have cleared £40,000 a year. The governor forwarded a despatch to Earl Grey, shortly after the discovery of gold, which graphically describes the state of the country:—"It is quite impossible for me to describe to your lordship the effect which these discoveries have had upon the whole community, and the influences which their consequences exercise at this time upon the position of every one, high and low. Within the last three weeks the towns of Melbourne and Geelong, and their large suburbs, have been in appearance almost emptied of many classes of their male inhabitants; the streets, which for a week or ten days were crowded by drays loaded with the outfit for the workings, are now seemingly deserted. Not only have the idlers, to be found in every community, and day labourers in the town and the adjacent country, shopmen, artisans, and mechanics of every description, thrown up their employment, and in most cases leaving their employers and their wives and families to take care of themselves, run off to the workings, but responsible tradesmen, farmers, clerks of every grade, and not a few of the superior classes have followed; some, unable to withstand the mania and force of the stream, or because they were really disposed to venture time and money on the chance; but others, because they were, as employers of labour, left in the lurch, and had no alternative. Cottages are deserted, houses to let, business is at a stand still, and even schools are closed. In some of the suburbs not a man is left, and the women are known for self-protection to forget their jars and to group together to keep house. The ships in the harbour are in a great measure deserted. Fortunate the family, whatever its position, which retains its servants at any sacrifice, and can further secure the supplies for their households from the few tradesmen that remain."

A license fee of thirty shillings a month was exacted from the diggers, and it produced the large sum of £580,616. Still the expense of officials, escorts, and constabulary was so great, that the governor contemplated doubling the fee, so as to induce the less fortunate diggers to return to their former employment; but if this had been carried out there would doubtless have been a rebellion. Poor Mr. La Trobe had no easy time of it, and at length he sent in his resignation, which was accepted.

Sir Charles Hotham arrived in the colony as governor in 1854. In November of that year, 800 diggers united together and determined not to pay any license fee. They armed themselves with rifles and revolvers, formed an intrenched camp, called the spot "Eureka," and raised the flag of independence, making a fire of their old licenses. Troops were sent from Melbourne, and an engagement took place in which fifty miners were killed and wounded. Peace was then restored. The license fee was afterwards abolished, and an export duty of half-a-crown an ounce put on the gold.

Vast numbers of those who now had money wished to invest at least a part of it in the purchase of land, and a long and loud cry arose to "unlock the lands." This was naturally opposed by the squatters, who claimed a pre-emptive right under the "Orders in Council," and much ill-feeling was engendered.

In 1852 the value of the gold exported was nearly eleven millions of pounds sterling; in 1853, nearly thirteen millions; in 1854 nine millions and a half; and in 1855 it rose to upwards of eleven millions. "Gipps' Land" was found to contain a fine gold-field—"Omeo," and this discovery has led to the opening up of this magnificent country, which up to that moment had been but partially known.

It was said of Mr. La Trobe that he was too easy in his administration; of Sir Charles Hotham they said just the contrary. The difficulties of his position brought on paralysis, of which he died on the last day of 1855.

Major-General McArthur, son of the Mr. J. McArthur who introduced the Merino sheep into Australia, administered the government for a year. At this time the new constitution was inaugurated, the colony receiving full power of self-government. Every male adult has a vote for the colonial House of Commons. Manhood suffrage and vote by ballot are in full exercise.

Victoria was just twenty years old when she attained her majority. Rapid indeed had been her growth, and she goes onward at a rapid pace, and promises to maintain the rich expectations formed of her in her youth. At first great opposition was made to the admission of the Chinese. But after a time it was found that they were harmless and industrious, and so the taxes were taken off them, and they have the same privileges as other people. Many of them are very wealthy, and have intermarried with some of the Irish orphan girls. In the year 1855 it was found that there were 1,893 manufactories in the colony.

Sir Henry Barkly was the first governor under the new constitution, and he arrived at the close of 1856. He had been originally a West Indian merchant, and afterwards the governor of a West Indian colony. His salary and allowances were equivalent to £20,000 a year. He was most favourably received; his duties were comparatively easy and pleasant, and so he retained his popularity. In 1850 the gross revenue of the colony was £259,433; in 1854 it reached £6,154,928. It fell gradually from this enormous sum. But for the next ten years it averaged three millions; one-third of which is expended in roads and bridges and public works, which items alone have cost £20,000,000, all paid by the people themselves. But now the colonists are not satisfied with ordinary roads, they must have *railways* and electric telegraphs. A public debt of £8,000,000 of money was created, and the money expended in the construction of about 200 miles of rail. You can now go to Ballarat, or even to the Murray, as easily as from London to Liverpool. Ballarat is a wonderful place. A few years ago and nothing was to be heard but the bleating of sheep. Now the great works are carried on by machinery—blasting and crushing the quartz rock. The old system of gold digging has quite disappeared. It is now *regular mining;* and machinery of great value is employed. Some idea of the value of the Ballarat mines may be formed from the fact that up to the end of 1866, 31,731,344 ounces of gold had been obtained from them, worth £126,925,376.

After a seven years' tenure of office, Sir Henry Barkly was relieved, and proceeded to the Mauritius as governor, and was succeeded by Sir Charles Darling in 1863. Sir Charles was a nephew of a former governor of New South Wales. The subject of the unlocking of the lands was being continually brought before the legislature, and change after change took place respecting them. It was a short time before Sir Charles Darling's arrival that a comprehensive measure was passed. It is called the "Land Law of 1862." The government re-appropriated all the agricultural lands of the colony, giving the squatter the use of them on sufferance till they were wanted. But these lands could not be invaded by the intending purchaser until they had been surveyed and proclaimed open to purchase without auction. The price was to be twenty shillings an acre; the area from 40 to 640 acres. They could buy one-half their section at a pound an acre, and leave the other half, paying half-a-crown a year per acre for it for eight years, when the grant would issue without further payment. Thus, if a man wanted 640 acres, he could pay £320 and have the whole land at once, paying £40 a year for eight years. Then he would have a freehold of 640 acres. As the yearly payment was really only a *fair rent*, it follows that he *virtually* got his land in fee-simple at ten shillings an acre. The following was found to be the state of the case as regarded the waste lands of the colony. There were about fifty-five and a half millions of acres, of which four and a half millions had been sold; half a million occupied by gold diggers; two millions granted as commons; and thirteen millions of waste and sterile land. There remained ten and a half million acres suitable for agriculture, and twenty-five millions more fit for pasturage.

The western district of the colony deserves special notice at the hands of those who are seeking for good land, in a mild and comparatively cool climate. It is the volcanic region of the country; extinct volcanoes, with the craters and their ashes, are to be found in all directions. The soil is very rich; it is in fact the granary of the colony. In crossing the vast plains between Mount Elephant and Mount Shadwell, one of the natives in the early times said that, " Long while ago, Mount Elephant spit fire at Mount Shadwell;" this was his idea of the two great volcanoes. Portland *was*, I suppose I must say *is*, the chief sea-port on the coast; it was laid out at the same time as Melbourne and Geelong, as we remarked before. It is most beautifully situated on rising ground looking down upon the bay. The scenery around it is charming. Its great distance from the capital, and the fact that it is surrounded by a dense forest for some miles before you come to the good land has retarded its progress; instead of advancing, it is I fear going back just now. It was proposed some years ago to form a tramway through this forest, in fact it was commenced but was not carried on. And whilst it has been stationary, Belfast and Warrnambool on the same coast, and Hamilton and other townships inland, have been going rapidly ahead, and threaten to leave Portland behind in the race for distinction. In 1800, Lieutenant Grant, in the *Lady Nelson,* sighted this fine harbour, and called it "Portland Bay," after the Duke of Portland, one of the Secretaries of State at the time. It was he who named the Capes Northumberland and Bridgewater; and also Mount Schank, Mount Gambier, Lawrence Rock, Julia Percy Island, Cape Otway, &c. The bay was in those days much frequented by seals and by whales. Major Mitchell, of whom we have spoken before, was surprised when he got near this place, where he thought the white man's foot had never trodden, to come suddenly on *an old shoe;* and the Hentys' shepherds (to one of whom probably this old shoe had belonged) seeing a body of strange men coming down upon them, made sure that they were bushrangers from New South Wales, and got their arms ready for defence; but instead thereof, it turned out to be the surveyor-general of New South Wales. In speaking of this place in his work, he says, "The situation of Portland Bay is a most eligible one for the site of a town." And it was thought that it would become a second Melbourne. In 1840 the upset price of town land was £100 an acre, and it fetched £300. As early as 1842 the clip of wool was 3,000 bales; and in 1846 it had two newspapers. Its first ship direct from England arrived in 1850. The climate is delightful. The mean thermometer 58°; the highest in February being 80°, and the lowest in May being 44°. It is not therefore subject to the same extremes of heat and cold as Melbourne, Geelong, and the interior, which range at times from 30° to 120°. Portland is the "Brighton" of Victoria; and as our citizens retire from the active pursuits of life, and seek for quiet resting-places, I know of no prettier and healthier spot than this; and I believe the day will come when it will be a favourite resort to which "paterfamilias" will take his wife and his little ones to for their "outing" at the sea-side.

In keeping along the coast, and going eastward, at a distance of 50 miles you reach Belfast. I shall not soon forget one of my earliest bush journeys between the two places. There are several rivers to cross, and of course there were no bridges. I was accompanied by a clergyman from a neighbouring town who knew the tracks better than I did. He was on horseback and I was driving in a buggy. When we came to one of the rivers, there were two ways of getting over it. You could either go to the mouth of it, where there was a "bar" at the point of its entering the ocean, or, higher up, there was what was considered a good crossing-place. We agreed to try the river higher up. "But," said he, "take care to keep to the *right*, for there is a deep hole, in which you will be lost with your carriage if you get into it." I quietly suggested to him, that as he knew it so well and was on horseback, it might be as well that he should save his archdeacon from the chance of a ducking by going in first. To this he most kindly agreed, and went in; I following very timidly in his wake. But presently there was a great splash, which frightened my horses sadly, and lo! my friend had gone right down into the hole, and nothing was visible but his hat. Profiting by his mishap, I avoided the hole and escaped the ducking. On returning by myself a few days afterwards I was afraid of meeting with his or a worse fate, and determined on going through the surf. But I had been warned that I must be careful, for that at the mouth it was a quicksand, and if the horses got frightened and stood still I should sink. I went in, and when a huge wave came rolling in with a white crest and the spray struck the horses, they quivered like an aspen leaf, and stood stock still. I shall never forget the sensation. When the wave receded I heard the wheels grinding down into the quicksand, and felt that we were sinking, and looking out to sea, I saw another great wave gathering itself up to pounce upon us. My coachman used his whip most unmercifully, and I belaboured the horse on my side with a stick, and by dint of his lashes, my cuts, and our united loud shouts, we roused the horses, and thank God escaped.

Belfast is the town of a "special survey." Its bay is called Port Fairy. In the year 1840 this system came into operation. Capitalists were permitted to purchase a block of 5,000 acres at twenty shillings an acre, without competition. In 1834

Mr. Atkinson, a lawyer in Sydney, heard that there was good country in the land now called Victoria, and he went to England and interested some capitalists in his scheme. They applied for a few hundred thousand acres, at five shillings an acre; but before anything was settled, Batman had gone to Port Phillip, and Governor Bourke had reported the matter to the Colonial Office, and so the bargain was not struck. But, availing himself of the special survey system, Mr. Atkinson secured 5,280 acres at Port Fairy. He was a native of Belfast, and called his new town after his native place. He sent a ship-load of people down from Sydney, most of whom were Irish, and located them on what were to be afterwards farms. He supplied them with tools, seed, and rations. Their rent was to be paid in kind, and ranged from one to two bushels of wheat to the acre. At first no land was sold; afterwards it was slowly brought into the market at high prices. One quarter of an acre in the town sold, I know, for £1,000. Belfast stands on the river Moyne, which has a sufficient depth of water for steamers and ordinary vessels to go up to the wharves in the centre of the town, but their doing so was prevented by the usual obstacle—a bar harbour, which nothing but boats could cross, and they at times with difficulty, if not with danger. The government have lately taken in hand the useful work of removing this bar, and so directing the current as to keep the passage clear. It is expected that these works will be finished during the present year; and if the success be as complete as it is expected to be, it will be the commencement of a new and most important era in the history of the place. There is a handsome English church; the Roman Catholic one is very pretty, and is nicely situated; there are also Presbyterian and Wesleyan churches. In Australia, where religious equality exists, they are all styled "churches." This town has three banks, two newspapers, a mechanics' institute, and an active and enterprising population.

Perhaps the most interesting feature in the district is "Tower Hill," situated midway between Belfast and Warrnambool. It is an island encompassed by a moat. The land in the neighbourhood is extremely fertile, the country beautifully wooded, and the extinct volcano rises to so great a height, that from its top you catch a fine view of the sea to Portland. The rapidly rising township of Koroit, the centre of a rich agricultural district, is in its immediate neighbourhood. And as you look towards the sea, you will observe a remarkably rich stretch of arable land. This is the "special survey" of W. Rutledge, Esq., a name well known in the history of the colony from its very commencement, and who lives in the midst of his numerous tenantry much respected for his kindness and liberality.

After crossing the Merri River, we come to the township of Warrnambool. When I lived at Belfast, the infant township formed a part of my parish, and

I occasionally went over to take service. It was necessarily in an evening. The people were very few indeed, and scattered. The service was held in a private house. Partly to enable me to steer clear of "wombat" holes, and partly in order to advertise the time for holding the service, I carried a large lantern in my hand. It had for many years formed the heifer station of a neighbouring squatter. It is now a large and thriving town, having churches for all denominations, banks, merchants' stores, steam-mills, &c. This, and nearly every town of any size in the country, has a hospital, supported partly by the government and supplemented by local subscriptions. The banks of the Hopkins, in the neighbourhood, are very beautiful, and the town itself is prettily situated. On the first occasion of a visit to this little place by the Bishop of Melbourne, we had to go down the river in a boat so leaky that the bishop was set to the ignominious post of "baling out" with a tin pannikin, and I was stationed in the bows to look out for snags in the river. Those who were pulling us did not seem to know much about their work; and at last the bishop, who doubtless had known on the banks of the Cam something about an oar, took one and showed them how to manage it. When we landed, a little black boy was picked up to carry the episcopal bag, and thus we entered the quiet little place. All I could do was to get together a congregation of *seven* persons to hear the bishop. What a change has taken place. Now there are many handsome churches filled with large congregations.

This district has of late years been literally dotted over with government townships. In some cases they consist of a public house, and perhaps a blacksmith's shop. But other places have become, or are rapidly becoming, large centres of population. Hamilton is one of these. It is in a most central position; and if the plan talked of be carried out, viz., carrying a railway to it, it will have the effect of diverting a great part of the traffic from the seaport towns. It is situated on the Grange Burn. The Wannon Falls in this neighbourhood are pretty, and at the right season well supplied with water. The Wando Vale, the Valley of Cashmere, and that loveliest part of Victoria, the Valley of the Wannon, and in fact the whole country round, must be seen to be appreciated. When Major Mitchell traversed this part of the country, which was then in a state of nature, he said, "It is an open grassy country, extending as far as we could see; hills round and smooth as a carpet; meadows broad, and either green as an emerald or of a rich golden colour, from the abundance of a ranunculus-like flower. Down into that delightful vale our vehicle trundled over a gentle slope, the earth being covered with a thick-like matted turf, superior to anything of the kind previously seen. That extensive valley was enlivened by a winding stream, the waters of which glittered through trees fringing each bank."

The township of Coleraine, about twenty miles from Casterton, has made great progress of late years. Between the two places there is a stretch of good land, as there is also about the Green Hills and Branxholme. Proceeding from Hamilton towards the little village of Dunkeld, which is almost as charmingly situated as the place whence it took its name, you see to great advantage the two southern hills of the Grampian Range—Abrupt and Sturgeon. The River Wannon flows at the foot of Mount Sturgeon. In the early days I was staying at a settler's hut there, when an old shepherd took me to a cave, and told me that they had had heavy work there once. The sheep were depasturing in the neighbourhood, when a tribe of blacks came down and killed many of them. They gorged themselves with mutton, and then brake the legs of a great number, as was their habit, to prevent their straying from them, and afterwards went into the cave to sleep off the effects of their meal. The enraged shepherds came out, and seeing what had been done, they went to the cave's mouth and *shot every one of the natives*, and threw their bodies into the Wannon. The whole range of the Grampians is extremely beautiful.

In former days the settlers in this district had very large runs. In some cases they hold them still, having bought up the freehold. One gentleman, at whose station the Duke of Edinburgh stayed when in this part of the country (Mr. Moffat's, of

Hopkins' Hill), has 500 miles of fencing on his estate, which cost £75 a mile. Thus the mere fencing of his property had cost £37,500! And he is not singular. There are many of the old race of gentlemen squatters, who are now the proprietors of large estates. We have thus the foundation of a landed aristocracy—a kind of "upper ten thousand." And this will form a conservative element in the state, if the owners of these noble properties identify themselves with the country, and become resident on them. But very generally in this colony the proprietors go home and live at ease, and merely draw their incomes from them. If this be the case of the majority, we shall ultimately have all the evils of the "absentee landlord" system, which has wrought so much mischief in Ireland. It appears to me that in New South Wales and in Tasmania a greater proportion of the original settlers, and of their children after them, remain on the spot where their fortunes were made, than is the case in Victoria. True, it is but a young country, and we can hardly judge of the two cases together; but I fear the tendency is in the direction indicated. People look upon this colony as a means to an end. They go to it, and work hard and make money, and run away from it. The Bishop of Melbourne, utterly unable to take the oversight satisfactorily of the whole country, has sought for a long time to get an endowment, so as to enable him to subdivide the diocese, but he has not succeeded. In Sydney, on the contrary, the new bishoprics of Goulbourn, Grafton and Armidale, and Bathurst, have all been recently formed and suitably endowed. It is greatly to be desired that the Bishop of Melbourne's efforts in this matter should be successful. In a former chapter we spoke of a single individual in Tasmania erecting a handsome church and endowing it with £400 a year. Will not some of our large landed proprietors and merchant princes in the colony strengthen the good bishop's hands in this work, which he has we know greatly at heart; and may not some of those in England, to whom God in his providence has given great wealth, and a desire to expend it to his glory and for the spiritual good of their fellow creatures, be found who, when they know the crying need there is of this subdivision, will help him in accomplishing it. It is proposed that the head-quarters of the new see should be at Ballarat.

"State aid to religion" still exists in Victoria; but a Bill has recently passed the Lower House by which it is proposed to do away with it in five years. And on this plan: on 1st January, 1870, to be reduced to four-fifths; 1871, to three-fifths; 1872, to two-fifths; 1873, to one-fifth; 1874, to nil. The annual grant is £50,000, divided amongst all the denominations, according to the census. It will, however, be observed that the gross amount receivable will not amount to two years' purchase of the existing grant, while payment is to be spread over four years. It will be a great loss to the colony if this Bill become law. The money has been most carefully expended. Help has been given in the erection of churches and parsonages, and in the maintenance of clergymen, in the infancy of the different townships, but it has been withdrawn or greatly diminished so soon as the material fabric was erected and the people able to provide for their own wants. And if it be taken away altogether, I do not know how the different denominations will be enabled to minister to the wants of the thinly inhabited villages and the scattered populations of the interior. The Church of England is by far the largest body. Her proportion of the grant is £23,000, or between one-half and two-fifths. Half of the sum is devoted to buildings, the other moiety to the stipends of ministers. After passing this Bill the Lower House has just carried another, for the payment of members. The sum granted is to be £30,000 a year; the allowance to each member £300.

In the year 1852, Mr. Gladstone proposed to pass through the Imperial Parliament a general measure, under which the Church of England in all the colonies might act in one prescribed manner; but it was opposed and abandoned. In 1854, an Act of the Legislature of Victoria was obtained, constituting the Church of England in the colony a legally recognised body, with its own tribunal, and disciplinary and other powers. This required the royal assent. In 1856 a ratifying Act was passed and assented to; and in October of that year the first assembly of the Church of England in Victoria took place. It is an assembly of all the clergy, and of lay representatives elected by the members of the Church in their respective parishes. They meet in one house, but vote separately. The temporal affairs are managed by the bishop and a "Council of the Diocese," composed of clergymen and of laymen, who report to the Church assembly. The system is working admirably, and is the strength of the Church. The patronage question is thus settled: In all new parishes the bishop has the first appointment of the clergyman; but he invariably consults the congregation. In the two next vacancies the people, by their representatives (who form a Board of Advowson) have the nomination, subject to the bishop's approval.

Formerly there were two systems of public education supported by the State—the denominational and the national. But in 1862 the two boards were abolished and one general and national system was introduced. It provided that the public money should be spent in giving secular and unsectarian teaching during four hours in the day, without interfering with any other teaching that the different parents or clergy might see fit to impart.

In the year 1853, at the instance of Mr. H. C. E. Childers, who was formerly an inspector of schools in Victoria, but who now holds the distinguished post of First Lord of the Admiralty, the Melbourne University was established. It is quite unsectarian in its character. The buildings are very fine, and were opened for the reception of students in 1856. The University stands on 40 acres of ground, which are tastefully laid out. It is endowed with £9,000 a year out of the public revenue. There are four professorships, each having an income of £1,000 a year, besides rooms. Excellent grammar schools, identified with each religious body, train the youth for the university curriculum, which is fully equal to that of the English universities. It is making not rapid but sure and most satisfactory progress. The Imperial government have conceded to the degrees of this and of the Sydney University a status of equality with those of their elder sisters in England. Mr. Westgarth, in speaking of the rapid progress of the colony, thus describes the spot where all these fine buildings now stand : " About twenty years ago," he says, " the author happened to return late one evening from the house of a friend, situated several miles in a northerly direction out of Melbourne. It was quite dark, being near midnight, as he approached the town. There were no gas lamps in those pristine days, nor indeed lamps of any kind, and the roads from the nascent metropolis still partook mainly of the random character of 'bush tracks.' Feeling therefore rather uncertain of his whereabouts, he partook himself to a source of information that was all of a-piece with the other characteristics of that early date of the settlement. This was the encampment of a tribe of aborigines, to which he had been guided by the fires that flickered in front of their rude wigwams. Some lay asleep, rolled up in their opossum rugs; one was sick, and a ghastly and comfortless spectacle he appeared; while others were still busy over the tobacco and other spirits of the day gathered in the town. The site of that native encampment is now that of the Melbourne University. The reminiscence possesses a charm in its freshness and reality, because it is rare indeed that such extremes of condition in a country's history are brought within the compass of so few years, or even within the experience of a single life." This spot and scene, so graphically drawn by Mr. Westgarth, are well known to me. It appears to have been a favourite camping place of the natives. Late one night, in 1839 or 1840, I was taken to the same spot, and there I witnessed a "corroboree" of these sable natives of the forest.

During Sir Charles Darling's administration there occurred a "crisis," into which we cannot enter here, but which did the colony a great deal of harm in the estimation of those who were living in England, and who could not understand the collisions which were almost sure to arise between the two branches of a legislature which were both anxious to maintain their respective privileges. The "deadlock" caused extreme inconvenience to many persons, and injury to others. But after a long period of angry opposition, the Gordian knot was cut by Sir Charles Darling declining the proposed grant.

The present governor is Viscount Canterbury (formerly Sir C. Manners Sutton). Up to the present time his popularity has received no check, and we trust that it may receive none.

Although for the present free passages are only granted to single females, and to a few married couples, yet the terms on which assisted passages are granted are so favourable, that few of those who have friends in the colony may not hope through their help to procure a passage. The following are the latest regulations which have been issued on the subject:—

"Emigration to Victoria, Australia, is governed—for the present, and pending the issue of further instructions—by regulations, dated Melbourne, July 10th, 1865, which provide as follows:—

"1. *Free Passages.*—The only persons eligible for free passages are single females, under the age of 35, who have been accustomed to domestic service, and who can produce certificates of good character. They must be free from any mental or bodily infirmity.

"Emigrants of this class are assisted to reach the port of embarkation at the cost of the Government.

"The Agent-General is authorised to select a few married couples to act as mess constables for the single females, and to grant them free passages.

"Applications for free passages must be made upon printed forms, which can be obtained from the Agent-General, or from the local agents appointed by him.

"2. *Assisted Passages* are granted to persons in the United Kingdom who have been nominated by their friends in Victoria, upon the payment, to the Government of Victoria at Melbourne, of deposits, according to the following scale:—

"*Scale of Payments by Depositor at Melbourne.*—Under fifteen years—male, £2, female, £1. Fifteen years, and under forty—male, £5, female, £2. Forty years, and upwards—male, £8, female, £5.

"Passage warrants are issued to the depositor in favour of the person nominated by him. The depositor forwards the warrant to the nominee in the United Kingdom, who, upon delivering it to the Agent-General, 8, Victoria Chambers, Victoria Street, Westminster, and being approved by him, is provided with a passage, subject to certain regulations, which can be ascertained upon application.

"Passage warrants are available for nine months from the date of their issue. If not used by the nominee, a passage warrant may be exchanged, upon application to the Immigration Agent at Melbourne.

"All communications relative to Emigration to Victoria should be addressed to

THE AGENT-GENERAL FOR VICTORIA,
8, *Victoria Chambers, Victoria Street,*
Westminster, S.W.,

from whom Forms of Application and all other information may be obtained.

"Persons communicating with the Agent-General should give their name and address in full, and plainly written.

"G. F. VERDON, *Agent-General for Victoria.*"

We give below an interesting leader from a late *Melbourne Argus*, on the subject of increased postal and telegraphic facilities between England and Australia:—

"While Earl Granville is doing his best, by a policy which is either unintentionally maladroit or perversely offensive, to repress the loyalty and alienate the affections of an important member of this group of colonies—New Zealand, to wit—the Australian dependencies are moved by a common impulse to draw nearer to the mother country, and to improve and multiply their means of communication with her. They neither undervalue nor desire to relax those ties of sentiment, family, and interest, which bind them to the parent state; and although it is to be acknowledged and deplored that the fiscal legislation of two or three of the colonies has taken a shape as hostile to English commerce and manufactures as it is detrimental to the substantial progress and prosperity of ourselves, yet the enlightened portion of the community everywhere recognises the mischief and folly of protection, and the duty and advantage of promoting to the fullest extent a free commercial intercourse between all parts of the empire. We look to Great Britain as the most profitable outlet for the product of our gold, silver, and copper mines, our surplus wool, wheat, and wine, and for our superabundant flocks and herds. We cannot be blind to the fact that her coal measures, her iron and tin mines, her machinery, skill, capital, and labour, qualify her to produce numberless articles of manufacture better and more cheaply than we can hope to do for a century to come, and that the exchange of these commodities for those which we possess in excess is a transaction by which both parties must be benefited, and in the effecting of which numerous subsidiary and intermediate industries are called into profitable exercise.

"Actuated by these views, the eastern colonies of Australasia—New South Wales, Queensland, and New Zealand—are simultaneously directing their attention to opening up more frequent and more rapid mail communication with Great Britain. During a recent visit of the Premier of New South Wales to Queensland, the basis of an arrangement was arrived at on the part of the Governments of the two colonies, in virtue of which a monthly mail is to be established to Galle *viâ* Torres Straits, its arrival and departure being so timed as to secure the advantages of a fortnightly mail to most of these provinces. It is proposed that the steamer should receive mails at Cape Moreton (near Brisbane), Rockhampton, and Bowen, and should coal at Cape York, the most northerly point of this continent. This would bring the outposts of settlement in Queensland nearer to England, as regards postal communication, than any other of the settled districts, and this circumstance could scarcely fail to operate beneficially upon the flow of immigration thitherward. The terms upon which the subsidy is to be contributed are these :—New South Wales is to pay one-half, Queensland two-sixths, and New Zealand one-sixth. It is proposed to withdraw altogether from the Peninsular and Oriental Company's contract, so soon as the latter expires; it being considered that the advantages derivable from it can be obtained by giving the southern and western colonies the use of the Torres line as an equivalent. Concurrently with the establishment of this route, the Queensland Government undertakes to extend its line of telegraph to the Gulf of Carpentaria, from whence a submarine cable will connect it with Java, and thus bring it into relation with the Indo-European service, towards which the government of New South Wales will grant a subsidy.

"On the other hand, the Legislature of New Zealand has signified its intention to discontinue its contribution to the Peninsular and Oriental Company's contract, so soon as the latter expires, and has authorised tenders to be invited for a monthly steam service between San Francisco and that colony. A glance at the map of the world will show that this is the most direct line of communication between the mother country and the "Great Britain of the South," as Sir Robert Peel called it. The opening of the Pacific and Central Union Railways having brought San Francisco within fifteen days of London, and the eastern ports of New Zealand being within twenty-one days' steaming of the Californian capital, our brethren in the islands are naturally eager to avail themselves of the opportunity of getting their letters from England only five weeks' old, instead of nearly eight weeks, as at present; the more especially as it has been ascertained that the cost of such a service will not greatly exceed the quota now contributed by New Zealand to the Peninsular and Oriental Company's subsidy. For passenger traffic, the proposed line will offer many inducements to persons in good circumstances, since a voyage across the Pacific is attended with an amenity of climate and a freedom from cyclones which have obtained for that ocean the appellation which it bears; while the opportunity of seeing every phase of settlement and civilisation, from the Indian wigwam to the marble palace, and from the forest clearing to the swarming "empire city," which will be afforded by crossing the North American continent, is one which will not be undervalued by either outward or homeward bound travellers belonging to a colonising nation.

"Thus it will be seen that for the time to come, the Australian group of colonies will separate themselves, for postal purposes, into two divisions; the eastern despatching their mails by way of Torres Straits in one direction, and California in the other; while the southern and western—Victoria, South Australia, Tasmania, and Western Australia, will adhere in all probability to the present route as the most direct and expeditious for them. And to render it more so for the transmission of telegraphic intelligence, the Government of South Australia is considering a scheme which has been submitted to it by an English company for the extension of the wires by a land line from Port Augusta to King George's Sound, and from thence by a submarine cable in two sections, *vid* Keeling's Island, to Ceylon. The projectors of this scheme ask for a guarantee from the South Australian Government of six per cent. upon an estimated outlay of £800,000; but they anticipate that the net subsidy would not exceed £8,000.

"An alternative telegraph line is also engaging the attention of the South Australian Government. This would pass through the northern territory of that colony to Port Darwin, and thence by submarine cable to the south-western extremity of Java, where it would unite with the lines already in course of construction to India and China. Transmitted by either of these lines, a message, as Captain Osborn points out, 'would probably be in Ceylon from Australia in half the time and with a tenth of the risk it would have in reaching Singapore through

Java.' On the whole, the line across the continent to Port Darwin appears to be regarded with the greatest favour in South Australia, and if it should be adopted, the northern terminus on the main land could be readily brought into communication by way of Burke Town or Norman Town, on the Gulf of Carpentaria, with the present northern terminus of the Queensland lines at Rockingham Bay."

"The statistical annual registers for 1868 of New Zealand, South Australia, Queensland, and Tasmania have just been published. Those of New South Wales are not yet forthcoming, but information so far as Victoria is concerned is accessible in various scattered documents, and with that before us we can form a fair estimate of the progress made last year in regard to population in five of the Australian colonies. In Victoria the increase was 24,429; in New Zealand, 7,586; in South Australia, 3,438; in Queensland, 7,578; in Tasmania, 2,251. Of the five colonies enumerated, two—New Zealand and South Australia—appear to be slackening speed, while the other three—Victoria, Queensland and Tasmania—are experiencing a revival."

"At a recent meeting of the council of the Acclimatisation Society, the secretary read the report of his mission to Hobart Town, whither he had been sent for the purpose of bringing over to this colony some trout ova, for the stocking of the Victoria water-courses. He stated that, within 60 hours of the ova being taken from the ponds at New Norfolk, having been carried a distance of eight miles on foot, then by steamer to Melbourne, and 60 miles into the interior of Victoria by carriage, these 2,000 young trout in embryo had been deposited in the breeding-ponds in perfect condition, only four being dead. The president was able to announce at subsequent meetings of the society that nearly all the ova had been successfully hatched. Out of the 2,000 ova, only a few had proved bad, the loss sustained being less than 2 per cent. The young fry are in the most satisfactory condition, and will be ready for liberation in a few weeks. It was announced, also, at a recent meeting, that

Captain Edward Jones, of the *Superb*, had brought over to this colony the largest number of pheasants ever imported at one time into Victoria. The society propose to liberate them in the ranges, where suitable cover and food will be available."

"The satisfactory intelligence received by the last few mails respecting the disappearance of the prejudice once existing against Australian preserved meats as an article of food has not only led to the formation of several new companies, but has encouraged manufacturers at present in the field to extend their operations. The Melbourne Meat-preserving Company have found it necessary to enlarge their works on the Saltwater River, in order to keep pace with the increased demand for their meats. The extensions are now in course of construction, and, when completed, the manufacturing power of the company will be increased one-half; and whereas they can now turn out about twenty-six tons of meat a week, when the additions are finished they will be in a position to preserve forty tons in the same period. Since the company re-commenced operations in June last, they have shipped 300 tons of meat in tins, and not only has the whole met with a ready sale, but the agent at home has considerably oversold the shipments forwarded. Recent advices show that the retail selling price of tinned meats is 7½d. per lb., while the best joints of butchers' meat fetch 10d. per lb., so that the advantage obtained by the purchase of the former is very apparent. The wholesale price of the company's meat is from 6d. to 6½d. per lb. The stock markets are very favourable just now to large buyers. The progress made by the Victorian Meat-preserving Company, of which Mr. R. Caldwell is the managing partner, and Mr. M'Cracken the practical manager, is also very satisfactory. The company have experienced considerable difficulty in overcoming the prejudice against their meats, owing to the supposition that the process they employed was a new one. The process is, however, a very simple one. The meat (beef and mutton) is preserved in a raw state. The bones, sinews, &c., are taken out, the meat lightly cured, rolled up, and packed in casks with refined melted fat. By thus excluding the air, the meat is found to retain all its excellence for years. Shipments of meat thus preserved have been made to almost every market in the world, and many experienced and intelligent sea captains have testified as to its fitness for ship's use. The Lords of the Admiralty have sanctioned its use for H.M. ships under the command of Commodore Lambert, in the Pacific. The French Government of New Caledonia have ordered largely of the meat for that colony, after a careful trial for twelve months. The troops in India have used it with much satisfaction. The new settlement in Northern Australia, which is an Indian climate, has been supplied largely with this meat, and it has there been preferred to the very excellent tinned meat with which the settlers are also provided. The process employed by the company is not only a thoroughly economical one, saving everything from the animal, but it has been proved to be one of the most certain in its results, and though the meat is now being sold in London at 4½d. per lb., a fair profit is left to the manufacturer and the shipper. Several other companies are preparing to commence operations. Mr. A. Morris, who went to England as Mr. Mort's agent in connexion with the freezing process, has recently returned, and has brought back with him much valuable information respecting the preservation of meat. Several specimens of meat preserved by him by different processes, and under most unfavourable circumstances, in London, in May last, and since brought out to New South Wales, were tested a few days ago, and pronounced to be excellent in almost every particular."

The establishment of another novel industry is foreshadowed in the following paragraph from the *Mount Alexander Mail:*—

"Messrs. Thompson and Co., calculating the extra cost to which the colony is put by importing starch that might be produced of the best quality from local flour, made the experiment of making starch, and so well did they succeed that they are encouraged to hope that a good industry may be opened up in this direction. They have given the project due consideration, and as it looks practicable, they are on the look-out for a skilled person to conduct a factory on their account."

"The soil and climate of Gipps' Land," says the *Times*, "have long been known as well adapted for the growth of hops and tobacco, and a very good proof of this fact was presented to us at Stratford. Mr. Writlemin, who came out from Switzerland some time ago to cultivate the white mulberry, at which he has had twenty-five years' experience, has about six acres of land, taken up under the 42nd clause, under tobacco cultivation at the Top Plains. He has handed us a bundle of cigars made from his own tobacco of last year's growth. They are fine flavoured, smoke well, and can be manufactured at £5 per 1,000.

"The erection of a cheese factory on a large scale at Allensford, near Warrnambool, is being rapidly proceeded with, and is expected to be finished by the 1st of October, when cheesemaking operations will be commenced. There is some probability of another being established at Mamba, in Gipps' Land."

"The revenue returns of the colony of Victoria, for the three, nine, and twelve months ending the 30th of September last, has been published in the *Government Gazette*. Compared with the preceding year, there is an increase on all three periods. That on the quarter amounts to £101,603 12s. 3d.; that on the nine months to £267,161 5s. 2d.; and that on the year, to £396,139 4s. 6d. Taking the year, the increase in customs amounts to £153,782 7s. 2d.; in the territorial revenue, to £141,479 18s.; in the railway income, to £47,906 8s. 7d.; on water supply, to £8,236 9s. 3d.; in the electric telegraph department, to £2,745 11s. 5d.; on tonnage, to £3,082 3s.; and on postage, to £8,995 17s. 11d. Analysing the Customs returns, we find that towards the increase, spirits contributed £37,956 19s. 5d.; wharfage rates, £18,423 13s. 1d.; and 'all other,' £94,899 5s. 3d. With the solitary exception of pastoral occupation there is an increase in every item which appears under the head of 'Territorial Revenue.' The decrease on that one account amounts to £11,396 7s. The increases on the other items are as follow :—Sales by auction, £101,641 4s. 5d.; rents and selections, £32,899 0s. 1d.; rents and licenses, £8,298 8s. 9d.; miners' rights, £2,499 0s. 1d.; business licenses, £763 10s.; leases of auriferous and mineral lands, £6,680 7s. 6d.; and water-right and searching licenses, £94 14s. 2d. Taking the returns as a whole they are more satisfactory than they have been for some time past, and they appear to indicate that the colony is gradually recovering from depression."

The new Land Bill has now become law, and it is of a most liberal character. All the pastoral leases expire on the 31st December, 1870. But the new Act authorises the re-issue of yearly leases for pastoral purposes for ten years more, which is the period fixed for the duration of the measure.

As regards *bonâ fide* settlers, the terms on which they can procure a freehold are exceedingly advantageous. A man may only select 320 acres under the Act, but of course he can purchase at auction any additional quantity he may require. The 320 acres he may select just where he pleases—reserves only excepted—and pay for them in ten years without interest, at the rate of 20s. an acre. That is, he pays a rent of 2s. an acre, and gets the freehold for nothing.

The *Melbourne Argus*, with its usual ability and care, lately produced an article on the subject of the demand for labour and the rates of wages, from which we gladly make the following extracts :—

"For the information of our readers in Great Britain, numbers of whom we hope to include among our readers in Victoria, we have been at some pains to collect from independent and authentic sources the rates of wages actually current at this moment in Melbourne. They will be found in another column, and it will be seen that for skilled labour generally—for artisans engaged in the building trades, for example—the rate is 10s. per diem, the working day being limited to eight hours. For cabinetmakers, ironfounders, and mechanical engineers, this may be taken as the minimum, the maximum ranging from 12s. to 14s., according to the quality of the work to be performed and the special capacity or technical skill demanded for its performance. Builders' labourers receive 7s., and pick-and-shovel men 6s. per day of eight hours. Good tailors are said to be scarce, and can earn from £3 to £3 15s. per week, but in the factories they do not average more than from £2 10s. to £3. Tailoresses earn from 30s. to 40s., and machinists from 20s. to 30s. For girls the rate varies from 12s. 6d. to 17s.

"The wages of farm labourers fluctuate according to the period of the year. During the last month, when the ingathering of the hay and corn harvests have both been actively proceeded with, harvestmen have refused to go to work for less than £2 a week and their rations, which mean three substantial meals a day, with meat at each; and in some of the remoter districts the farmers have had to succumb to a demand for £3 a week and rations, or run the risk of seeing the over-ripe corn shed its grains upon the ground before it could be hastily cut and garnered. This, of course, is an exceptional and temporary state of things; but so much land has been taken up by men who in former years were farm labourers themselves, and so much more is likely to be entered upon under the new act which was passed last week, establishing free selection over the whole of the colony, that a steadily growing demand for agricultural labour is likely to exist for years to come. Irrespectively of which, tenders will be shortly invited for the construction of a trunk line of railway from Melbourne to the north-eastern boundary of the colony, and this will constitute a serious drain upon the local labour market. Two other main lines are projected, and will be proceeded with so soon as the position of our finances will admit of it. Thus it will be seen that besides the ordinary demand for labour, which is mostly in excess of the supply, and, as such, has a tendency to check speculative enterprise, because an element of uncertainty enters into all calculations based upon a prospective rate of wages, there will arise during the next few years a competition between the Government and the private employer which will be necessarily favourable to unskilled labour more especially. Add to this the general progress of settlement, the multiplication of wants arising out of a more consolidated state of society, the accumulation of capital, and the gradually decreasing rate of interest which its possessors feel themselves compelled to acquiesce in, and most reflecting men will acknowledge that the prospects held out in Victoria to industrious immigrants were never so numerous or so encouraging as they are at the present time.

"It must also be remembered that a wage-rent of 10s. a day represents a far greater purchasing power, with respect to all the necessaries of life, than the same sum does in England. The best wheaten bread is sixpence the four-pound loaf, beef is from threepence to sixpence, and mutton from three-halfpence to fourpence per lb., fresh butter is from ninepence to a shilling, and cheese from sixpence to tenpence per lb.; all kinds of garden and orchard produce are cheap and abundant; tea, sugar, and coffee are cheaper than in the mother country, and wearing apparel is probably as reasonable in price, and is certainly as good in quality in Melbourne as in London; while it is the artisan's own fault if, with the aid of a building society, he is not the owner of the house he occupies.

"With respect to female immigration, a single incident will suffice to exhibit the magnitude of the demand for and the insufficiency of the supply of domestic servants. On Friday last it was notified that twenty-three young girls who had just arrived by the *Charlotte Gladstone* would be open to engagement at eleven o'clock in the morning, at the Immigration Depôt in this city. Five minutes sufficed to procure situations for the whole of them at wages averaging from £20 to £30 per annum. There were about 160 heads of households applying for domestics, and it was stated that at least 300 female immigrants of the class above referred to could have met with immediate engagements, if such a number had been forthcoming. As a general rule, domestic service in this colony is less onerous, while it is much more liberally remunerated, than in Great Britain. Most houses consist of a ground-floor only, or of two storeys at the most, and are conveniently planned. Fires are not required for more than four months in the year, and the winters are mild and genial. Hence domestic servitude does not imply, as it too often does in the mother country, domestic suffering, and the position of our Abigails and Bridgets is sufficiently independent to exempt them from the necessity of submitting to the arbitrary exercise of authority, to caprice of temper, or rigorous limitations of personal liberty, should these be manifested towards them by harsh and exacting mistresses.

"If we wished to strengthen the inducements which present themselves to industrious men and women to emigrate to Victoria, we might refer to the large sums deposited in the savings banks and invested in building societies and other prudential associations by the wage-earning classes. But to persons of average intelligence, the particulars as to wages and expenditure which we have furnished above, and the accuracy of which may be thoroughly relied on, will suffice to enable them to form their own conclusions as to the advantages which will result from transferring their labour from an overcrowded to an imperfectly supplied market. They must not imagine that by so doing they will be dispensed from the exercise of diligence, frugality, temperance, perseverance, and forethought; but with these, they may confidently calculate upon achieving an amount of worldly prosperity in Australia which they could never hope to attain to in Europe."

"The Labour Market.—During the last month the demand for house servants, both for town and country, has far exceeded the supply, and rates have ruled correspondingly high.

NEW HOMES.

In fact, very little hiring has been done in this branch of labour, servants preferring generally to remain out of place until the holidays are over. The difficulty of obtaining house servants has of late been so great that in small families it is seriously considered if it would not be better to do without them altogether. Good servants for the country are greatly wanted. First-class married couples without children can command almost any price, as much as £100 per annum having been given for a first-class married couple lately. This, of course, includes board and lodging. Mechanics connected with the building trades have been kept fully employed, the contractors often finding it difficult to get a supply of good workmen. As usual at this time of the year, agricultural labourers are in great demand, and the supply is very short. In some districts men for harvest work are getting as high as 10s. per day and their food, while in others the rate is from 6s. to 7s. per day. The following rates have been taken from the largest and best establishments of their kind in Melbourne, and where the work is regular. For tradesmen in every case, except where otherwise mentioned, the day's work is eight hours. For country and house servants the average rate is taken, as the last month's rates are exceptional, and not for a permanency.

"The usual weekly rations allowed in Victoria are 10 lb. to 12 lb. of meat (beef or mutton), 10 lb. flour, 2 lb. sugar, and ¼ lb. of tea. The following servants are fed and lodged by their employers, receiving rations as above:—Shepherds (first-class), £35 to £45 per annum; hutkeepers, £25 to £30 per annum; lads for the country, 10s. to 12s. per week; general farm labourers and station hands, 15s. to 20s. do. Married couples for out stations £40 to £55 per annum. The following servants are fed and lodged with the employers' families:— Grooms, for country, 20s. to 25s. per week; men cooks, for hotels, £1 to £4 do.; female do., £40 to £80 per annum; married couples, for country (first-class), without encumbrance, from £65 to £85 per annum; female house servants, for country (first-class), £35 to £45 per annum; do. do. (second-class), £30 to £35 do. ; laundresses £35 to £45 do.; nurse-girls, for town, £25 to £30 do.

"The following wages for skilled labourers and other tradesmen are without rations, unless where specially mentioned:—

"Tradesmen.—Among stonemasons, bricklayers, plasterers, and carpenters an arrangement has been made with the employers that the rate of wages shall be 10s. per day; builders' labourers (hodmen), 7s. per day; pick and shovel men, 6s. per day.

"Tailors.—In first-class establishments good men are scarce, and constant work is to be had at the average of from £3 to £3 15s. per week. In second-class establishments the average earnings are from £2 10s. to £3. In factories, tailors, best hands, average £2 10s. Tailoresses can earn as follows:—Trouser and vest hands, 30s. per week; coat do., 35s.; pressers, £2.

"Clothing Machinists.—Best, 30s. per week; ordinary, 20s.; shirtmakers (machinists), girls, 12s. 6d. to 17s.; cutters, 15s. 6d. to 30s.; finishing, 2s. to 6s. per doz.

"Bootmakers.—In the best establishments for bespoke work the rates paid are as follow:—Wellingtons, 14s. 6d.; elastics, 12s.; closing, 8s.; riding boots, back strap, 24s. In factories good workmen can earn from £2 to £2 15s. per week at slop work. Ordinary hands earn £2 per week.

"Cabinet-makers.—In the best shops the average earnings of good tradesmen is 12s. per day and upwards, according to ability; polishers, 10s. to 11s. In second-class establishments and factories first hands make 10s. per day, and for cabriole work 12s.; upholsterers, 9s. to 10s.; polishers, 8s. to 9s.; sawmill hands, 10s. to 12s. per day of eight hours.

"Iron Founders, Smiths, &c.—Smiths are paid per hour, and good men can earn on an average 10s. to 14s. per day; fitters, 9s. to 12s.; turners, 14s.; moulders, 11s. to 14s.; pattern-makers, 10s. to 13s.; mechanical engineers, 12s. to 14s.; shoeing-smiths earn on an average £2 10s. per week of 10 hours per day.

"Stevedore's Men.—Lumpers and wool-stowers are paid 12s.

per day; foremen, 16s. The rate never alters, but there is often a good deal of broken time. Donkey-engine drivers, about £4 per week; engineers in tow-boats, £16 per month.

"Painters.—Ordinary hands get 8s. per day, but work is not very steady in this trade.

"Watch Jobbers.—Advertisements have appeared for steady men in this trade at £4 per week; this may be taken as the ordinary rate.

"Bakers.—First-class workmen (foremen) average £3 per week; second hands, £2 to £2 5s. The work in this trade is 10 hours per day.

"Gardeners.—First-class men (without rations) for situations near town, get 50s. to 60s. per week, but the demand for best hands is very limited. Do. for country, 50s.; second-class do., near town, 36s. to 42s. per week; third-class, for country (with rations), 15s. to 20s.

"Grooms in livery-stables get from 30s. to 40s. per week.

"Saddlers and Harness-makers.—The best hands in this trade earn £3 per week—time, 10 hours per day; second-class (mostly young men), 25s. to 30s."

And these high wages are to be obtained in a country where all the necessaries and many of the luxuries of life are to be readily obtained at cheap rates; so that if the emigrant will but be steady and economical, success will undoubtedly reward his labour.

The following account of the retail markets is extracted from the *Argus:*—

"RETAIL MARKETS.—Eggs maintain late quotations and butchers' meat is unaltered in price. Poultry is in demand, and the feeling of the market is firm, but butter is plentifully supplied, and rather dull of sale at slightly reduced rates. The current prices are as follow:—Beef, 3d. to 6d. per lb.; mutton,

1½d. to 4d. per lb.; veal, 6d. per lb.; pork, 8d. per lb.; fowls, 5s. to 6s. 6d. per pair; geese, 8s. to 11s. do.; ducks, 6s. to 7s. do.; turkeys, 12s. to 20s. each; cheese, 6d. to 1s. 4d. per lb.; eggs, 10d. to 1s. 2d. per dozen; butter, 10d. to 1s. per lb.; bread, 8d. per 4 lb. loaf; milk, 6d. per quart; hams, 1s. 2d. to 1s. 4d. per lb.; bacon, 1s. to 1s. 2d. per lb.

"Hay Market.—Mr. James Fenton reports:—'The market has been deluged with new hay of an inferior quality all the week; indeed, the supply of good is very limited. There has been very little enquiry for old hay, and prices are not so firm. Quotations are:—Old hay, £8 10s. to £9 5s.; new, £3 to £4 15s.; straw, £3 10s. to £5.' Messrs. Butler and Moss report:— 'This has been a very dull week, large arrivals and few buyers occasioned to some extent by the holidays. We expect a more regular sale next week, even if prices are no better. We have sold—Old hay, £8 10s. to £9 5s.; new hay, £3 to £5; straw, £3 15s. to £5 5s.'

"Eastern Market.—There was a heavy supply of cabbages and new potatoes brought to market this morning, and sales were very dull and at low prices. Peas were in request at an advance, other descriptions of vegetables being the same as last week. In fruits, strawberries were in active demand and cherries of prime quality sold readily, but many of them this season have suffered from hailstorm, and are very inferior. In dairy produce butter was heavy, and lower rates were gladly accepted, but eggs were firm at last week's quotations. Pigs and poultry were well represented. The following were the prices ruling:—Vegetables—Jerusalem artichokes, 1½d. to 2d. per lb.; asparagus, 6d. to 2s. 6d. per 100; basil, 1s. per dozen bunches; beans, broad, 1d. per lb.; beet, 6d. to 9d. per dozen bouquets, 3s. to 8s. per dozen; cabbages, 3d. to 1s. per dozen; carrots, 6d. to 8d. per dozen bunches; cauliflowers, 6d. to 2s. per dozen; cress, water, 6d. to 9d. per dozen bunches; cucumbers, long spine, 2s. 6d. to 4s. per brace; horseradish, 3s. to 6s. per dozen bunches; leek, 9d. to 1s. per dozen bunches; lettuce, 4d. to 1s. per dozen; marjoram, 9d. per dozen bunches; mint, 6d. to 9d. per dozen bunches; onions, dried, 8d. to 9d.

per lb.; do., green, 6d. to 10d. per dozen bunches; parsley, 6d. per dozen bunches; parsnips, 9d. to 1s. per dozen bunches; peas, 1¼d. to 2d. per lb.; old potatoes, 5s. to 5s. 3d. per cwt.; new do., 6s. to 10s. per cwt.; radishes, 4d. to 6d. per dozen bunches; rhubarb, 1s. to 2s. 6d. per dozen bunches; sage, 9d. per dozen bunches; spinach, 1d. per lb.; thyme, 8d. to 9d. per dozen bunches; turnips, 6d. to 1s. per dozen bunches. Fruits. —Cherries, 9d. to 1s. 3d. per lb.; gooseberries, 3½d. to 4d. per quart; strawberries, 1s. 3d. to 1s. 9d. per lb. Dairy Produce.— Butter, 8d. to 10d. per lb.; cheese, 6d. to 8d. per lb.; ducks, 5s. 6d. to 6s. per pair; eggs, 10d. to 1s. per dozen; geese, 8s. to 10s. per pair; hens, 5s. to 6s. per pair; honey, 6d. per lb.; pigeons, 2s. to 3s. per pair; pork, 6d. to 7d. per lb.; rabbits, 2s. to 4s. per pair; sucking pigs, 8s. to 12s. each; turkeys, 11s. to 19s. per pair; hams, 1s. to 1s. 2d. per lb.; bacon, 1s. per lb."

A copy of the statistics of Victoria for the year ending 31st December, 1868, has been just received from the Agent-General. We make a few extracts therefrom. During the year 32,805 emigrants arrived, including Chinese, only 8,522 of whom were females. During the same period 25,552, including Chinese, left the colony. The population amounted to 684,316. On the 30th September, 1869, the population had increased to 703,817. There are nearly 90,000 more men than women. Those employed in the gold-fields number 271,788. The estimated value of the rateable towns and boroughs is £21,503,942, their revenue £500,323, and their expenditure £398,386. Of the electors for the Legislative Council it was found at the last election that not more than about 53 per cent. exercised their privilege; and for the Legislative Assembly 61 per cent. The net revenue for the year was £3,022,922, and the expenditure £2,263,831. The public debt is £9,417,800. The total military force in the colony was 483, and the expenditure under this head £59,537. The Victoria volunteer force amounts to 4,002, and the expenditure on their behalf to £25,558. Immigration cost £23,131. The expenditure on public works was £103,136, and on roads and bridges £76,072. The imports for the year were £13,320,661, and the exports £15,593,990. The value of the preserved meat exported came to £28,565, of gold to £7,843,197, and of wool £4,567,182. The number of vessels that entered inwards was 2,067, of the tonnage of 653,362 tons; and outwards 2,172, of the tonnage of 685,207 tons. There are 633 post-offices through which there passed in the year nearly ten millions of letters, and five millions of newspapers. There are now 86 electric telegraph stations, 3,171 miles of wire, and the revenue from this source was £31,058. The colony has now 271 miles of railway opened, the total cost of which has been upwards of ten millions of money, being at the rate of £37,331 a mile. The passage rates are: first-class, 3¾d.; second-class, 2¾d. a mile. The total receipts for the year have been £712,765.

The lands sold during the year were 275,648 acres, at the average price of £1 6s. 1d. The total quantity of land sold in the colony is 6,675,246 acres, and the total extent of unsold land now is 48,967,803 acres. There are 1,050 runs held by the squatters, covering an area of 27,034,785 acres. The cultivated land is 712,865 acres, of which 259,804 acres are under wheat and 36,204 under potatoes. There were upwards of four million bushels of wheat and eighty thousand tons of potatoes. There are nearly eight millions of vines.

The return of sheep and cattle is as follows: sheep, 9,756,819; cattle, 693,682; horses, 143,934; and pigs, 136,206.

The number of buildings of all descriptions used for public worship by the chief denominations is thus given: Wesleyans, 392; Presbyterians, 383; Church of England, 340; Roman Catholics, 294. There is accommodation in all the places of worship for 286,760, with an average attendance of 180,721.

The Melbourne University has now 253 graduates. There are 1,430 public and private schools, attended by 97,884 scholars. Sabbath schools number 1,201, with an average attendance of 83,627 children.

There are eighty public libraries or mechanics' institutes, twenty-six hospitals, six benevolent asylums, six orphan asylums, four hospitals for the insane, six industrial schools, one deaf and dumb institution, a Magdalen asylum and a refuge, two benevolent societies, and a Jewish philanthropic society. A mint for Victoria is in course of erection in Melbourne. It is to be under the charge of Colonel Warde, who held a similar post a few years since in Sydney.

This is an age of statistics. We may confidently refer to the above as demonstrating most clearly the rapid progress and the financial prosperity of Victoria.

From what has been said about this colony the reader will have gathered the following facts: that there is no room for men wishing to take up new runs for sheep or cattle. The only way to obtain such property now is by purchase. For those, however, who wish to find everything ready to their hand the terms for purchasing are very favourable, as stations are selling at a low rate. There is ample room for men of small capital desirous of buying a homestead and commencing farming operations. We believe that in this colony "squatting" will die out, and we shall see a large body of men, like the farmers in England, combining within a limited space agricultural and pastoral pursuits. And such a class is a most valuable one for any country, and of their success there can be no reasonable doubt. Mechanics in moderation, and labourers in any number, and female servants without limit, will find remunerative employment in a land like "home."

Chapter VI.

SOUTH AUSTRALIA.

BY "South Australia" we should naturally expect to find that country which was farthest from the tropics, but such is not the case, for the whole colony of Victoria is to the south of Adelaide. The title is therefore a misnomer. And more so now than formerly, for great part of the most *northern* portion of the island is now included in *South* Australia. In fact it goes through the whole land from north to south, and thus constitutes the largest of all the British colonies. As originally established, its area was estimated at 300,000 square miles, or 192,000,000 acres, being more than twice the size of Great Britain and Ireland. In 1861 it was further enlarged by the addition of a territory called "No Man's Land," a district situated between South and Western Australia; and in 1863 the great "Northern Territory" was temporarily annexed to it. Its northern boundary is now the Indian Ocean, and the southern boundary the Southern Ocean, and it covers an area of 750,000 square miles.

So far back as 1831 a number of gentlemen of

high standing in England formed a company for the purpose of colonising this distant land. But after a lengthened negotiation with the government they failed to obtain their charter, and the project was abandoned. But it was revived in 1834, and a Bill passed both Houses of Parliament and received the royal assent, enabling the projectors to carry out their plans under certain regulations.

In 1827 it was proposed to appoint a select committee of the House of Commons on emigration. On that occasion Colonel Torrens explained the novel principles to be pursued. "I am not merely prepared to show," he said, "that emigration would cost less than maintaining paupers in their parishes at home, and would thus prove a measure of permanent economy and retrenchment, I am prepared to go much further than this. I am prepared to prove, both theoretically and practically, that emigration may be so conducted as to replace with interest the whole of the expenditure incurred in effecting it, and to aid the finances of the country by opening new and not inconsiderable sources of public revenue. Should any honourable member conceive that I am departing from the strict sobriety of fact, let him look to the United States of North America, and learn from the *practical* men of that untheorising country the gigantic scale upon which emigration and colonisation may be beneficially carried out. The population of the States is nearly twelve millions; it doubles in a period of about twenty-five years, and the main annual increase may be taken at half a million. Now of this half-million annually added to the population, the far greater proportion annually emigrate to the western territory. Here their capital rapidly accumulates, the forest recedes before them, villages and towns rise as by enchantment, and the unreclaimed and unappropriated lands bordering upon the perpetually extending scale successively acquire exchangeable value, and are sold by the government for increasing amounts. Will it be said that England cannot do in her colonies that which America is doing in her western forests? If an extensive emigration to New South Wales would, in the first instance, be more costly than one of similar magnitude to British America, the repayment would be earlier and more rapid, while the value which the influx of population and capital bestowed upon the fertile plains of Australia might be expected to open a source of very considerable revenue from the sale of crown lands. Such an emigration judiciously conducted would, I am fully persuaded, be the appropriate remedy, the true specific for the deep-seated disease which infects our social system. The expense of locating the able-bodied poor in the colonies would be less than that of maintaining them at home; the rapid reproduction of capital, when applied to fertile soil, would enable them in a short period to replace the expenses of their first establishment; *while the value which the influx of an industrious population bestowed upon the colonial lands, at the disposal of the crown, would become a permanent source of national revenue, and of clear and unbought advantage to the country.* In giving effect to extensive and improved plans of colonisation, we are multiplying the British nation, we are rocking the cradles of giant empires, we are co-operating in the schemes of Providence, and are its favoured instruments in causing Christian civilisation to 'cover the earth as the waters cover the sea.'"

The plan proposed to be adopted is generally known as the Wakefield system of colonisation—a plan which has been tried more than once and has failed. The new colony was to be self-supporting. The assumed principle was that land without labour is valueless; therefore it was proposed to raise a revenue by the sale of land at a price sufficiently high to pay for the passages of labourers to cultivate it. A board of commissioners was appointed to carry the proposed scheme into effect. The Act was not to come into force until £35,000 had been raised by the sale of land; and £20,000 of bonds were to be invested as a guarantee that the new country should not become a source of expense to England. They thought it wise to fix the price of the land high, so as to keep the labourer in his right position instead of becoming a landowner; and for the comfort of the settlers and the protection of the free labourer no convicts were ever to be sent to it. So that of all the Australian group

Victoria and South Australia alone were established on this basis. The "South Australian Company" purchased land to the amount required, giving £81 for one acre of town land and 134 acres in the country.

The new scheme was eagerly taken up, and as in the case of another colony, so desirous were some of the emigrants to be at their new homes, that three ships arrived there before the surveying staff. The emigrants were landed on Kangaroo Island, at the entrance of the Gulf. The survey party got there in August, 1836. The chief officer was Colonel Light. He knew nothing personally of the country when he arrived at Gulf St. Vincent. They found a harbour in a narrow inlet, and fixed the site of Adelaide on some rising ground seven miles inland. The city was divided into two unequal parts by a reserve of 200 acres of land, which was kept for a park, and the River Torrens runs through it. The town was surrounded by a park about 500 yards wide; there were six squares, a reserve of ten acres for the government domain, and sites for botanical gardens, a hospital, and public cemetery. The streets run at right angles with each other, and are from 60 to 130 feet wide.

The first governor was Captain Hindmarsh. When he arrived he did not approve of the site selected for the town, and great misunderstanding arose. There appears in fact to have been a mistake in the arrangements as made at home. There was a resident commissioner to represent the company, and a governor appointed by and in the interest of the crown. Great delays took place in the surveys, and the colonists were reduced in many instances to considerable difficulties. When the clashing of the rival parties as to the site of the city and other matters was brought under the notice of Lord Glenelg, he recalled the governor and the commissioner in 1838, and sent out Colonel Gawler, who in his own person united both offices. Still the people came, and still the difficulty continued—that the lands were not surveyed. The new governor found things in a sad state. The public offices were in great confusion, no records had been kept, very little progress had been made in the surveys, the expense of transporting goods from the anchorage to the city was ruinous, and the ready money was sent out of the country in order to purchase necessaries in the older colonies.

Colonel Light, the head of the survey department, resigned; and under his successor, Captain Frome, the surveys were rapidly proceeded with, and the people settled on their lands.

Centralisation instead of dispersion seems to have been Colonel Gawler's favourite plan, as indeed it was Wakefield's. In 1840 the population was 14,610, and nearly 9,000 of them were within the municipal district of Adelaide. The governor gave the men employment on public works there instead of in making roads and bridges, which would have opened up the country. He had a kind of authority to draw on the Home Government in case of absolute necessity. In 1840, the income was about £30,000, and the expenditure £170,000; and in the next year, with a revenue of £26,720, the outlay had been £104,471. In the former of these years a hundred sovereigns were paid for a ton of flour, and bread rose to famine prices. The 4 lb. loaf was three shillings and sixpence.

Of course this continued overdrawing of accounts did not last long. The governor was recalled in 1841, and Captain Grey, who had formerly been in Western Australia, succeeded him. If Colonel Gawler had been lavish, his successor went almost to the opposite extreme. The estimates were reduced by £60,000. With the sudden stoppage of the large expenditure of government money, came bankruptcy amongst the employers of labour, and want of work among the labouring classes. At this time two thousand people, out of the eight thousand in the town, were thrown upon the government for support as absolute paupers. Threatening language was used. The contractors, having shared among them in the year before about £150,000, which was spent on the government buildings, prayed that the works might be resumed; but the governor was firm, and would only meet the difficulty by giving the men work on the roads at low rates of wages.

At the time when there was so much want and so much insubordination in Adelaide itself, those who had got possession of their lands in the country were reaping a golden harvest. The soil and climate of South Australia appear to be peculiarly adapted to wheat. Its flour may be considered as the best in the world. It took the prize medal at London in 1851, and at Paris at the last Exhibition. As soon as the residents in the town saw the success which attended agricultural pursuits, they gladly followed in the steps of those who were succeeding so well. One-third of the houses in the town then became empty, and landlords were in despair. One-third of the public-houses also were closed, provisions became cheap, and the colonists were eating their own breadstuffs instead of importing them. Dispersion succeeded where centralisation failed.

From this time the colony adopted agriculture as its chief pursuit, and it has done so ever since. Its progress was very rapid indeed. Thus, in 1840, there were 2,503; in 1841, 6,722; and in 1842, 19,790 acres under cultivation. The next year it was nearly 29,000! But then another difficulty arose. How were they to get in this great harvest, for the hands were very few, and the climate so hot and dry that it must be cut and thrashed speedily. Thanks are due to a South Australian colonist (Mr. Ridley), who, in 1843, invented a reaper which goes by his name. It is drawn by a couple of horses, and is managed by two men, and it gathers the ear and thrashes out the grain in one operation. It reaps ten acres in a day. The grain is just passed through a winnowing machine and bagged, and is ready for market. There are now not far short of 500,000 acres of wheat grown in the colony, and at least four-fifths are cut and thrashed by these machines. The farmer requires no barns, but sends his grain from the harvest-field direct to the railway station or to the merchant's store. The machines are not expensive. Almost every farmer has one of them, and each town has a maker or repairer of them.

Everything now was going on most prosperously. In 1844 there were 450,000 sheep, 30,000 horned cattle, 2,150 horses, 12,000 pigs, and the exports amounted to £82,268.

As in later years New South Wales and Victoria were startled from their quiet pursuits by the discovery of gold, so in 1843 a new and great source of wealth was found in South Australia. The colony appears to have been indebted to some German immigrants in this matter. They had worked in the mines of their native country, and so were on the look-out for metals. They found lead ore (galena) on the slopes of Mount Lofty. Some settlers purchased a section of land where these specimens were most abundant, and sent some of the ore to England for analysis. This colony has from the commencement had a great advantage over its neighbours in that no reserve is made by the Crown of metals or minerals. In 1842, pieces of stone were picked up with blue and green streaks in them; a boy took some of them home to his father, and shortly afterwards an overseer looking for lost sheep kicked against some of the same stones, and knowing something of mineralogy, he told his employer, and on going to the spot they found in all directions a great deposit of the copper ore. The master was Captain Bagot; the overseer, Francis Dutton. This turned out to be the "Kapunda Mine," out of which they amassed large fortunes. Within eight years of its discovery, copper ore of the value of half a million sterling was procured, and it has gone on increasing ever since. Kapunda is the name of a township, having about 3,000 inhabitants, and it is the present terminus of the Northern Railway. It has just been lighted with gas. This mine was worked in 1843, and was the first that was discovered. Gawler Town is in the neighbourhood of this place, at which there are two very powerful steam mills, from which large quantities of. flour are sent to Adelaide and exported. Mr. Duffield's residence is not far from this rich part of the country. It is called "Para Para," and is considered one of the finest houses in the colony. The Duke of Edinburgh visited him when he went to the Kapunda mine. The soil and situation are well adapted for the vine, and the vineyards belonging to Mr. Duffield are said to produce the finest of those wines for which this colony is rapidly acquiring a reputation.

In the following year (1844) the great Burra Burra mines were discovered by the accidental turning up of the ore by the wheels of a bullock dray. The Kapunda mine was private property, at which many of the people were so chagrined that they petitioned for a survey of twenty thousand acres, that each might have a chance of getting a slice of the rich country. This was granted, but all the purchasers were bound to pay for their lots in hard cash. Ready money was very scarce in those days, and it is said that many a man had to thank his wife for her careful habits, when she relieved him of his difficulty by bringing forth her "old stocking"—her prudent provision against a rainy day. This large block of land was divided into two portions. The scrip of one of them was worth about £12 in the year 1850, and the £5 share of the Burra Burra was eagerly taken at £290. Kapunda is about forty-eight miles from Adelaide, through the centre of a rich wheat-growing district. It was in 1858 that the first railway, seven miles long, was constructed from the Port to Adelaide; thence it was extended to Kapunda, and there is now an authorised continuation of it to the Burra Burra mines, which are nearly one hundred miles from Adelaide, and fifty from Kapunda, passing still through a very large area of wheat-producing lands. There is also a line of rails, twenty-three miles long, which when completed will connect another large agricultural district with the sea at Port Wakefield; and a third, connecting Strathalbyn, which is the centre of the eastern districts, with Port Victor, on the south—Port Victor being the outlet for the River Murray traffic. The ore at the Burra mine was found near the surface. Within the first three years copper to the value of £700,000 was raised, and for many years afterwards the average annual yield was nearly double that large sum. Of course as soon as these rich discoveries became generally known there was a mania for copper and lead mining, second only to the intoxication caused soon after in the neighbouring colonies by the gold. Men who had previously ridiculed the whole thing were to be seen, hammer in hand, chipping the hard rock in the hope of hitting upon malachite, or green carbonate. In the year 1850, there were fifty-two mining associations floated, and forty out of them never gave a shilling of return either of principal or of dividend. A large body of Cornish miners were sent for, a class of men who at first did a great amount of good to South Australia, and who were invaluable in Victoria when the gold was discovered there. English capital was attracted to the colony, and Adelaide presented an exciting scene, and a cheering one too, for they were times of real not fictitious prosperity. Had things gone on thus, Port Phillip might have been left behind in the race for population and for wealth.

Colonel Robe succeeded Captain Grey as governor in 1845. He became very unpopular by two acts. The first was imposing a royalty on all minerals raised within the colony. This was so strenuously resisted that it had to be abandoned, being contrary to the conditions on which the purchasers of land had obtained their grants. The second was the indiscriminate endowment of all religious bodies. This was likewise opposed, but not so violently, and it lingered on until a representative legislature was established, and then all State aid was abandoned.

In the year 1850 the population had reached 63,000, and there were nearly 60,000 acres under crop. At this early period nearly 300 acres of vineyard had been planted, and this industry has been going on ever since, and there can be no doubt of the adaptability of the soil and climate for the growth of the vine, so that it is but a question of time and care and skill, and the wines of this colony will form a considerable item in its exports.

But the next year came, 1851, and there was the news of the gold discovery in New South Wales. This was a subject of deep interest to the skilful Cornish miners, and the colonists generally were looking on somewhat in dread as to what effect it would have upon their prospects. But Bathurst was so remote that it did not greatly unsettle the mining population, nor injure South Australia. But almost before they had time to congratulate themselves on this, the news spread like wild-fire that still richer gold-fields had been found in the colony adjoining their own—Victoria—whose western boundary was not more than 150 miles from their eastern frontier. Copper was very well, but gold was better.

And so within six months half the adult population of the whole colony had quitted it for Ballarat, Mount Alexander, and Bendigo. They left their wives and families behind as pledges for their return. And return they did, especially all the skilled German and Cornish miners, and brought their "piles" with them. If Victoria's lands had been unlocked then, and sold, a vast addition would have been made to the permanent population. Nay, it would have been well for the colony if she had *given* an allotment to every man who came to make it his home. The South Australian government acted with great wisdom at this critical juncture; they helped instead of impeding this migration. They marked out a road, dug wells, made bridges—which would assist the people, not only in going to *but in returning from* the diggings. And they established an escort, which brought the gold belonging to the colony to Adelaide. There it was melted, assayed and stamped, and declared to be a legal tender in all transactions with the government. It was during Sir Henry Young's tenure of office as governor, who succeeded Colonel Robe, that the Australian colonies were convulsed by the discovery of gold. Sir Henry's name is chiefly identified with the great interest which he took in opening up the navigation of the Murray.

Still the Adelaide people wished to have a gold-field of their own. Very naturally. And the legislative council, which had been recently established, co-operated with the government by offering a reward of £1,000 for the discovery of a gold-field which would be of real value to the country's exports, and Governor Young assented to this. In 1852 specks of gold were found on the Onkaparinga River, but they were only specks. For ten or twelve years after this there were frequent rumours of the finding of the precious metal, but nothing of much value came to light. In 1864 the government invited Mr. Hargreaves, the first discoverer of gold in New South Wales, to survey the north and the south portions of the vast territory. He spent half a year in the search, but did not succeed. And up to this time the colony remains without a gold-field. There is, however, a well founded expectation that as the northern part of the country becomes more extensively known, the hopes of the colonists will ultimately be realised.

Sir Henry Young was succeeded by Sir Richard Macdonnell, who arrived in 1855, and who gave place early in 1862 to Sir Dominic Daly. Before quitting the colony Sir R. Macdonnell, in a valedictory speech to the legislature, briefly enumerated the principal changes which had taken place during the seven years of his governorship: " Had I time, it would be interesting to recall to your recollection the most salient points in the history of that epoch. This, however, is not a moment to attempt such a task, though I cannot but remind you that when I landed here in June, 1855, there was not a mile of railway opened in the colony, and yet there are now 57 miles in use, over which annually rolls a traffic of more than 150,000 tons and 320,000 passengers. Your coasts have been lit with three additional first-class lights, and three additional harbours have come into extensive use. Your population has grown from 86,000 to nearly 130,000; whilst the exports of colonial produce have risen from less than £690,000, in 1855, to £1,808,000 for the year ending the 30th of last June. When I landed there was scarcely sixty miles of made road in the colony, whereas now, independent of those in the city, there are nearly if not over 200 miles; and instead of 160,000 acres in cultivation there cannot be less now than 460,000, a number greater in proportion to the population than obtains in any other portion of Her Majesty's dominions, or indeed in any other part of the world with which I am acquainted. It is moreover since 1855 that the first telegraph post was erected in the colony, and yet you already possess 600 miles of telegraphic communication, and nearly 1,000 miles of wire, together with twenty-six stations. It is also since 1855 that the explorations of Mr. Stuart and others have added so much to our geographical knowledge, filling up the large blank spaces which had so long defaced the map of South Australia, and usefully opened up the country for further settlement. Above all, it is since my arrival here that the great experiment has been tried of entrusting the general mass of the people, through their immediate representatives, with power to control completely the taxation and expenditure of the country and direct its general legislation. I am bound to say that, although such an experiment must be more or less hazardous anywhere, there is less risk accompanying it in South Australia, owing to the character of the people and the division of property here, than would attend it in almost any other country. I may add that if I were to select any one reason, as the paramount cause of responsible government working hitherto with so great a measure of success, I would attribute it to the fair and equitable view which generally prevails as to the mutual and necessary dependence of the various great interests of the colony one on another. The sentiments avowed on that subject at public meetings, and in the debates of Parliament, form not merely a pleasing and healthy contrast with what takes place in other colonies, but give the best and strongest guarantee that society here will continue united for the advancement of the common weal, and will thereby have the greatest chance of promoting the general prosperity."

Disappointed in their hope of a local gold-field, the colonists bravely set to work to make the most of of the rich resources which they had within their reach, and specially to the increased growth of the vine, both for table use and for wine. In 1863 there were nearly *six millions of vines* in the colony, and nearly 500,000 gallons of wine were made from those which were in bearing. There is also a large export of very fine grapes to the other colonies. Grapes of the best kinds can thus be bought at a penny or twopence a pound. And though Adelaide had not gold, she made indeed a golden harvest of her wheat and flour. The people of Victoria were too busily engaged in digging for gold to care about ploughing, sowing, and reaping their lands; and so the Adelaide farmers became rich by supplying cereals to their neighbours. In 1863 the wheat produced amounted to 3,841,824 bushels. Each person in the colony had on an average more than eighteen acres of freehold land, and the sheep produced 13,229,009 lbs. of wool. The imports and exports combined reached, during the year 1864, the large sum of nearly six millions, leaving a considerable balance to the credit of the colony. In that year £70,000 were voted for immigration purposes, and during the next five years 33,420 persons were brought into the colony by means of the government grants. The disproportion of the sexes is less in South Australia than in any other of the Australian colonies.

As we remarked before, the early settlers were at first greatly disheartened, but they soon rallied. In Capper's "South Australia" some interesting accounts are given in letters to friends, which were never meant for the public eye, and which detail the troubles of colonial life at first, and the way in which these troubles are soon surmounted. An emigrant and his wife thus address a relative in Scotland: "We left Blackwall, London, on the 24th August, 1837. We were well used on board, had a very fine captain, and a most excellent man for a doctor. We had more rations than we could use. We lay seven days at Kangaroo Island, and got ashore one day and had a look at the settlement there. The soil appears to be good, but there is no fresh water. I have seen onions selling in town, which grew upon the island, the largest I ever saw. We left that on the 8th December, and arrived at our destination, Holdfast Bay, on the 9th. We had two weeks' rations allowed us after coming to town, and a free house, in which we lived six months. My first work was to drive bullocks, but I did not like them; so I commenced, under a carpenter, fencing and jobbing at five shillings and sixpence a day. I left him and commenced taking jobs with an Englishman who came out in the ship with us. We did very well, making from eight shillings to ten shillings a day. Now Bell and I have engaged with a Joint Stock Cattle Company, to have charge of a dairy for one year at £80, and to be found in provisions. The company consists of eighty shares at £25 a share. I have taken one share, and think I will take another. I have also bought half an acre of land adjoining the town, so I consider I have made a good change by coming here. We are living quite happy, and I consider that an industrious man with a good steady wife may be independent in a very few years. For our own part we have saved more cash since we came here than we ever could have done in Scotland. This is a most delightful country; the climate is hotter than that of Scotland, but I have never found the heat oppressive." A second man writes thus: "After landing, I went to work at thirty shillings a week. My wife goes out washing two days a week, for which she has four shillings a day and her keep; the remainder of the time she takes in washing, at five shillings a dozen, so that we are doing quite well. It far surpasses my expectations. I have reason to bless God that I ever came to South Australia, in respect of temporal blessings. It is of no use for a man or a woman to think of coming to Australia to be lazy, for they will be miserably mistaken, as it is downright hard work here; but a sober, steady man may do well." We must just give one more example. Stephen Goldsack and his wife write to a friend, who was a wheelwright at the Royal Arsenal, Woolwich, thus: "I engaged at once with a baker at £2 10s. a week, and bread, flour and potatoes. I stayed with him until last week, when I left him, after having had built for myself a good stone house and bakehouse. I can and do clear with ease £1 5s. a day, and don't mean to see the inside of my bakehouse on Sundays. We board and lodge a gentleman for £1 6s. a week—washing, &c., extra. Jane has more work in dress-making than she can attend to, at her own price. I must confess that I should be extremely glad to see you—yes, all of you—out here in this fine and thriving country; yet I will write nothing but truth, and you may please yourselves. However, God willing, we will some day see you all again—in England, if we cannot out here; for the colonists of South Australia are licensed by destiny to work only from eight to twelve years before saving a good fortune. I mean such as are industrious, eat and drink of the best, *and keep from drunkenness*, the curse of all new settlements. I suppose you think yourself too old now to do any good? Well, that excuse is better than a worse. But I tell you that, as sure as I breathe, there are people in Adelaide, whom I know well, *as old as your father*, who left England two years ago not worth ten shillings, and now, through nothing but industry, they have each several good stone houses and several acres of town land. Ten hundred pounds would not buy them, if you produce it in gold. Jane sits at my elbow and says, 'Tell him he must come out, and must bring Marion with him, and Betsy, and the family.' Children of all sizes and of both sexes are worth here 350 per cent. I hope that by the time you get this Jane and myself shall have something less than a dozen."

We have made these extracts from the letters of successful emigrants, because they contain evidence of the elements which make the prosperous man:

industry, steadiness, and a regard to God's blessing. And though time has passed by since they were written, and the colony has progressed to an extraordinary extent, yet even now men possessing these characteristics need not fear. They would be sure to get on, and in the long run attain to independence.

South Australia was the first of the colonies visited by His Royal Highness the Duke of Edinburgh, and here, as everywhere, he was most enthusiastically received. The early croakers against a settlement in Australia, because it would rapidly throw off the yoke of England and become a nest of pirates, were far from correct in their predictions. Her Majesty's dominions are widely spread, for the sun never sets upon them; but amidst them all, none are more loyal in their devotion than the Australian colonies. The Gawler Institute had given a prize for the production of the following verses, or "Song of Australia," and it was most enthusiastically sung by the Sunday school children in the Duke's presence:—

> "There is a land where summer skies
> Are gleaming with a thousand dyes,
> Blending in witching harmonies;
> And grassy knoll and forest height
> Are flashing in the rosy light,
> And all above is azure bright—
>   Australia!

> "There is a land where floating free,
> From mountain top to girdling sea,
> A proud flag waves exultingly;
> And Freedom's sons the banner bear,
> No shackled slave can breathe the air;
> Fairest of Britain's daughters fair—
>   Australia!"

It was during the administration of Sir Henry Young, in 1851, that the first representative constitution was granted to this colony. It consisted of a single chamber of twenty-four members, eight of whom were appointed by the Crown, and the rest elected by the people. When two years later a new Act was passed whereby the government was to be vested in a double chamber, the members of the upper one being nominees for life, so much dissatisfaction was expressed that, in 1856, a second Act received the royal assent. The government is now vested in a Legislative Council, and a House of Assembly, the members of *both* being elected by ballot. The Council is elected by the whole province as one constituency, and it cannot be dissolved by the governor. There is no property qualification for a seat in the Upper House. The only requisites are, that a candidate must be thirty years of age and have resided in the colony for three years. A voter for the Council must be of age, have been on the electoral roll for six months, and have a freehold of £50 value, or a lease of the value of £20 a year, or occupy a house of the rental of £25. The number of voters for the Council is about one-third of the adult male population. A member of the Lower House needs no qualification beyond that of being of age, and that his name has been on the roll for six months.

The author of the "Cruise of the *Galatea*," writing in 1867, has the following interesting remarks on the subject of the working of this new system of government: "During the past eleven years everything has advanced at a rapid pace. The area of occupation has been extended many hundred miles into the interior. Thousands of immigrants have been imported annually at the public expense. The extent of land sold is reckoned by millions of acres, and the annual produce of the colony by millions of bushels of wheat, millions of pounds of wool, and thousands of tons of copper. Public works have been prosecuted in a most liberal spirit, and on a large scale, until the colony is traversed in every direction by good macadamized roads, supplemented in some districts by well-constructed railways for horse or steam power. In the higher branches of government education, sanitary affairs, &c., the example of the mother country has been closely and not unsuccessfully imitated. The economical principles of the government are sound in the main. The system of taxation is free from the protectionist fallacies common in other colonies. The commercial code, though far from methodical, is liberal and judicious in its aims. The laws of property, especially those of them which are embodied in Torrens' Real Property Act, have been recognized by eminent legal authorities at home as an improvement on many parts of the Imperial statute book. The results of the eleven years' legislation, which has taken place under the Constitution Act of 1856, comprise, amid many superfluities and much that is susceptible of improvement, a number of measures that have been eminently beneficial. The moral influence of the legislature on the people has as a rule been healthy. By triennial elections they have been trained to feel a genuine and permanent interest in public affairs. By the use of the ballot-box they have learned how to conduct even the most exciting election with all the order and decorum of ordinary business, at the same time almost wholly avoiding the tendency to bribery and corruption which is so common a feature of elections elsewhere. Through an extensive network of district councils a spirit of local self-government has been diffused among the settlers. The breadth of the suffrage, though enabling some incompetent men to get into Parliament, has in some measure compensated for that evil by bringing a very strong public opinion to bear upon the course of legislation."

This is high praise indeed. The question appears to have arisen in the author's mind as to whether the double chamber, constituted as it is, is suitable for the present circumstances of the colonies, and also as to whether the system is not cumbrous and expensive.

In the extract given above reference is made to what is called "Torrens' Act." Very great credit is due to Mr. Torrens for this. In the year 1858 he succeeded in carrying a Real Property Act. It has been found to work remarkably well, and has been adopted in consequence in other colonies. Its main features are as follow: A Land Title Registration Office is established; the owner of freehold land goes to it and deposits his costly deeds, has his name registered in a book, from which the transfer is copied on a certificate that costs only a few shillings. It fixes by the stamp of official authority every transaction in land under its provisions, thus doing away with the necessity for investigating the prior title and long and expensive abstracts of title. It appears so far to have given complete satisfaction, and in many cases capitalists refuse to lend money on the mortgage of property which has not been brought under it. Mr. Torrens received the thanks of both Houses of Parliament in South Australia for this admirable land and conveyance system, and all the great colonies have adopted it.

In 1851 State aid to religion was abolished. The voluntary system is therefore in full play there. The Church of England is by far the largest body; the Roman Catholics are the next, but their number is not one-half as many; the Wesleyans are nearly equal to the Romanists, who are followed by the German Lutherans, and then by the Presbyterians. It is a great place for Sunday schools; and so active have they been in church building that there is accommodation for nearly every man, woman, and child above fourteen, in the colony. Miss Burdett Coutts, in her well-known liberality, endowed the see of Adelaide. The bishop is the Right Reverend Dr. Short. The legislature refused to recognise the church by a special act of incorporation. The bishop, clergy and laity have therefore entered into a consentual compact, declaring their unity with the Church of England, and their agreement with her in doctrine and discipline. To obviate difficulties which may probably arise, the Synod first summoned in 1855 has expressed a wish to have in its own hands the appointment to the bishopric whenever a vacancy may occur. And this will probably be granted. Great liberality has been displayed by the members of all the denominations in the erection of churches, parsonages, and schools. A citizen of Adelaide has lately given property valued at £20,000 towards the endowment of the Church of England College. The bishop has lately laid the foundation stone of his cathedral, but many years must elapse before it can be completed.

The author of "Greater Britain" says, "The capital of South Australia is reputed the hottest of all the cities that are chiefly inhabited by the English race, and as I neared it through the Backstairs Passage into the Gulf of St. Vincent, past Kangaroo Island, and still more when I landed at Glenelg, I came to the conclusion that its reputation is deserved." It is indeed very hot, hotter a good deal than Melbourne. This applies to Adelaide itself, which is very sandy; but the heat is more bearable than in other places, such as Sydney. The houses are built with a view to protection from the sun; the people rise early, and do not spare water in the streets. Men dress coolly, but ladies, says the author quoted above, persist in going about in shawls and coloured dresses, "And," he adds, "might they but see a few of the Richmond or Baltimore ladies in their pure white muslin frocks, and die of envy, for the dress most suited to a hot dry climate is also the most beautiful under its bright sun." The hottest months are December, January, February, and March. In these months in the neighbourhood of Adelaide the temperature is frequently from 100° to 115° for days together. The hot winds generally last for three days; the wind then veers round gradually to the south-west and a most refreshing cool sea-breeze sets in. And thus throughout the summer months hot and cool weather come alternately. But although the heat is really great, it is of such a dry character that it is not overpowering. Men do not lie by in the middle of the day, but pursue their out of door labour as they do in England, and the settler thinks nothing of riding forty or fifty miles in a hot wind. The extreme healthiness of the climate is attributable to this dryness of the air. The weather from the end of March to the end of October, that is for seven months, is really delightful. The mean temperature at Adelaide of the six summer months is 70·96; of the six winter months, 56·46. The barometer rises with a south wind and falls with a north wind.

Speaking of the aborigines, of their general condition and disappearance as civilisation advances,

Sir Dominic Daly, the late governor, thus writes: "It is the melancholy and all but unanimous testimony of the early settlers, and of others best qualified to form an opinion, that the aboriginal population is fast dying out; but there are no records from which to ascertain the rate of decrease. The causes of the decrease are disease, sterility of the females, and infanticide, which it is believed is a crime of very frequent occurrence. From evidence given before a select committee of the Legislative Council in 1860, it appears that the natives in general have been in no way benefited by being brought into contact with Europeans. But I think this view is open to modification, since it cannot be denied that the squatters, who are justly called 'the pioneers of civilisation,' treat them with much forbearance and kindness, and encourage the natives to remain upon their 'runs' for the sake of their services. The young men especially soon become useful as shepherds, shearers, reapers, stock-keepers, colt-breakers, and the *lubras* as washerwomen and in other domestic occupations. About a fourth of the able-bodied males were employed by the settlers in 1861, and the proportion is now (1863) probably greater. Generally they were well remunerated, and some of them obtain as high wages as the best white labourers. It is pleasing to be able to inform your Grace (the Duke of Newcastle) that the reports of the missionary establishments at Poonindie and Point Maclcay are encouraging. At Poonindie there are thirty-six natives who receive careful religious and moral instruction, and who are trained to habits of industry. The experiment there may prove in its results the possibility of the civilisation of the race, and confirms the opinion so often expressed by missionaries, that Christianity is the only efficient instrument for its accomplishment. Dr. Walter, the Protector of Aborigines, to whom I am chiefly indebted for this information, informs me that the beneficial effects of the religious instruction imparted to the natives is apparent without as well as within the establishment at Point Macleay. Many of their superstitions have been abandoned, their character for honesty has improved, they observe the Sabbath as a day of rest, and a considerable number appear at morning and evening service neat and clean, and conduct themselves with great propriety. That the capacity of the young to receive instruction is beyond dispute, and that from frequent and personal examination, he is of opinion that they make as rapid progress as the average of white children. The crime of infanticide is also less prevalent. A sum of money is annually put in the estimates and voted by the legislature for provisions, blankets, medical attendance, &c., for the aborigines. The amount voted last year (1861) was £3,195. Depôts have been formed in the localities where the natives are most numerous, and flour, tea, blankets, &c., are distributed amongst the infirm and destitute, according to their necessitics." The testimony borne to the capacity of the young to receive instruction is beyond doubt the truth. Englishmen amongst the early settlers were very unwilling to believe this. They used to say that they were only a step above the brutes, and could not be taught; and a clergyman once gravely told me that he regarded them as animals, and he did not consider that they had souls. But all this was a mere attempt to justify the treatment that was too often dealt out to them, and perhaps to drown the voice of conscience, which would at times make itself heard, and plead for the poor creatures. Many years ago a benevolent lady had taken great interest in some native boys, and coming to live on an island which then formed part of my parish, she asked me to give religious instruction to them. I gladly did so, and these young men used to pull over in a boat to the mainland, and walk up to my house weekly with their Bibles in their hand, and they listened with marked interest as one great truth after another was unfolded to them; and they read and delighted to read the word of God, and to hear of Him who came "a light to lighten the Gentiles," and to be for salvation unto the ends of the earth. On another occasion a young man was brought to me for baptism. He also had been carefully trained up by a Christian lady on a station. I examined him as to his knowledge of the Scriptures, and took pains to ascertain that he had an intelligent knowledge of what he was engaged in, and I can assure you that his answers would have shamed many a white man. All honour to those noble women, who amidst the domestic trials incident to life in the bush, in the early days, still found time to instruct and to train for eternity some of the children of the natives. And who can tell what would have been the result if this plan had been more generally pursued.

Many of the governors of the Australian colonies have died at their posts. And this was the case with Sir Dominic Daly, who so hospitably entertained the Duke of Edinburgh. He died, much and deservedly respected, on the 19th February, 1868. The present governor is Sir J. Ferguson, Bart.

After the discoverers had passed right through the vast island continent from south to north, Sir Charles Nicholson, so well and so favourably known both in the colonies and in England, addressed a communication to the Colonial Office in 1862, recommending the formation of a crown colony in that northern territory which was subsequently annexed to South Australia. From that communication the following extract is made: " From its geographical position the territory referred to enjoys advantages such as are possessed by scarcely any of the other colonies of the Australian group. It constitutes, in point of fact, that portion of the continent of Australia nearest in a direct line to Great Britain. It is in close proximity to Java and the islands of the Eastern Archipelago, and is within a few days' reach of China and Japan. Its physical capabilities are also, according to the evidence of Mr. Gregory and those by whom it has been explored, of a very superior kind. The whole of the northern coast is indented with deep bays, accessible to large vessels, whilst the Victoria River is represented as one of the largest navigable streams in Australia, the tide rising some thirty feet at its embouchure in Queen Charlotte's Channel. Mr. Gregory, the distinguished explorer and present surveyor-general of Queensland, represents the whole of the valley of the Victoria River as being of the most promising description, well adapted for grazing purposes, and no doubt admirably fitted for the growth of all tropical produce, such as cotton, sugar, rice, and coffee. Horses, the race of which has become so prolific in the other colonies that they are of scarcely any value, would here speedily constitute an article of export to India of the greatest importance, both as affecting the colony itself and as regards the Indian government in the supply of cavalry. Certain localities may also be indicated on the banks of the Victoria and Alligator Rivers which must become the sites of large and important towns, great metropolitan centres of trade and commerce. The only difficulty that presents itself is the mere initiation of the colony. Once set on foot it would find within itself sources of vitality and growth that would render it independent of all external aid, and one of the most important and thriving."

The colonial secretary of the day, instead of acting upon this recommendation, communicated with Sir Dominic Daly, the governor of South Australia at the time, in order to ascertain the wishes of the government, and on hearing from him, instead of founding a crown colony he annexed a portion of the northern territory to South Australia, which took prompt measures for "settling" the new acquisition. A surveying party was organised and sent forth, and land sales were ordered to take place in London and in the colony. A "North Australian Company," under the auspices of a former governor, Sir R. G. Macdonnell, was formed, and all seemed to promise success. But difficulties and disappointments arose. Large blocks of land were sold both in England and in the colony, but the surveys were not completed so early as the holders of the land-orders expected. To compensate them for this delay an Act was passed at the end of 1868, whereby the holders of preliminary land-orders were at liberty within five years to select 320 acres for every 160 acres to which their orders entitled them; and the colonial government in January of last year addressed the following despatch to the agent-general in London, for the information and satisfaction of all persons interested. This territory is so vast and its successful colonisation so deeply important, that we think it of sufficient consequence to print at length the following papers which have been obligingly placed at our disposal by the agent-general, Mr. Dutton.

The author of "Greater Britain" does not appear very sanguine of success. He says: "It would be as cheap to colonise equatorial Africa from Adelaide as tropical Australia. If the northern territory is ever to be rendered habitable it must be by Queensland that the work is done. It is not certain," he goes on to say, "that North Australia may not be found to yield gold in plenty. In a little-known manuscript of the 17th century the north-west of Australia is called 'The land of gold;' and we are told that the fishermen of Solor, driven on to this land of gold by stress of weather, picked up in a few hours their boat full of gold nuggets and returned in safety. They never dared repeat their voyage on account of their dread of the unknown seas; but Manoel Godinho de Eredia was commissioned by the Portuguese Lord Admiral of India to explore this gold land and enrich the crown of Portugal by the capture of the treasures it contained. It would be strange enough if gold came to be discovered on the north-west coast, in the spot from which the Portuguese reported their discovery."

"Despatch from the Government of South Australia to the Agent-General in London, on the subject of the Northern Territory, and extracts from the Adelaide Papers relating to the Surveyor-General's Expedition to survey that Territory :—

"TREASURY OFFICES, ADELAIDE, 5th Jan., 1869.

"SIR,—In my despatches per last mail, I had the honour to inform you that this Government were preparing to complete the survey of the Northern Territory, and that although the term prescribed by the Act would not expire till March, 1869, yet it had been decided that a double area of land should be given to each order-holder as a compensation for the delay in completing the survey. Copies of the amended Act and notices were sent per last mail.

"It must, however, be remembered that this delay was in a great measure caused by undue anxiety to prove by further exploration whether any better land was available for the purpose of the settlement.

"You will now be pleased to learn that the Surveyor-General (Mr. Goyder), with an efficient staff, and *six* complete double survey parties, amply equipped, sailed in the *Moonta* on December 27th, for the purpose of completing the survey without any delay. Ample stores and field equipment have been provided, and the schooner *Sea Ripple* will follow in about ten days, with further supplies.

"This latter vessel has been purchased, and will remain under the orders of the Surveyor-General.

"The well-known energy and perseverance of this gentleman are guarantees for the due completion of the work he has undertaken, and *here* all question or excitement on the subject has ceased.

"A list of the officers and men of the expedition is enclosed.

"The London holders of Northern Territory land-orders may now be informed that the preparations for the occupation and utilization of their property will be proceeded with without delay.

"In order that the views of this Government may be fully understood, I append the following concise recapitulation:—

"1st.—This Government sold lands on the Northern Territory to be surveyed and selected within five years.

"2ndly.—The Surveyor-General with six double survey parties has proceeded to complete the survey.

"3rdly.—All order-holders will be entitled to receive double the amount which they purchased. This is a liberal compensation for the delay which was principally caused by the action of order-holders themselves, or their representatives, in this Colony.

So far from repudiating their contract, the Government are giving twice the area of land which they would be obliged to do by the terms of agreement.

"4thly.—The idle cry of repudiation has been raised by those order-holders who wish to reclaim their money and repudiate their obligation.

"5thly.—Could the money be returned to any number of order-holders, still the Government would not be released from the obligation of surveying the Territory for the benefit of those who prefer to have their land.

"The arrangement will be completed by this Government with the strictest good faith.

"The statement on flyleaf hereof will show the action taken by the South Australian Government with a view to settling the Northern Territory.

"I have the honour to be, Sir,
"Your obedient servant,
"H. KENT HUGHES, *Treasurer.*"

EXTRACT FROM THE "ADELAIDE REGISTER."

"ADELAIDE, *Tuesday, January* 5, 1869.—The starting of another survey party for the Northern Territory, is the answer of the South Australian Government to Mr. Elder's writ of attachment. Mr. Goyder sailed in the *Moonta* on the 27th December, and if land surveying be not wholly incompatible with the 'starting point of civilisation,' the order-holders will receive their double allowance of land within twelve months. Meanwhile, the one-sided, underhand use which has been made of the London Press to damage the reputation of the colony, has not at all promoted the chance of an amicable issue. However great the mismanagement of the Northern Territory scheme may have been, South Australia is able to abide the consequences, and will meet them openly if they present themselves openly. However much the speculators in land at seven and sixpence an acre may be disappointed in not finding it already worth as many pounds, they have no cause, legal or moral, to whine as they have done in the *Times* about repudiation.

Whatever their grievance may be, they have no right thus to prejudice their own case, or to pretend that the door is closed against redress. Their worst obstacle has alone been among themselves, in so far as they cannot agree about the kind of redress they will accept. The order-holders here insist on getting their land; the order-holders in England clamour for their money back; and if both cannot be instantly satisfied, we are to be the repudiators! If, believing as we do in our own national honesty, we could be put into hysterics by such slander, should we not also be fools?

"THE NORTHERN TERRITORY SURVEY.

"We have already announced that the Government some time ago decided upon sending Mr. Goyder, the Surveyor-General, to the Northern Territory to survey the land intended for the order-holders. The whole of the arrangements were left in his hands, and were carried out with great rapidity. The vessel selected to convey the members of the expedition is the *Moonta*, 627 tons, which has been placed on the Slip, and thoroughly examined, and the survey proved satisfactory. She is well known, and hailed last from Newcastle, having brought a cargo of black diamonds very recently. A goodly portion of the between decks will be required to accommodate 40 to 50 horses, now being purchased; and the fodder and water for these and a few bullocks will also take up considerable room; but store cattle and sheep not being intended to be taken, space will not be greatly cramped. The party have passed through the ordeal of a strict medical examination, army fashion. The schooner which has been purchased for exploring purposes is the *Sea Ripple*, which is shortly expected to arrive from Melbourne. The *Moonta* was handed over to the Government on Thursday, December 17. She has been undergoing overhaul and survey on the Dunnikier Slip, but was launched on December 15, and at once moored alongside the Copper Company's Wharf, for the discharge of about 70 tons coals which she had on board, and to take in a small quantity of ballast and about 150 tons of water in tanks. The *Moonta* is one of Simpson's

Black Diamond Liners, and as the result of the survey has proved, is a most seaworthy vessel. Her register tonnage is 627; but as she has carried 1,000 tons of coal, she will only be in ballast trim with all the stores and stock on board. She has spacious 'tween decks, the after part of which will be separated by a bulkhead, and with the cabin will supply the necessary accommodation for the party. Captain Barneson has been for a length of time in the same employ, and has been favourably known in the coasting trade for several years. For the conveyance of the Northern Territory party the amount to be paid is about £3,000. The Government have purchased a small steamer at the Port for the use of the Surveyor-General on reaching his destination. The passage will be by way of the Leuwin, and it is anticipated will be accomplished in four or five weeks. The lay-days at the Northern Territory amount to 21. In the survey yard, on Wednesday, December 16, the major portion of those who are proceeding with Mr. Goyder assembled, and the rates of wages, not previously stated, were then announced, from which it appeared that cooks and chainmen are to receive 5s. per day; headsmen, *alias* axemen, and trenchers, 5s. 6d.; provision being made for overtime payments. From the Victorian Meat Preserving Company 10,000 lbs. of beef and mutton, prepared according to Ritchie's process, have been procured, and the other supplies have been bought in Adelaide through one or more brokers.

"On Wednesday, December 23, the *Moonta* went to Light's Passage, and on the following Sunday evening, December 27, set sail for her destination. In accordance with official notifications the men intending to proceed by her left Adelaide so as to arrive alongside shortly after two o'clock, and the trains throughout the day carried to the Port immense numbers of friends and relatives with ordinary sightseers, who thronged the platform of the Railway Station, and besieged the ticket office. Arrived at the Port, a scene of great bustle and indescribable confusion presented itself to bewildered onlookers, who saw trucks of goods coming on the wharf up to about seven o'clock, in addition to earlier consignments of drays, waggons, and lighter vehicles, for use at Port Darwin. Slinging the horses and bullocks, and depositing them in the 'tween decks attracted much notice, and was efficiently managed under the superintendence of Mr. Formby; 24 horses occupy stalls on the main deck and 20 are placed down below. Mr. Goyder arrived from town by the train following that which had conveyed the greater portion of the party, and he was actively engaged for several hours in overseeing the operations which were going forward. On board everything appeared in a delightful state of confusion consequent upon a large quantity of stores and baggage arriving late and being heaped together preparatory to stowage when leisure could be found. The heat all day was excessive, and in the experience of members of the Expedition they were melting moments caused by temperature as well as partings. Iced drinks were in constant requisition where obtainable. For several hours under a scorching sun the men strove to maintain an existence, or getting beyond that state, and, regarding the weather as a foretaste of the tropical heat, amused themselves as best they could, or whiled away the time under cover. Tea, *sans ceremonie, a la* mug and pannican, was served at 6 in a large store, and at 7.20 a bell, rung on board, summoned the entire party to the wharf alongside the *Moonta*, when Mr. Goyder called the roll of officers first, and then of men, each one passing up the gangway when summoned. Nearly all answered to their names, but two or three were unavoidably absent, having, it is understood, received the well-meant but not welcome attentions of bailiffs, who required Adelaide to be revisited. At 8 o'clock, steam having been got up on board the tug, the *Moonta* was towed into the stream, and proceeded on her way to Light's Passage. Before casting off, the tanks were filled up with water, a 60 days' supply being taken. As the ship sheared off she appeared to literally swarm with men, who crowded the deck and darkened the rigging. Cheer upon cheer was given on board, and re-echoed from the wharf by the immense concourse gathered there; and as the ship glided out and was towed away, the moonlight view was very fine, and her outline was better seen. The last train to town conveyed back a large number of visitors who had bid good-bye for a time to friends, brothers, husbands, or fathers, and in some cases the separation appeared to produce gloomy feelings; but on the whole, a buoyant spirit was manifested in those who went and those who stayed.

"Little more, however, appears necessary to be said respecting this new chapter in the history of Northern Australian exploration and surveying, the commencement of which is before us, but the end hidden. News will reach the colony once in two months from head quarters, as it is intended that the *Sea Ripple* shall run across to Koepang, bringing and taking mails, and be otherwise usefully employed. A good many tons of hydraulic-pressed hay, bran, and other cargo will be left for the schooner to carry. She will also take two boats, which have been bought in Port Adelaide, and the captain of the *Sea Ripple* is, as previously noted, empowered to select the seamen required. It is not likely that the schooner will convey any supplementary baggage for the men, as space is limited, and they have been confined to the contents of a sailor's canvas bag, with slight additions; officers also taking a zinc box, of regulation size. Documents, forms, and papers have been packed in similar boxes. Here we may note that the leading photographers have succeeded in taking portraits of the greater number of the officers and men, and the likenesses seen are clear and faithful, giving on the whole the same favourable impression as to the *personnel* of the surveying force as was produced on seeing them step one by one on board. Doubtless there are some of the body hardly fitted for the rough, hard, and hot work before them, and some appointments may possibly be considered open to objection by outsiders; yet, taken as a whole, the force is a good one; and contains several of the best of those who have figured in previous adventures of the same kind. In addition to a number of well-known colonists and members of both Houses who were at the Port on Wednesday, the Attorney-General was at the scene of operations for several hours, and the Commissioner of Crown Lands remained till the last. Considerable benefit may reasonably be expected from

U

the investigations of Messrs. Schultze and Homeyer, whose labours as naturalist and assistant will probably be productive of practical results. These gentlemen have been provided with ample appliances for use in the pursuit of their researches in various departments, and we have received a copy of the instructions to the botanical collector issued by Dr. Schomburgk, Director of the Botanic Garden. The sheets or botanic notebooks issued with these instructions specify the several particulars required in each case as descriptive of the specimens. These are—where found, description (tree, shrub, &c.), height, colour of stem, colour of leaves, calyx, petals, stamens, filaments, stygma. A column is open for remarks, and may be made to embody a large amount of valuable information. The reason for requiring such minute data as to colour, is obviously because that the appearance and tints of botanical specimens would be liable to material change, and a record of the state when collated will thus be preserved.

"Mr. F. G. Waterhouse, the Curator of the Adelaide Museum, has supplied a long and formidable 'List of birds, most of which are peculiar to Northern Australia,' giving the numbers affixed in Gould's Handbook, 1865. He also furnishes a list of 'Mammals peculiar to Northern Australia,' and adds a few lines suggestive of other classes in natural history which it is desirable should be sought after and preserved.

"When visiting the *Moonta* on Thursday we found that the members of the party were gradually settling themselves down, and making themselves 'at home' on board; and all in excellent spirits, although somewhat disappointed to think that ·hey should be compelled to spend their Christmas on board whilst the vessel was detained in the river. Boats were constantly to and fro between the port and the ship during the day and Christmas day. On Thursday evening Mr. Goyder mustered his party, and told them off in watches for the voyage, at the same time pointing out to them the necessity of all working amicably together, so as to secure comfort and safety during the voyage."

FROM THE "SOUTH AUSTRALIAN ADVERTISER."
6th January, 1869.
"THE EXPEDITION AFLOAT.

"Punctual to the day appointed Mr. Goyder and his party are afloat, and will shortly be on their way to the Northern Territory. With reference to the survey and settlement of the north part of Australia, we have now reached the beginning of the end. It would be neither wise nor useful to recall here the disastrous history of our former attempts to accomplish the work which Mr. Goyder has now started to complete. We should only have to recount a history of mismanagement, disorganisation, and waste, which our readers have heard enough of. We are now, however, starting afresh, and we ought to let 'the dead past bury its dead.' Nothing that the colony has ever done is more creditable to it than this last attempt to retrieve past blunders, to vindicate its aspersed honour, and to do what is fair and right to those who put faith in the integrity of the colony. We made a bargain with those who purchased our land-orders to give them possession of the land surveyed within a period of five years, and although by no fault of ours, but by misfortunes which we could not control, we have not been able to fulfil our part of the bargain within the time fixed, we have done our best to compensate those who put confidence in us for the apparent breach of faith on our part. We have at some inconvenience to ourselves sent out the best man we had in the colony to complete the work of survey; we have furnished him with a sufficient outfit for the work, and with a sufficient body of men to assist him; and, more than this, we have doubled the area of land to each purchaser, which will be more than a compensation for the short delay which has been occasioned by past failures.

"We know it will be asked by those who know little of the colony, what security they have that Mr. Goyder will succeed where his predecessors have so wofully failed. And our simple answer to this question is, our security is in the character of the man who is at the head of the expedition. The Surveyor-

General is not a man to fail in any work which he undertakes, and having, in full view of the responsibility he has undertaken, agreed to do the work, life being spared, he will accomplish it. Then, the greatest care has been taken to avoid the blunders which were previously committed. Mr. Goyder possesses supreme and undivided authority. He has had the sole selection of the men who accompany him. No person, however high his influence may be, has been able to force men upon him. From the highest to the lowest the men have been chosen because of their fitness for the positions to which they have been appointed. Nepotism, favouritism, and patronage have been firmly put aside, and persons have been chosen, not because they had influential connections, but because, as far as could be judged, they were able to do the work which has to be done. This is one of the best features in the expedition. Mr. Goyder himself has chosen men to be his assistants in whom he can place confidence. He has not only selected his men but his stores. No one knows better than Mr. Goyder that the health and cheerful working of his party will depend to some extent on the way in which they are kept, and he has made every possible provision for having the stores of the expedition of the best quality, selected under his own eye, or the eyes of those in whom he could place full confidence.

"Then, again, no outsiders are allowed to be of the party. Persons who go on their own account, or as agents for others, may, without intending it, do considerable mischief on an expedition like this. In the very nature of things they can have but little to do, and idle persons are apt to grumble, and grumblers often do mischief in breeding dissatisfaction and attempting to interfere with the plans and operations of the chief, who is responsible to the government alone. None of this class have been allowed to go with Mr. Goyder's party. All who accompany him are placed directly under his control, and are subject to his orders. It is difficult to estimate how much an arrangement of this kind will contribute to the success of the expedition. Every man who accompanies Mr. Goyder will have to work, and to work hard, and there will be no time for grumbling or fault-finding.

"Mr. Goyder, too, is fortunate, we think, in the doctor whose services he has obtained. We know Dr. Peel only in his public character, and as a public man he has won golden opinions from all sorts of people. While he was House Surgeon at the Adelaide hospital he was held in high esteem for his kindness and skill; and during his residence at Mount Gambier, where he occupied a similar position in the hospital there, he won for himself many friends, and secured a high reputation. He is a man of energy, and will doubtless be a useful coadjutor to Mr. Goyder.

" We understand that the instructions given to the Surveyor-General are of a very general character, leaving a great deal to his discretion, as was necessary. He thoroughly understands the wishes of the Government, and the nature of the work which is expected from him. He will land his party at Port Darwin, and will commence the work of survey without delay. We believe arrangements have been made by which the Government will have frequent progress reports from Mr. Goyder; and it is expected that if all goes on well the whole work will be completed in twelve or eighteen months from the time of departure. The expedition carry with them the best wishes of the colony. High anticipations are cherished of the success of Mr. Goyder's work in the Northern Territory, and we trust these anticipations will not be disappointed. The Government, we believe, have given him all he asked for; he goes to his work in the prime of life, with all his physical and mental powers in full maturity, and with an experience acquired by many years' labours; and according to the usual course of events, failure under such circumstances is hardly possible—certainly not probable. We hope the holders of land-orders in England, who have not treated us fairly in this Northern Territory matter, will now believe that as a colony we are intensely in earnest to fulfil our engagements to them. We have never for one moment wished to act unjustly towards them. Our anxiety has been to give them the land which we covenanted to give for the money we received from them; and because we could not give them this land exactly at the time we expected to do, we have now given them ample compensation by doubling their acreage. No one can say that these gentlemen are in a worse position now than if we had been able to hand over the land surveyed to them in March next, when by waiting just one year longer they will get for the delay twice the quantity."

FROM THE "AUSTRALIAN AND NEW ZEALAND GAZETTE."
August 14, 1869.

"THE NORTHERN TERRITORY OF SOUTH AUSTRALIA.

"We have received Mr. Goyder's report of his operations at the Northern Territory, addressed to the Government, which we give in full:—

"NORTHERN TERRITORY, FORT POINT,
"PORT DARWIN, *May* 3, 1869.

"SIR,—I have the honour to forward in separate parcel duplicates of letters, &c., sent per mail by ship *Moonta*, and herewith 26 plans and diagrams of the principal and two minor townships at Fort Point, on the Elizabeth, and in the fork at the junction of the River Darwin with the Blackmore; diagrams of 43,000 acres of land, surveyed into sections of 160 and 320 acres, and the completion of which has been properly certified; a plan of the township at this place, and a general plan showing the position of the lands surveyed and natural features of the country, so far as such have been ascertained by personal inspection and fixed by the respective surveys; pay-sheets for the months of March and April; list of orders issued for the same periods; progress reports, so far as such have been sent in from the field; 13 boxes from the naturalist, containing specimens of plants, animals, shells, reptiles, and seeds; two live pigeons, a native canoe, paddles, spears, throwing-stick, and a few trifling curiosities as per debited lists; copy of rough journal; copy of letter from Dr. Peel respecting the health of the party; meteorological observations at Fort Point during March and April, and requisition of provisions, tools, &c., required for the use of the party, and which should be sent without fail by the schooner on her return trip. The *Gulnare* arrived here on the 27th

March. Beyond delaying the work and a little anxiety, no other inconvenience resulted from the condemnation of the *Sea Ripple*. Captain Sweet reports his voyage protracted to 42 days by calms in the tropics. He is an able, active, energetic officer, and did all in his power to facilitate my plans. He is also an expert photographer, and has taken several views in the locality, of which I am glad, as Mr. Brooks has been fully occupied preparing plans and documents for the field parties during the past two months. We have here a splendid harbour, suitable to vessels of the largest tonnage, deep water, and good holding ground. At a trifling cost jetties or wharves might be constructed, and the place is healthy, and the sites of the townships here and elsewhere the most healthy the country affords. We have also obtained good roads thence into the interior, and lands varying in character from light sandy loam to rich black and chocolate-coloured soils, with water and grasses in abundance—the quality of the pasture improving towards the south, south-west, and south-east. I believe, from the experience of others and what I have seen, that this harbour is the best in the locality, and, with its high lands and deep waters close to the points of landing, estuaries radiating towards the interior and navigable to lands suitable to the growth of any product adapted to the climate, with first-rate pasturage for large stock and supply of water, though in the dry season, except in watercourses or water-tables (this will have to be obtained by sinking below the surface), most suited for the purpose of commerce and likely to lead to the satisfactory settlement of the country. I look, therefore, on the object of the expedition as gained, and consider that the quality of the land under survey—the timber, vegetation, and conveniences for traffic—equals, if not surpasses, the most sanguine expectations of the land order-holders and those interested in the development of the country. It is to be borne in mind, however, that so far our experience only extends to the rainy season and the early portion of the dry, by the end of which grass that is now green will be dry and the earth in many places look parched and dusty, but that is common to all countries in this latitude. Indeed, the same may be said of the greater portion of South Australia. My first impressions in its favour, as detailed in my previous report, are only confirmed by more extended travel, and I trust that but a short time will elapse before it is occupied. Apart from the suitability of much of the soil for the growth of cotton, sugar, rice, &c., it is invaluable for breeding large stock, and horses or cattle could readily be shipped and conveyed to India. It is true the heat is great and the climate for at least six months in the year oppressive, and for Europeans it is as bad as some portions of India, and the same amount of work cannot be done as in South Australia without great determination and exertion; but, again, our experience is that of men new to the locality, and much may be done by acclimatisation, but labour can be readily obtained from the adjacent Islands.

"I expect the survey to be completed, at latest, by 1st of October of the present year, when the party will be prepared to return, and have sent the schooner back direct to Adelaide with the mail and instructed Captain Sweet to bring back necessary stores, tools, &c., and to call for letters at Timor on his way back to this place.

"We have carried on operations thus far without collision with the natives. There are about 60 in the locality, many of whom hang about the fence round the camp from daylight till dark. They brought in some weeks ago two Malays, the survivors of a proa which they state was wrecked two years ago. The names of these two men are Sennam and Salammo, natives of Maccassar. They state the captain of the proa was named Di Sorrie, the proa *Lambazay Senkang*. She was trading between Maccassar and Marragie, and had on board 103 piculs of rice and 43 hands. She carried three guns and five muskets, and was owned by a Chinese named Ka-soo-ah, who does business in Campou-mals-Koo, Maccassar. All perished but these two men, who were suffering from incipient scurvy, and were fed out of the camp and attended to by the doctor. As they expressed great anxiety to get to Koepang, where one has a wife and family, I have instructed Captain Sweet to make them useful on board and land them there on his way back. Their present story is essentially different to that first told by them, but this may arise from the more perfect knowledge of the language attained by R. D. Burton, who conversed with them, though at first with great difficulty. Then they spoke of half the crew being drowned and the remainder speared by the natives, their lives only being spared at the instigation of Mira, who protected and subsequently brought them here from Escape Cliffs, and to whom I gave a ration for his humanity, after having the reason fully and clearly explained to him by Burton, who understands a good deal of their language. The land upon the Adelaide Plains is still under water as far south as the latitude of Fred's Pass. It will not be dry for two or three months yet. I do not purpose surveying any of this land, although doubtless of good quality. It is only prevented from constant inundation by the greater height of the land on the bank of the river, and will require to be properly drained before it is available. When this has been done, it will probably yield a larger price and profitable returns, but it would be premature to survey such allotments at the present time. The above remarks only apply to the land north of the latitude of Fred's Pass, and extending northward to the Narrows near Escape Cliffs and to the east of the Daly Range. After personal inspection of the locality, I have altered the site of the proposed township there from the low bald rises formerly spoken of, and which, during the rainy season, are surrounded by water, to a preferable site on the east slope of the range nearer the pass. All the party are in good health.

"I have the honour to be, Sir, your obedient servant,
"G. W. GOYDER, *Surveyor-General.*"

"CROWN LANDS OFFICE, ADELAIDE,
"*June* 21, 1869.

"SIR,—I am desired by the Honourable the Commissioner to inform you of the arrival of the *Gulnare* on the 6th instant, and to acknowledge the receipt of your letters, progress reports, and plans, &c., as well as the cases of specimens and miscellaneous articles forwarded in the care of Captain Sweet.

"The continued energy displayed in the prosecution of the work and the absence of severe illness and accident are sources of great gratification to the Government.

"The requisition for stores has been placed in Mr. Turnbull's hands for execution, and that for medicines, &c., in Messrs. Faulding's hands, after due consideration of your minute thereon as to the latter being only required for the service of a permanent staff.

"The cases and miscellaneous articles have been divided between Dr. Schomburgk, of the Botanic Gardens, and Mr. Waterhouse, of the Adelaide Museum, and have given considerable satisfaction.

"With reference to the more important topics, viz., the appointment of a Government Resident and a permanent staff and the bringing away of the present survey party under your command, I am to inform you that these have been carefully and anxiously weighed by the Commissioner and his colleagues.

"They feel that it would be premature at this moment, notwithstanding the large amount of work accomplished by you in a very short time and your estimate of the time required for completion of the survey, to appoint a Government Resident, or to despatch another party and to incur the expense of a steamer on the supposition that the party can leave on the 1st October next.

"They are accordingly fitting up the *Gulnare* with stores which would last until the end of the year, and in doing so are providing articles which considerations of climate and health may render of value to you, in addition to the few bare necessaries included in your requisition.

"Without positively controlling you in your disposal of the *Gulnare* or in your course of action, they consider that your best way will be to despatch her back direct to Port Adelaide, so soon as you are able to send plans of the surveys of five hundred thousand (500,000) acres in addition to the townships, and a certificate that the lands have been actually marked out on the ground in accordance with such plans.

"No steps will be taken towards the selection of the land until such certificate has been received.

"Such alterations have been made in the *Gulnare* as will enable her to bring back yourself and some of your surveyors, should you think it right to accompany her on that trip; or consider that from economical and other motives the officers might be reduced in number. It is understood, however, that the doctor must not leave the settlement.

"The party then remaining at the Northern Territory should continue the survey of another one hundred thousand (100,000) acres, or one hundred and fifty thousand acres (150,000); and be employed in such works in the harbour or in other improvements as you may think desirable.

"I am to impress upon you that should you desire to return by that trip, that is, after five hundred thousand (500,000) acres have been surveyed and plotted, you are to be guided entirely by your own wishes in the matter and by considerations of health.

"In the selection of any subordinate officers for return passages you are unfettered, merely bearing in mind the necessity for careful deliberation in appointing your successor should you, as you probably may, return for the purpose of reporting fully to the Government.

"On the arrival of the *Gulnare* with yourself or your report of the townships and 500,000 acres having been actually surveyed, the Government will take immediate measures to arrange for the selection of the land and for despatching some vessel (probably a steamer) to take up persons desiring to select lands or settle in the Northern Territory, and to bring back such of the party as do not remain either in Government service or private capacities.

"The interval between the departure of the *Gulnare* from the Northern Territory and the arrival of the large vessel will probably be from ten to twelve weeks, but the arrangements on this side will be as rapid as possible.

"The field parties employed in surveying the extra 100,000 acres should be within easy reach of the port, certainly at the end of ten weeks.

"The above are the leading features of the plan in the minds of the Government, but are of course subject to alteration by you in the event of any unforeseen emergency arising on your side of the continent and requiring the *Gulnare* to visit Timor or Batavia.

"As a permanent settlement will have to be maintained in the Northern Territory, you can recommend such members of your party as may be desirous of obtaining suitable appointments there, but they must most distinctly understand that the rate at which their services will be remunerated must be left to the Government.

"I am, Sir, your obedient servant,
(Signed) "JAMES N. BLACKMORE, *Secretary.*
" G. W. Goyder, Esq., Surveyor-General, Port Darwin."

FROM THE "SOUTH AUSTRALIAN ADVERTISER."

" The *Gulnare* will sail next Wednesday and take important despatches to Mr. Goyder from the Government. We do not profess to have an exact knowledge of their contents, but we believe the general purport of the instructions to be something like the following:—As soon as 500,000 acres are surveyed, Mr. Goyder is to certify to that fact and forward plans to the Government. The *Gulnare* is to return to Adelaide immediately that Mr. Goyder is in a position to announce that he has accomplished the above, and he may, if he think fit, return by her himself; but this will be optional on his part. What the Government require is simply this—that the *Gulnare* shall return to Adelaide as soon as 500,000 acres are surveyed. The party is not to be broken up, but will go on surveying 150,000 acres more, so that there shall be 650,000 acres to choose from. In the event of all this being accomplished sooner than anticipated, the party will be employed in effecting any improvements that may be deemed desirable in the new settlement. On the return of the *Gulnare* with the Surveyor-General's certificate of the completion of the survey, the Government will immediately arrange for a permanent staff to administer the affairs of the infant colony; and here will begin the most critical part of their duties and responsibilities. It has always been laid down as a fundamental principle, and asserted by successive Governments and by leading politicians of all parties, that the Northern Territory is not to be a charge upon the general revenue of this province; in other words, that it is to be self-supporting, and there is no doubt that it can be successfully developed on this principle. But the Government must beware of the temptation to create a host of billets. When the revenue raised in the Northern Territory is equal to the maintenance of a 'staff,' and when the settlers who raise that revenue declare that they want a 'staff,' by all means let the most improved official machinery be erected. But, until the actual necessity for expensive government arises, let us carefully avoid it. Of course a Government Resident must be appointed, and we do not know a better title than that just mentioned, as it can be made to cover everything. A Government Resident may be Governor, Judge, Special Magistrate, Military Commandant, Collector of Customs, Harbour Master, and ever so much besides, with just a clerk or two to assist him in clerical work. One thing the Government will have to see to is, that there shall be no necessity to send prisoners to the Supreme Court in Adelaide for trial. This will be rather too costly a luxury, and one that may be very well dispensed with, at least for some years to come. Of course, at first one supervising and superintending head ought to be sufficient, and Ministers will find that the truest economy will consist in the appointment of a Government Resident able, by habit, experience, and education, to preside over the general administration of the young settlement without the expensive encumbrance of a host of subordinate officers. We hope the Ministry will be as successful in the inauguration of government in the Northern Territory as Mr. Goyder appears to be in the survey of the country.

"We should add to the foregoing that after the return of the *Gulnare* facilities will be afforded by the Government for the passage to Port Darwin of land purchasers, or their agents, who may be desirous of going out to look at the country and making arrangements for settlement; but until the survey is completed no persons other than those engaged on the official staff will be permitted to take passages by the Government vessels. The

Gulnare will take out a supply of various sorts of vegetables and other requisites for the use of the expedition over and above those for which Mr. Goyder has specially applied.

"ARRIVAL OF THE 'GULNARE.'

" When the English mail came in, people eagerly inquired for news from the Northern Territory, although it was not likely that there would be any by that medium. However, the *Gulnare* has opportunely turned up, having sailed on the 5th May and reached Port Adelaide on Sunday, the 6th June. Full particulars of her trip will be found in our shipping columns. The party are in good health and good spirits, excellent discipline prevails, and the work of surveying proceeds vigorously. The accounts of the country are as favourable as those by the *Moonta's* advices; and neither climate, rain, nor natives have as yet given the expedition any trouble. We have several letters, but for the present must content ourselves with publishing the following, which is the most circumstantial. It is dated April 30, but we have one from the camp at head-quarters dated 3rd May. At the later date all were well and everything progressing satisfactorily. Mr. Goyder informs the Government that the survey will be completed by the 1st October, and we believe he is careful to state the latest date to which he expects his task can extend, for private advices mention August as the time at which the work of the expedition will be over. We now append the letter :—

"'PORT DARWIN, N.T., *April* 30, 1869.

"'There is not much news to communicate this mail, but the little there is will no doubt be welcomed with satisfaction by the people in Adelaide. When the *Moonta* sailed in the beginning of March considerable progress had been made with the survey of the town at Port Darwin, and by the 25th of the month every portion of the work, including wharfage allotments, was completed and eight parties had been started on the rural surveys. The remaining four parties were also away at the end of the month. There are now three camps of four parties each, working in different directions through the country—one lot at the head of the south arm, one at the east arm, and another further to the eastward on the ridge between this and the Adelaide River. Large townships have been surveyed on each side of the arms, and though it is difficult to say exactly, I think the quantity of country work done may be estimated at between 50,000 and 60,000 acres. By the time this reaches you over 200,000 acres ought to be ready to select from. Of course everything depends upon the continuance of the advantages which the surveyors have enjoyed up to the present time in good health, fine weather, capital country, and freedom from annoyance by the natives. In any case, however, there is, I think, every probability of the work being got through before next wet season; and those who have friends up here may fairly expect them back to dinner on Christmas Day next. The Surveyor-General appears to have little spare time on his hands. He is nearly always away from here, either exploring, examining the coast, or visiting the different camps. At the beginning of the month he started overland for the camp on the south arm, which he reached in about ten days; having visited Fred's Pass, near the Adelaide, and examined the country in its vicinity, a first-rate route was found through well grassed and wooded country, watered by fine fresh-water rivers and creeks. On returning to this camp he only remained a day or two before he started up the south arm again, to make further explorations to the southward and westward, where good country was also found.

"'The *Gulnare* did not arrive until the 27th March, three weeks after the departure of the *Moonta*, and during that period serious fears were entertained for her safety, or rather for that of the *Sea Ripple*, for of course we were not then aware that that vessel had been condemned. Her appearance in the port dispelled a great deal of anxiety, for she had the greater portion of our stock of meat on board, and we had already been put on rather short allowance in anticipation of her non-arrival. She had also several drays, without which the transport of the camp equipages and stores about the country would have been almost an impossibility. The little steamer *Midge* has proved exceedingly useful in keeping up communication with the river camps, and carrying stores, &c. The Northern Territory Fund has never been better expended than in her purchase.

"'The weather has been extremely favourable. The change of the N.W. monsoon took place about the middle of March, and during that period we were visited with several heavy thunder-storms and squalls; but there has never yet been sufficient rain to stop the progress of the work for one day. The weather now is really delightful—fine breezy days and cool, or rather cold nights, for the thermometer has stood below 60 deg., rendering the use of a rug necessary as the rule. This, together with a good country and mosquitoes and sandflies in the minority, helps to render existence even in the Northern Territory not altogether unenjoyable. Under these circumstances, it is no matter of surprise that the health of the party continues good. Of course the sick list is not always empty; such a thing could not be expected out of 130 men; but the doctor has not yet, I think, been troubled with anything like a serious case of illness.

"'On the 13th March a party, under charge of Mr. Burton and including several members of the former expeditions, started for Escape Cliff in two boats and returned on the 18th, bringing back with them two bullock drays, a quantity of ironwork, bananas, chilis, and several plants. They found the place in nearly the same state as when it was left by Mr. Manton, old Mira having continued to carry out strictly his protective policy. The old chief was away at the time turtle-fishing on one of the adjacent islands; but he had left a number of natives in charge under another chief named Miranda, who made the party welcome and showed by every means in their power their pleasure at seeing the white men amongst them again. They did not seem, however, to relish the removal of any of the things, and if Mira had been there a difficulty in that respect would probably have arisen. As an instance of how jealously the things are guarded, it was gathered by some of the party during their stay that since the settlement was deserted a large number of blacks from the Alligator River visited the place for the purpose of burning the houses, but were stoutly resisted and were driven off after a sharp encounter. Two of the large wooden houses were found to be in nearly as good a state as when first erected. The majority of the huts were also sound. The graves of the men who died there were overgrown, but the railings around them and the headboards were still standing, the inscriptions on the latter being perfectly legible. The principal object of the party was to ascertain the condition of the boat *Julia*, and if she was seaworthy to bring her round here, but she was found sunk at her moorings, and every portion of her except the hard-wood with which she was repaired up there completely perforated by worms, and of course she had to be left. Her anchor and chains and one or two of her spars were, however, recovered. From the accounts given by the natives, it would seem that the horses and cattle which were turned adrift on the west side of the Adelaide have been breeding largely, and are now running near the narrows in considerable numbers. There was some talk of sending a party from here to drive them in, but it has not been spoken of lately, and the idea will not, I suppose, be carried out unless it is found absolutely necessary to increase the number of horses in the expedition.

"'The natives here have up to within a week or two been very quiet, but lately their numbers have been augmented by a large body from the Escape Cliff side, headed by Mira; and finding that their demands for *ton ton* (their name for food) are not supplied so liberally as when the survey parties were camped here, they are commencing to act in a manner that is not altogether unlikely to end in a quarrel. A few days ago one of them raised his spear to Mr. Schultze, the naturalist, simply because he refused to give him something or other that he asked for. I understand that none have yet been seen at any of the survey camps; and it is remarkable that Mr. Goyder did not come across any on his journey to the south arm, or during any of his other trips.

"'Two or three persons are leaving the party, I hear, and return to Adelaide by the schooner, but their places will in some measure be filled up by two Malays, who have been brought amongst us by rather strange circumstances.

"'About a fortnight ago one of the boats was round at Shoal Bay with the naturalist, when these poor fellows came down the beach to the party and asked to be protected from the blacks, who were trying to spear them. They were brought here, and on being questioned by one of the party who is acquainted with the Malay language, it was found that they had belonged to a large proa which sailed from Maccassar with a crew of upwards of forty men for the purpose of fishing on this coast, and which was wrecked somewhere near here. The rest of the crew were either drowned or speared by the natives. They appear to be very grateful at the kind treatment they have received from us, and are willing to do whatever is asked of them.

"'It is rumoured that in order to save the expense of chartering another vessel, the party are to be taken back to Adelaide in the *Gulnare*, but I cannot think it possible that such a thing could have been thought of for one moment. Apart from the meanness of such a course, it would be an act of gross injustice to those who returned to subject them, after their hard labours, to the sufferings they would have to endure if cooped up during a long sea voyage on board of such an undersized craft.'

"With regard to the wreck of the Malay proa, we are informed by another writer that it was wrecked off Escape Cliffs with 44 hands on board, of whom 30 were drowned, 12 were killed by the blacks, and 2 were brought to Port Darwin by the chief Mira, and are now in Adelaide, having been sent to the Dutch Consul here by Mr. Goyder. One of them is in a bad state of health, and will probably be removed to the hospital. As respects our correspondent's fear that the whole party will be brought back in the *Gulnare*, there is little danger of anything of the kind being done, or attempted to be done. The health and comfort of the expedition must be as carefully studied in the arrangements for the homeward voyage as in those for the voyage out.

NEW HOMES.

"To a correspondent at the Northern Territory we are indebted for the following:—

"'Since the departure of the *Moonta* we have been going ahead in first-rate style. There is none of the idleness, drunkenness, and disorganisation which so strongly marked the career of the previous parties here, but every one works cheerfully and willingly, and with a desire to complete the surveys before the next wet season sets in. At present everything promises that this end will be attained. The town at Port Darwin and two outlying townships on the east arm, or Elizabeth River, and the other on the south arm, or River Darwin, are completed, and the rural surveys are now in full swing. I cannot tell you how many acres are already knocked off, but by the time this reaches you a pretty good hole will be made in half the area. There are twelve field parties at work, and I think between them they will manage to get over 120,000 acres per month, or close upon it. We are now scattered over the country in all directions. Four parties are working from Fort Point towards Fred's Pass, along the ridge to the westward of the Adelaide River; four are on the Elizabeth, and four on the Darwin. To give you some idea of our work, I will tell you what was done to-day. The cook of our party was called at 4.30 A.M., the men at 5; and by 6 breakfast was over and all hands started for the field. A walk of about two and a half miles brought them to their starting-point, from whence they surveyed, pegged, and trenched two miles of line; and then had over a mile and a half to walk back to camp, which they did not reach till 4.30 P.M. Sometimes the walk to work and back is not so long, but sometimes it is longer, and the above may be taken as a very fair average day's work. You will, I think, agree that it is not a bad one, especially when I can tell you that officers and men have also to take their turn in watching the camp during the night. Strange to say, the natives have not yet visited any of the outlying camps, but they may do so at any moment, and we have always to be on the look out. No man ever goes out from the camp unarmed. The natives at Fort Point are, I believe, getting rather troublesome, and they have recently had their numbers increased by a batch from the Escape Cliffs. We have had splendid weather since we have been here, and we expect it to continue for seven or eight months longer. The country is also first-class, and we have nothing to complain of, except that the provisions are not quite up to the mark. We get rather too much salt meat and not quite sufficient vegetable food. The authorities in Adelaide will, I hope, send us out by the *Gulnare* a good supply of potatoes and onions. The more I see of this country the better I am pleased with it. I was out exploring to the eastward yesterday, and saw some of the finest land I have ever seen. We are to survey some 60,000 or 70,000 acres to the eastward, camping out on the work at night, without moving the bulk of our equipage. Then we shall go southward.'

"In addition to numerous letters from private members of the Northern Territory Expedition, the public have now had an opportunity of perusing Mr. Goyder's official report. It is very brief—quite the antipodes of the Cadell style; but Mr. Goyder went out to do the maximum of work in the minimum of time, and, consequently, has no leisure for rounding fine sentences or elaborating picturesque descriptions. His statement, coupled with those of the various other persons who have written, will be regarded as eminently satisfactory by the general public. There are mosquitoes, no doubt, although they seem to prefer some skins to others, or else it must be that some people are more irritable than others and make more fuss about a common annoyance."

"SURVEY OF NORTHERN TERRITORY.

"*Ordered by the House of Assembly to be printed*, 23rd *November*, 1869.

"COPY OF SURVEYOR-GENERAL'S REPORT ON SURVEY OF NORTHERN TERRITORY.

"Fort Point, Port Darwin, 27th *September*, 1869.

"Sir,—I have the honour to acknowledge receipt of your letter of the 21st of June, which arrived here per *Gulnare* on the 24th August, after a rough passage of fifty days from Port Adelaide, *viâ* Timor Koepang, to Port Darwin.

"Capt. Sweet reports experiencing heavy weather and adverse winds for the first three weeks of his voyage. He brought with him a supply of fruit, vegetables, fowls, a few goats, buffalo, and sheep from Timor, which, with the potatoes from Adelaide, were highly acceptable, as symptoms of incipient scurvy began to show themselves in some of the officers and men. These symptoms you will be glad to learn have since entirely disappeared.

"The survey of nearly six hundred thousand (600,000) acres of land of the required area was completed upon the ground by the end of August. Taking into careful consideration, however, the various subjects named in your letter, coupled with the facts that the draftsmen and most of the senior officers would be actively employed for the succeeding four weeks in preparing the necessary plans, diagrams, and records of the work done, and the necessity of certain repairs and alterations in the schooner, which required a thorough overhaul after her late trip, I decided to employ the parties of the officers engaged upon the plans and records of survey in prosecuting necessary and indispensable works to the new settlement, and to send the remaining parties into the field to complete the survey of the additional area required, so that a proper connexion of the survey might be secured, and the plans, diagrams, and fieldnotes of the whole reach you at one and the same time with the requisite certificates. This course appeared to me the more desirable, inasmuch as the heat is rapidly increasing, rendering field-work more trying to the system; whilst those employed near Fort Point during the hot season, having less walking and better accommodation, will be in a better position to carry on the work during the allotted hours for labour. I carried out this determination, and the survey of the extra lands was completed, and the respective parties returned to Fort Point by the 25th instant.

"As there were many reasons why I should personally confer with the Honourable Commissioner as early as possible, I accepted the permission accorded to me in your letter, and propose returning to Adelaide by the *Gulnare*, which leaves to-morrow morning, and have arranged for the prosecution of the works at Fort Point during my absence, or until the arrival of the steamer, in terms of correspondence appended. In taking this step I have every confidence in the officers and men, and feel assured that everything will be carried out in accordance with my instructions.

"In my last report I was happy in being able to congratulate the party upon the entire absence of serious casualties, and I did fervently hope that I might be permitted to return to Adelaide with my party safe and well. In this, however, I am disappointed; and it is with extreme regret that I have now the painful duty to report the death of Mr. J. W. O. Bennett, one of the draftsmen of the expedition, who died on the 28th of May, from spear wounds inflicted by the natives at Fred's Pass, when Mr. Bennett was off his guard, on the 24th of the same month. It is with unusual hesitation that I enter upon this subject, as I had personally remonstrated with him for his persistent familiarity with the natives, and had written a special memorandum upon the subject.

"Mr. Bennett, it will be recollected, formed one of the members of the previous expedition, and was highly spoken of by Mr. Finniss, on that gentleman's return to Adelaide. He understood much of the language of the tribe, and intended constructing a vocabulary: which so far as compiled by him, is appended hereto, with other papers, and which give, so far as can be obtained, particulars of the attack.

"Laborer Guy, who was with Mr. Bennett at the camp, and was also speared by the natives—though dangerous, fortunately not mortal—has, at my request, sent in a statement, so far as his memory served him, in the enfeebled state to which he was reduced by loss of blood and subsequent suffering, by which it will appear that, despite my remonstrance and written orders to the contrary, Mr. Bennett continued to trust to the natives implicitly, even allowing them to paint him after their manner. Indeed the poor fellow considered himself perfectly safe amongst them, and others of the party supposed him a source of protection from attack. The sequel proves how little they understood the treacherous nature of those with whom they had to deal.

"The organization and equipment of the respective parties on their leaving Fort Point, was such as to preclude, with a very small amount of care, the possibility of such an attack succeeding in its object; but the apparent friendliness of the natives so deceived the officers and men of the respective parties, that my instructions were departed from, the men going out without arms, and the camps being separated instead of remaining together for mutual assistance and defence. I was absent exploring at the time, and did not hear the particulars of the attack until my arrival at Wood's camp on the Upper Manton, on my way back to visit the parties, when I insisted upon the immediate consolidation of the respective camps, as originally arranged, which effectually prevented a repetition of the attack. When returning some weeks later to the depôt at Fort Point, with a party of four, the natives surrounded, and did all they could to suffocate us, by firing the long grass in advance, on either side, and behind us; we could easily have shot one or two of them, as three were visible at one time, within twenty yards of me, but in the position of Protector of Aborigines, as well as that of Surveyor-General, I knew that these miserable specimens of humanity were only following their savage instincts in doing what they did; and whilst ever ready for the worst, we abstained from injuring them so long as there was a possibility to avoid bloodshed. By the coolness of my men and our knowledge of the country, we were enabled to avoid the effects of the fire, to the yelling disappointment of the blacks, without firing a shot—though the escape on one occasion was extremely narrow, owing to the difficulty in getting the frightened horses, fatigued by a long journey, through the burning grass, the flames of which, rising to a great height, roared and crackled sufficiently to confuse the poor brutes, apart from the heat and smoke which necessarily accompanied the burning. The natives kept firing the grass near and in advance of us for a distance of eighteen miles. But we got to Fort Point all right, where I was surprised to find the old native hangers-on at the camp about as usual, though they knew of all that had transpired. They were ordered off at once, and have not since been permitted to approach.

"No act of aggression has been perpetrated by the expedition against the natives, who had been invariably treated kindly up to the time of my return. Since then they have been kept at a distance, and they are well aware of the reason. It is a mistake, however, to suppose that because the natives do not show themselves, that there are none near: as, when they were allowed to assemble near the respective camps, all my movements were reported by them to the officers and men, though I was many miles away, and this with astonishing celerity and accuracy. This is the more surprising as, up to the time of the attack upon Bennett and Guy, I had seen no natives during my journeys inland.

"Both officers and men were naturally indignant at Bennett's murder, and, had the order been given for retaliation the punishment of the natives would have been a simple matter with a party so armed; but I considered the attack upon Bennett and Guy the results of feelings of revenge on the part of those who had probably lost relatives in some previous contest with the whites, the more so as we were informed on arrival of the *Moonta*, by the blacks here, that those on the Adelaide, or near that locality, intended to kill two of our party. To retaliate therefore, even could we have identified the murderers, would have been to secure to our successors, less able to defend themselves, a debt of lives to be paid for our act of reprisal, unless we had annihilated the tribe, which was not to be thought of. I had also to bear in mind that we were in what to them appeared unauthorised and unwarrantable occupation of their country, and where territorial rights are so strictly observed by the natives, that even a chief of one tribe will neither hunt upon nor remove anything from the territory of another without first obtaining permission, it is scarcely to be wondered at if, when opportunity is allowed them, they should resent such acts by violence upon its perpetrators. Since they have been ordered from the camp there has been no trouble with them. Our relations with the natives are peculiar. We are liable to the consequences of their sudden and treacherous attacks; yet retaliation on our part would, by many—and, I do not say without some show of justice—be looked upon as little short of murder, as we have no right to take the lives of these men without such be done in actual defence, or by the laws of our country. An appeal to such laws, however, would have been useless. We might have surrounded and captured the murderers of Bennett and sent them to justice, when from the evidence of witnesses and the declarations made, conviction and execution might have followed. But they could not have understood our language, nor could they have made themselves intelligible to us. The expense and trouble, therefore, would probably have been incurred in vain, and their subsequent experience, detailed to their tribes, might have given rise to other murders to ensure similar experiences. Persons coming here should be constantly and vigilantly on guard, and never without the means of defence. The latter is necessary even in mercy to the natives, as they rarely attack those prepared to receive them. Nearly all are alike treacherous. There may be a few better inclined—but they are few, and generally over-ruled by the general voice, which is for plunder and revenge, for which the occupation of the country is to them ample cause. Even the chief Mira had to be protected from the natives here by the men of the expedition, as spears were raised against him in the camp at Fort Point, because his policy was friendly to us; and this state of affairs must continue until the object and motives of the whites can be clearly explained in their own language, and the natives satisfactorily convinced of the futility and impolicy of opposition. The sooner, therefore, some one can be found willing and competent to learn their language, and undertake this mission, which might readily be carried into effect at Fort Point, the sooner will the great object of a peaceable and useful intercourse with the numerous native tribes in this locality be secured.

"It is with regret that I have also to report the death of Richard Hazard, a coloured man, and one of the cooks of the expedition, who died at Fort Point on the 9th of August, of premature decay. He was sent into the main camp on the 30th June, suffering from rheumatism; pleurisy succeeded, and as Dr. Peel dreaded from his early examinations during the first stages of Hazard's illness, was followed by serious effusion into the cavity of the chest, and death.

"The remains of Bennett and Hazard were interred in one grave, on the summit of the hill at Fort Point, and I caused a neat tomb to be constructed to their memory; in addition to which the officers propose to erect a further proof of their esteem for Bennett, on their arrival in Adelaide; and the men and officers subscribed over (£65) sixty-five pounds, which it is proposed to hand over to Hazard's widow on the arrival of the *Gulnare*.

"SURVEY OF LAND.

"The survey comprises a total area of 665,866 acres, including roads and reserves, viz.:—

	Acres.	Acres.
"1st. Principal Township at Fort Point—		
999 half-acre allotments =	499½	
Roads =	1,160	
Reserves =	27	
Park Lands =	730	
Cemetery and Cemetery Reserve =	90	
		2,506½
"2nd. Township on the River Blackmore—		
335 half-acre allotments =	167½	
Roads =	31	
Reserves =	8	
Park Lands =	252	
Cemetery and Cemetery Reserve =	40	
		498½

		Acres.	Acres.
"3rd. Township on the Elizabeth—			
313 half-acre allotments	=	156½	
Roads	=	76	
Reserves	=	8	
Park Lands	=	363	
Cemetery and Cemetery Reserve	=	25	
			628½
"4th. Township at Fred's Pass—			
207 half-acre allotments	=	103½	
Roads	=	18	
Reserves	=	1	
Park Lands	=	649	
Cemetery and Cemetery Reserve	=	23	
			794½
"5th. 1,708 blocks, each 320 acres	=	546,560	
"6th. 208 blocks, each 160 acres	=	33,280	
"7th. 330 blocks of irregular area	=	73,964	
"8th. Roads	=	7,554	
"9th. Reserves	=	80	
			661,438
"Total area surveyed			665,866

"The survey extends from Fort Point, in a south and south-westerly direction, as far as Fog Bay, Point Blaze, north of Anson's Bay; southerly, a distance of fifty-eight miles to the southern and eastern sources of the River Finniss; and easterly, to the swampy lands lying east of the Adelaide River. I did not survey any of the land on the Adelaide Plains, because most of them, as far south as Fred's Pass, are covered with water for eight months of the year; and, for a considerable distance to the south of the pass, the country adjacent to the river is impracticable for traffic most of the year—large paper-bark swamps existing between the west bank of the river and the higher lands flanking the plain. From latitude 13° south, however, east-south, and south-west of Mount Charles, there is over a million acres of land of fair average quality, some of it exceedingly rich, other portions equally poor and sandy, but most of it suited to the growth of tropical or semi-tropical products; the whole well grassed and watered, and admirably adapted for depasturing cattle or horse stock. To the south of the Finniss, and extending in the direction of the Rivers Daly and Victoria, the land, so far as our operations and examination enabled us to judge, continued to improve in character and quality, and running streams were more abundant; but my means, and the object of my journey, did not permit me an opportunity of examining its extent or detail—the horses being nearly all required by the field parties, and my presence being necessary at Fort Point to ensure the proper preparation of the records of survey, and to push on necessary works at that place prior to the completion of the duties required to be performed by the field parties; as it is, half my time here has been occupied examining the country in advance of the surveys, and in visiting the several parties.

"In fixing the sites of the several townships, I was invariably accompanied by one of the senior officers and the doctor; and, where such occurred upon a navigable stream, by a nautical man, by whose joint advice and judgment I was aided in the selection. The site first chosen on the Elizabeth was altered to a preferable one two miles further north, where vessels drawing six feet of water could approach the water-frontage allotments at all states of the tide—an impossibility at the first site, as low water springs exposed rock, which satisfactorily set the question at rest, though a good deal to my annoyance, as part of the survey had been completed before I discovered the mistake.

"The survey comprises portions of four native districts, viz., the 'Woolner,' 'Woolner-Larakeeyah,' 'Larakeeyah,' and 'Warnunger,' and is embraced within the limits of sixteen Hundreds —varying in area from one hundred and twenty (120) to one hundred and ninety-six (196) square miles, portions of which still remain unsurveyed lands of the Crown.

"The records of survey are contained in the field books, diagrams, data plans, Hundred sheets, townships, and general plans, as per detailed list appended, duplicates of all being left at Fort Point, for the use of the local Land Office, when such has been established.

"DESCRIPTION OF COUNTRY.

"The country in the neighbourhood of Fort Point consists principally of table-land of from sixty to 150 feet above the sea level, falling thence gently towards the sea, except upon portions of the coast between Fort Point and Point Emery, where it forms into cliffs of soil over a level bedding of indurated marl—with red and yellow stains from iron—over beds of slate and micaceous sandstone, very unctuous to the touch, and also containing a good deal of iron—these latter strata are nearly on edge or perpendicular, and run in a northerly and southerly direction. The cliffs, except at Point Emery and Point Elliot, where the land is more open, are fringed by a dense thicket from five to twenty yards through, of various sized timber, matted together by bamboo, convolvoli, and a variety of other vines and shrubs. The low lands near the sea—especially such as are under the influence of the tides—by dense mangroves of two or three varieties; these give place as you go inland and ascend to the higher levels, to paper bark (some of large growth), palms, fan and fern, screw pines, iron bark, gum, stringy bark, fig, cedar, cotton, and a variety of other trees and shrubs, forming an open forest. The grass over the whole, or nearly the whole of the surface of the ground, grows luxuriantly, from a rank species resembling holcus to the finer varieties—from all, or most of which, seed has been sent to Adelaide. The soil is mostly good, and of a dark brown colour, with small nodulous stones of ferruginous sandstone upon the surface; in places masses of this stone crop out, and about an acre is level and cemented into a surface resembling iron—broken only by timber growing through, but destitute of other vegetation. Near the sea, and generally upon a watercourse near its junction with the sea, swampy flats occur, containing timber of large growth and rank vegetation: but these being liable to inundation during the rainy season, have been excluded from the survey.

This general description of the country applies to all the table land as far south as Fred's Pass—the slopes and valleys being of better soil, and free from surface stones. The flats, on either side of large watercourses, also contain good soil; except where they join the higher land, where there is a narrow belt of a sandy character—poor to look at, though covered with timber and grass. I washed some of the poorest looking, and found it to contain but ten per cent. of earthy matter and ninety per cent. pure sand. From Mount Daly, westward, to the Blackmore, the same kind of open forest, undulating, and flat lands exist; at the Blackmore, however, from the Township to the tumbling waters, the soil changes suddenly upon the east side, from a dark brown to a very light loam, resembling fine white sand in appearance, but containing ninety-five per cent. of earth, and but five per cent. of pure sand. From thence the soil gradually improves to the south, south-east, and south-west, except where the ranges occur, and the size of the timber decreases, save on the watercourses, where there are fine specimens of the varieties named. The cotton tree, growing more abundantly upon the higher lands and low rises, and occasionally cork and other trees which I cannot now name. The cork near Mount Charles, abundant, and of large growth, and the bark apparently of superior quality. It was unfortunate that Mr. Schultze could not accompany me on my inland journeys—he being unaccustomed to horse exercise—a large amount of information was thereby lost to me, as specimens could not be carried by my party, and he could only identify specimens from which the leaves, fruit, seed, bark, &c., had been obtained. I endeavoured to counteract this loss, however, by sending him inland, on every opportunity, with the drays, when he generally reaped a rich harvest, and got into ecstacies with each new prize.

"The rocks in the various estuaries, said to be granite, proved, on breaking, to be either shales, slate, or micaceous sandstone, and the granite, so called, upon the ridges of most of the hills, a hard grey crystalline quartz rock, flanked by mica, schists and sandstone. A few miles north of, and for a considerable distance south of the Finniss, and upon its eastern and southern sources, two varieties of granite are met with— one grey, the other a flesh colour, in which the felspar predominates. The grey variety is compact, and of superior quality, and obtainable in large quantities. The schists on either side of these dykes are rapidly decomposing upon the surface, and easily crumbled by pressure in the hand. The ranges generally, so far as I have seen them, are mostly formed of crystalline quartz and rock on the ridges, cropping through slates, shales, or micaceous sandstone. I have seen no limestone in the locality, so that shells or coral, of which there is an abundance on the coast, must be its substitute. A diligent search for this useful material will, I trust, shortly prove successful.

"MINERALS.

"The minerals found by the party have been but few. They consist of the oxides of iron, protoxide of tin, carbonate of copper, and gold. The iron is extensively distributed; the copper was found near the river Finniss, to the north of the Giant Quartz Reef; the tin between the Celica and the Upper Darwin; and the gold at the Tumbling Waters, on the Blackmore; Section 618, west of the Blackmore; at and above the bar on the Charlotte, leading into Bynoe Harbour; on the Finniss, near Section 2130; Rocky Waterholes, Section 2193; and in the River Darwin. I had previously read of the discovery of gold in the Finniss, near the lower bar, by Mr. Litchfield; but I had also heard the alleged discovery discredited. I therefore determined to test its accuracy, and proceeded to the same spot from whence it was stated he obtained specs of the precious metal. We obtained, from a very hurried washing, three specs and a small round pellet of gold from the first four dishes, and subsequently we found gold in the same river, north of the Giant Quartz Reef. But one dish was washed from the bed of the creek, and two or three specs of gold were obtained. In justice to Mr. Litchfield, I am bound to state that gold does exist where he reported it was found, and that more importance might fairly have been attached to, and reliance placed upon, the description of the country travelled over by him, which, though only approximate as to the natural features, were altogether devoid of exaggeration as respects quality of soil, timber, vegetation, and apparently auriferous nature of the country.

"On my return to Fort Point, and after the horses had been rested, I sent R. C. Burton, with an efficient party, to search for gold; and, though he only obtained a little over three-quarters of an ounce, there is no doubt but that a more lengthened and detailed search would have developed a payable goldfield, if such may not have already been found. (See samples and correspondence, with Burton's report, in Appendix.) I also sent Mr. Schultze and his son with Burton's party; they returned with a large collection, and highly pleased with what they had seen, and the specimens sent will, I trust, be of use in determining the value of much of the country, both as regards its capabilities and natural productions.

"NATURALIST.

"In addition to the collection already sent by previous shipments to Adelaide, Mr. Schultze sends, per *Gulnare*, thirty-four cases, containing dry plants, seeds, birds' skins, skins of animals, crustaciæ, insects, snakes, fish, air-plants, sponge, coral, and live animals. This shipment makes a total of over eight thousand specimens. I have written to him acknowledging his assiduity, and expressing gratification that his efforts should have been so deservedly appreciated by those for whom they were obtained, and by whom they will be doubtless properly cared for and distributed. Mr. Schultze and his son remain for the present with the party, to augment their collection as far as such can be done.

"I append thirty-nine paintings, by Mr. Hoare, the Surgeon's assistant, of plants, flowers, seeds, insects, &c., &c., the colours of which fade too rapidly to enable them to be preserved by the Collector. They are mostly true to Nature, and very creditable to Mr. Hoare. I also append a few photographs to show the roads and buildings at the camp; but, as the negatives are being brought to Adelaide by Mr. Brooks, they will all be printed, and form the subject of a separate communication.

"An abstract of the improvements or works effected by the party at Fort Point up to this date will be found amongst other papers attached.

"The stock belonging to this party is in good condition and are doing well. That sent by previous expeditions has spread over the country, but will be got in before the end of the dry season. From the tracks seen they appear to have increased in number, and will doubtless prove a valuable addition to the settlement.

"The climate during the months of May, June, July, August, and September, has been very fine, and, generally, delightful—not too hot during the day, and invariably cool at night. The weather is changing now, however, the atmosphere becoming more moist and the heat more intense. Nearly all the men are well. Some of them stand the climate remarkably well, especially those of a spare habit. Personally I have not enjoyed good health, and twice acute and painful illness attacked me, which speedily succumbed to the care and skill of Dr. Peel, to whom I shall ever feel grateful for his unremitting attention to his duties to the officers and men of the expedition.

"I have the honour, &c.,

"G. W. GOYDER, *Surveyor-General*.

"The Secretary, Crown Lands and Immigration, Adelaide."

The latest statistical returns from Adelaide which have been yet received are up to the close of 1868, and the onward progress of the colony will be very apparent from them. The population was 176,298; there are 547 churches or chapels; the total number of places of worship is 754; 446 Sunday schools, attended by 28,719 scholars; the revenue from all sources was £716,004; the public debt was £3,727,500; the total imports were valued at £2,238,510 and the aggregate exports to £2,819,300; the export of wheat was 2,412,344 bushels, and of flour 43,703 tons. The value of the minerals for the year was £625,022; the export of wool was 29,629,525 lbs., of the estimated value of £1,346,323. The colony contains 4,987,024 sheep, 123,213 cattle, 75,409 horses, and 89,304 pigs.

The total area of land alienated from the Crown amounted on the 31st December last to 3,769,897 acres. There are $4\frac{3}{4}$ acres of cultivated land for each individual, or 14 acres for each male of 14 years and upwards. In Victoria there is but nine-tenths of an acre of cultivated land for each inhabitant; in New South Wales one acre; in Queensland only quarter of an acre.

There are 6,475 acres of orchards and gardens; and 6,209 acres of vineyard, having 5,869,406 vines in bearing, and 1,022,740 which are as yet unproductive. The aggregate quantity of wine made in the year is returned as 863,584 gallons, or nearly 5 gallons a head of the population. The South Australian vintage produced 140 gallons to the acre; that of New South Wales 106, and in Victoria 80 gallons.

The South Australian Government has added very greatly to her population by free and assisted emigration.

The following epitome of the regulations may hereafter be of use, but at this moment the Agent-General is not sending out any emigrants:

Settlers in the colony may obtain help out of the public funds to get emigrants out.

Married labourers and miners not above 45 years of age; single men or widowers not above 40; single females not exceeding 35; married mechanics (when required); single men, and the wives and children of married emigrants are eligible. The payment towards each passage is £4 for a man, and £3 for a woman.

In England assisted passages (when any are being issued) are obtainable under the following circumstances. When the applications from the colony are not sufficient in number, then the Emigration Agent in England can make up the deficiency, according to the above rules.

When private persons introduce suitable immigrants, they are allowed certificates equivalent to what it would have cost the government to introduce them, and these certificates are received as money in the purchase of Crown lands.

The expense of living in the colony is far from high. The following are about the rates of wages. They are not so high as in some of the colonies, but there are corresponding advantages which compensate for this. Masons, blacksmiths, carpenters, and general labourers, 6s. to 10s. a day; ploughmen, £40 to £45; shepherds, £40 to £50 a year, with rations; farm servants, 13s. to 18s. a week; housemaids, £20 to £27; general servants, £20 to £25.

"FARM AND DAIRY PRODUCE.—*Wholesale*—Bacon, 7d. to 8d.; butter, 9d to 10d.; cheese, 6d. to 8d.; eggs, 6d. to 7d.; hams, 8d. to 9d.; honey, 3d. to 3½d.; lard, 8d. to 10d.; new potatoes, 13s. to 17s. per cwt.; Warrnambool potatoes, including bags at the Port, £6 10s. to £6 15s. per ton; beeswax, 12d. to 14d. *Retail*—Bacon, 8d. to 10d.; butter, 10d. to 12d.; cheese, 9d. to 10d.; eggs 9d. to 10d. per dozen; hams, 10d. to 12d.; potatoes (new), 2d. to 2½d. per lb.; do. (Warrnambool), 7s. 6d. to 8s. per cwt.; lard, 10d. to 12d. per lb."

"Hay Market.—*Hindmarsh-square*. Hay—Best old wheaten hay, £7 10s.; do. new do. do., £6; good mixed do., £5 10s.; do. do., loose, from £4 5s. to £4 15s."

"Sheep Market.—*Adelaide*—The market to-day consisted of 6,720 sheep and 2,000 lambs. Sheep, from 5s. to 8s. 6d., according to quality; lambs, from 2s. to 5s. 6d., do."

"The Government have lately received (says the *South Australian Advertiser*) further despatches from Mr. R. D. Ross, giving an interesting and a hopeful account of his interviews and correspondence with the Indian Government and Stud Committee respecting a remount depôt at Port Darwin. On the arrival of the last mail we were able to inform our readers of the progress made by Mr. Ross in his mission. He had been favourably received by His Excellency the Governor-General of India, who had facilitated him in every way, and given him an introduction to the Stud Committee, before whom he had an opportunity of expounding his scheme. We also stated that so satisfied was the Governor-General with Mr. Ross's valuable information that he had recommended the Government to pay that gentleman's expenses back to Bombay or Ceylon. As Mr. Ross had determined, in accordance with his instructions, to return home by way of Bombay, he visited that Presidency, and writing from Bombay under date August 9, he states that he waited on Sir Seymour Fitzgerald, at Poona, on the 5th and 6th of that month, when His Excellency informed him that the Government of the Presidency would be prepared to take annually a certain number of horses for the army, from Port Darwin, whenever the remount depôt was established there. This, Mr. Ross regards as very satisfactory, but he adds that except the Bengal and Madras Governments come to a similar conclusion, the annual demand of the Presidency would not be sufficient to induce breeders to compete in the North Australian markets. Bombay is placed in a far more advantageous position than either of the Presidencies, so far as the Arabian, Persian, and Northern horse markets are concerned, and can always obtain its remounts on more reasonable terms. His Excellency, however, was fully sensible of the expediency of encouraging the Australian market, as it is one the Government of India could rely upon for certainty and regularity of supply. While at Poona, Mr. Ross had an interview with Lord Napier of Magdala, who was inclined to give the scheme a trial, and, in the event of the trial proving favourable, would advocate the Government having their own transports to perform the service between India and Port Darwin. We find that the Stud Committee in India were instructed to send in to the Government a separate report on Mr. Ross's scheme; so the matter is now fairly under consideration, and there is a prospect of something useful being done.

"While primarily seeking to interest the Indian Government in the proposed remount depôt, Mr. Ross has been also recommending the Australian preserved meats to the officials whom he met. He says Captain Robinson, the Superintendent of Marines, would be glad to receive a few sample cases, in order that they may be tested on board the transports conveying troops to and from Suez. If the reports were satisfactory he would recommend future supplies being drawn from Australia. The Commissary-General of the Bombay army informed Mr. Ross that the samples received *viâ* England had been commended for their quality; that large indents had been made on the India office to meet the army demands of the ensuing season; and that he would take care to recommend the supplies being obtained direct from Australia; but, in the first instance, some arrangements must be made with the War Office to obtain the assistance of the Imperial Commissariat Officers in the colonies in making such purchases. The whole question connected with preserved meats, jams, dried fruits, wine, and flour for the army in India, will be left for discussion with, and the decision of, the Home authorities.

"Mr. Ross was about to return to England by the mail steamer from Bombay, and before leaving he expressed his opinion that there was a prospect of a remount depôt being formed at Port Darwin, in which event, should the squatters take the matter up in a spirited manner, many years will not elapse before a large and valuable export trade in live stock will have been established, not only with India, but with the whole of the Eastern settlements, and a value given to large areas of land on the Australian Continent that otherwise would remain unoccupied for many generations.

"Mr. Ross has done his work well, and whatever may be the ultimate result of his mission, he deserves our thanks for the zeal he has displayed on behalf of this colony. By his position, intelligence, interest in and thorough knowledge of the colony, he was by far the best man we could have found to bring the subject before the Indian Government, and it is pleasant to know that he has made a favourable impression on the authorities there. We owe something, too, to His Excellency Sir James Fergusson, for securing for Mr. Ross an introduction to the Governor-General and to Sir Seymour Fitzgerald. Without such an introduction Mr. Ross's work would have been more difficult. A great deal will now depend upon the manner in which the matter is taken up by our squatters, who, we hope, will go into the thing with vigour."

"A movement of considerable importance has taken place under the patronage of His Excellency. A Committee has been formed to transmit samples of our colonial produce to India, with the view to introduce them in bulk to the Indian market. This is being vigorously carried out, and a vessel has been chartered to sail without delay with these samples. His Excellency has thoroughly identified himself with the movement, and there is no doubt that his personal influence with the Governor-General of India will at least secure a fair trial for our produce. Mr. C. H. T. Connor, who is a passenger by the present mail, will be in India when the vessel arrives, and will give his assistance in getting our produce thoroughly tested."

NEW HOMES.

"The Treasurer lately laid on the table his amended Ways and Means for 1870, which, however, he warned the House was to be regarded only as approximately correct. We subjoin an abstract which gives the Treasurer's estimate of the revenue and expenditure for the year :—

"ESTIMATED REVENUE.

Ordinary—
From usual sources £562,850	0	0
Additional license fees under Publicans' Act, as passed by House of Assembly... 2,400	0	0
Balance carried down, being probable deficiency 31st December, 1870 74,699	17	4
£639,949	17	4

"It is proposed to extend the payment of the actual ascertained deficit over—say, three years, by the issuing of short dated bonds, on the principle of Exchequer bills, and the levying of stamp duties.

"PROBABLE EXPENDITURE.

Estimated deficit on 1st January, 1870, arising from payments and liabilities on votes of Parliament, enumerated as 'Unexpended Balances,' 31st December, 1868 ... ... £82,836	18	7
Provision for excesses, 1869 15,000	0	0
Expenditure, 1870—		
Ordinary 459,512	18	9
District Councils and Corporations... 40,000	0	0
Roads—Maintenance or Construction 42,600	0	0
£639,949	17	4
Balance brought down as probable liability, 1st January, 1871 ... ... £74,699	17	4

"THE LAND FUND.

Estimated amount of sales £200,000 0 0

Bonded debt	£134,090 0 0
Drainage, South-Eastern District	4,000 0 0
Immigration Department	663 10 0
Land and Survey	14,565 0 0
Central and Local Road Boards	6,363 6 0
Road Construction	40,319 4 0
	£200,000 0 0

"REVENUE AND EXPENDITURE.

" The Treasurer's abstract of receipts and expenditure during the quarter ended September 30, exclusive of transfers in aid, appears in the *Gazette*. The statement is of course approximate, but it is sufficiently near the truth for all practical purposes. In Part I., Ordinary, the receipts amount to £127,902 2s. 9d., and the expenditure to £91,256 16s. 2d. In Part II., Public Works, &c., the income is £21,064 17s. 6d., and the expenditure £20,937 18s. 11d. In Part IIIA, Land Fund, &c., the income is £39,194 9s. 8d., and the expenditure £117,484 17s. 4d. In Part IIIB, Immigration Fund, the income is £19,191 3s. 4d., and the expenditure £255 14s. 9d. The total income for the quarter is £207,352 13s. 3d., and the expenditure £229,937 7s. 2d. This shows a deficiency in the receipts for the quarter of £22,584 13s. 11d., and does not seem to bear out the Treasurer's statement that the revenue was balancing the expenditure. The simple explanation of the matter, however, is that in this quarter *half a year's* charges on account of redemption of debt and interest appear, and these amount to £64,039. Fairly, therefore, only *half* this amount ought to be credited to the expenditure of the quarter. In addition to this there are also charges in this quarter on account of the unexpended balances of 1868. The public accounts for the quarter, then, are really in a better state than would appear from a cursory glance at the Treasurer's statement, and fully bear out what he has said in the Assembly."

The last mail brought the news that a new Land Bill, giving more liberal terms, and extending the time for credit purchasers, has passed through both branches of the legislature.

A meat preserving company has just been opened and is curing about 200 sheep a day. His Excellency the Governor and Lady Edith Fergusson have offered prizes for the curing of mutton hams and other useful manufactures.

The following announcement appears almost incredible, but we believe it to be true: That a mob of fat cattle from the Gulf of Carpentaria is now on its way to the colony, and may be shortly expected. It is evident, therefore, that an overland route from the extreme northern parts of Australia to its southern boundary is already practicable.

Had our space permitted, we should have liked to notice particularly the south-eastern part of the colony—the town and port of Lacepede, Guichen Bay, Robe Town, the Mount Gambier district, the lakes, and Port Macdonnell. We can only refer those seeking information on this portion of the colony to a series of papers written by Mr. Ebenezer Ward.

Our necessarily brief notice of South Australia must now be brought to a close. From its perusal, we do not doubt that the careful reader will see that this colony is steadily but surely progressing; not at the rate of Victoria, but very steadily and very surely. It has always struck me that one great element of success has been the numerous class of respectable yeomen, the holders of the 80 acre freeholds. The Northern Territory is as yet too new, and we know too little of it, to speak with confidence; but should we hear good accounts of it, it would seem to open a new field of profitable labour to a very large body of young and active men, who can bear a residence in a hot climate. It was but the other day that we knew anything practically about the land in the neighbourhood of the Gulf of Carpentaria, and that a mob of fat cattle should be traversing the vast continent from north to south speaks well for the climate, the soil, and the indefatigable energy of the Australian colonist.

Chapter VII.

QUEENSLAND (MORETON BAY).

THIS is the youngest of the Australian colonies, as it was not separated from New South Wales until 1859. But it was well known long before that period under the title of the Moreton Bay District. Captain Cook, just one hundred years ago, cast anchor in this bay, and named it after the Earl of Moreton, who was at that time the President of the Royal Society. Cook does not appear to have paid much attention to this fine bay. He thought the vegetation on the shore put him in mind of the West Indies, an opinion which was further strengthened by seeing turtles in the bay. Strange that, protected as this bay is from nearly every wind and from the heavy swell of the ocean by several islands, he failed to discover a river that pours a stream of water nearly a quarter of a mile wide into the centre of it. In the year 1799 the well known navigator, Lieutenant Flinders, was sent by the government of New South Wales to examine the north-east coast, to see if there were any rivers of sufficient size to permit the passage of small craft into the interior of the country. He examined Moreton Bay and also Hervey's Bay, more to the north, but he failed (somewhat strangely) in the object for which he had specially been sent out, and passed entirely by such rivers as the Clarence, the Brisbane, the Burnett, and the Mary. In another expedition he discovered Port Curtis, on a small river within which now stands the town of Gladstone, in the neighbourhood of which is a fine cotton and pastoral district. Things remained in this state for several years, and then, notwithstanding the formation of the penal settlements of Norfolk Island and Port Macquarie, and in Van Diemen's Land, the Home Government continued to send prisoners out to Port Jackson so rapidly, that fears were entertained of concentrating them to too great an extent; and so, in 1823, Mr. Oxley, the Surveyor-General of New South Wales was sent northwards, in the hope that he might discover some place to which the most abandoned of the convicts could be sent, and be thus far removed from the free population. In his outward trip he passed by Moreton Bay, but on his return a storm drove him into it. It was in this neighbourhood (says Mr. Wright in his "Queensland") that he met with some white men who had been carried in an open boat for many hundreds of miles, and after great sufferings had been cast upon this unknown shore. The natives treated them kindly. As Oxley's party were examining a number of the blacks who were coming down towards the cutter, they were surprised to see a man taller and lighter in colour than the rest in their midst. This man's name was Pamphlet. He told Oxley that four of them had been carried out to sea, and were for twenty-one days at the mercy of the winds and waves, till at last they were driven on shore at a distance of 500 miles from their starting place. They determined to endeavour to get back to Sydney overland, little knowing the difficulties which they must encounter. Pamphlet got disheartened and returned to the spot where Oxley rescued him; a second went back to the friendly natives, but was subsequently rescued; a third was heard of no more, and doubtless perished in the wild bush as so many of his fellows have since done. These two men, in detailing their attempts at escaping from the natives, told Oxley of a fine broad river which emptied itself into the bay not far from where they were lying at anchor. This was the Brisbane, so called after the governor at that time, Sir T. Brisbane. In the next year, 1824, Moreton Bay was constituted a penal settlement, and one of the two spots selected for the purpose was that on which now stands the city of Brisbane, fifteen miles from the bay by water. Brisbane has all the character of a tropical climate. The convicts, to the number of between two and three thousand, were employed in constructing roads and bridges and in erecting many substantial buildings in the infant settlement. For eighteen years this was the receptacle of the vilest of the vile; and scenes were enacted here both by bond and by free which if related as facts would not be believed. But all this is long past. In the year 1842 the settlement was proclaimed free and open for the reception of a free population. And very little indeed of its convict taint attaches to it now.

In 1857 the first steamer passed across the bay. But now the river steamers are to be seen daily between Brisbane and Ipswich; and there is constant communication by the same means between Sydney on the south and the ports on the north. Until 1859 the Moreton Bay District formed part of New South Wales, and was represented in her parliament first by one and afterwards by nine members. When the Port Phillipians obtained separation, Dr. Lang (a great friend of the district) began an agitation for the same boon for *it*. He was ably seconded in his efforts, and after eight years of struggling, Her Majesty not only granted their petition but bestowed on the new colony its present name—Queensland. Its boundaries at first were thus defined:—

Northward of a line commencing on the sea coast at Point Danger, in latitude about 28° 28′ south, and following the range thence which divides the waters of the Tweed, Richmond and Clarence Rivers from those of the Logan and Brisbane Rivers westerly to the great dividing range, between the waters falling to the east coast and those of the River Murray; following the great dividing range southerly to the range dividing the waters of Tenterfield Creek from those of the main head of the Dumaresq River, and following that river, which is locally known as the Severn, downwards to its confluence with the Macintyre River; thence following the Macintyre, which lower down becomes the Barwan, downward to the 29th parallel of south latitude, and following that parallel westerly to the 141st meridian of east longitude, which is the eastern boundary of South Australia, together with all and every the adjacent islands their members and appurtenances in the Pacific Ocean.

Since that day the western boundary of the colony has been extended to the 138th meridian, thus taking in a large and valuable country, the northern shores of which are washed by the waters of the Gulf of Carpentaria, comprehending the "Plains of Promise," which are already covered with thousands of sheep and of cattle up to the very shores of the Gulf, from a port on which direct shipments of pastoral produce have been made to England. The colony as originally constituted comprised 678,000 square miles, that is about six times as large as the area of the United Kingdom; and it is now calculated at nine times its size.

The first governor, Sir G. F. Bowen, who had previously been Secretary of the Ionian Islands, arrived at Brisbane on the 10th of December, 1859. He informed the inhabitants that "the name of Queensland was entirely the happy thought and inspiration of Her Majesty herself." And from that day forward, like all the rest of the Australian colonies, it has made rapid progress. It had some difficulties to contend with at first, from a prejudice against it on account of its earlier condition, and a fear of its climate; but these have been to a great extent dissipated, and it bids fair to hold no mean position amongst its elder sisters. The settlers have had periods of trial and of difficulty to pass through; but this has been the history of each of the colonies. And there seems to be such vitality in a new country, that it arises from these periods of depression endowed with fresh strength to aid it in its onward course.

In the year 1846 the population numbered 2,257; in 1856 it had increased to 17,082; in 1860 it had 28,056; in 1864 there were 74,036, showing that in three years the population had more than doubled itself; and on the 2nd March, 1868, it had reached 99,312! The gross revenue of the colony (including the land revenue) had increased from £178,589 in 1860, to £669,041 in 1867.

The first governor continued in office till January, 1868, and left for the governorship of New Zealand; and after an interregnum, during which Colonel O'Connell was the acting governor, Colonel Blackall relieved him, being the second governor. The Legislature is composed of the governor, as representative of the Crown; of a Legislative Council, nominated by the governor, acting under the advice of the Executive Council; and a Legislative Assembly, elected by the people. The exercise of the franchise is not so free as in some of the colonies, but still every industrious man, after a short term of residence, can qualify.

The increase of stock kept pace with that of the population. In 1860 there were: horses, 23,504; cattle, 432,890; sheep, 3,166,802; and pigs, 7,147. In 1862: horses, 35,625; cattle, 610,204; sheep, 4,345,901; pigs, 7,019. At the end of 1867 there were: horses, 53,146; cattle, 940,354; sheep, 8,665,757; and pigs, 18,142. In 1860 the export of wool was 5,007,167 lbs., of the estimated value of £444,188; in 1867 it was 21,554,557 lbs., valued at £1,462,209.

The inhabitants of Queensland are naturally taking great interest in the subject of the meat preserving process, for exportation to Great Britain. In fact very much of the success of the settlers in so vast a country must depend upon this. And each month's experience seems to warrant us in concluding with more certainty that they will not be disappointed. For some years past several establishments have been in full operation for salting meat for exportation, especially one on the River Bremer. But that system to which the Queenslanders are looking at most anxiously is "Mort's Freezing Process," which has been patented in Sydney, and by which it is confidently expected that meat slaughtered in the colony can be preserved fresh and sound for the English market. Hitherto there has been a great waste of animal food. Boiling down for tallow alone has been the only way in which the settler could get rid of his surplus stock. At the end of 1867 there were twelve boiling-down establishments, and in the year 95,804 sheep and 19,397 cattle had been boiled down, producing 34,859 tons of tallow.

The whole colony is divided into twelve districts: Moreton, Darling Downs, Port Curtis, Burnett, Leichhardt, Maranoa, Mitchell, Warrego, Kennedy, Cook, Burke, and Gregory. The first of these contains the metropolis of the colony, Brisbane, containing nearly 10,000 inhabitants, and also Ipswich, with about 5,000. The district of Moreton is bounded by the coast line for nearly 100 miles, and stretches inland to the dividing range. It is well watered, and contains much excellent agricultural land. The bar at the mouth of the Brisbane having been removed, large vessels can now go up to the wharves in the city. The distance between Brisbane and Ipswich is, by water fifty, and by land twenty-five miles. Steamers ply daily between them. There is a great deal of unoccupied land of good quality still to be obtained in advantageous situations. Cotton and sugar companies are established on the Barrow, the Albert, the Hotham, and other streams. Fish is plentiful; the chief kinds are the bream and mullet. Oysters, crabs, and turtle are abundant.

The public and many of the private buildings in

Brisbane are handsome in appearance, and are substantially built of stone and of brick. A public grammar school has been lately erected. In North Brisbane there is a School of Arts, and in South Brisbane an excellent Mechanics' Institution. All denominations have churches, some of which are fine buildings. The Right Rev. Dr. Tufnell was nominated Bishop of Brisbane in the year 1859.

The northern ports are reached by a fleet of good steamers, which ply regularly between the capital and Maryborough, Gladstone, Mackay, Port Denison, and Cleveland Bay. The neighbourhood of Brisbane is particularly pretty, and is charmingly situated for villa residences. The town is lighted by gas. There is one daily newspaper, one bi-weekly, and two weekly.

The terminus of the Southern and Western Railway is at Ipswich. This town also possesses many excellent houses, and amongst them the first grammar school established in the colony. Good coal is found in the neighbourhood, and is being extensively used by the Steam Navigation Company.

In the year 1827 the celebrated Darling Downs were discovered by Allan Cunningham. They extend for about 120 miles, with an average width of 50. It is the richest pastoral district in the colony, and is well watered by the Condamine River and by other streams. It is on the summit of the dividing range, and enjoys a fine climate; and although so much of it has been taken up, there are still many thousands of acres of rich agricultural soil thrown open to selection under the new Land Act. Toowoomba, at a distance of 85 miles from Brisbane, is the chief town, having, with the towns in the neighbourhood, a population of 6,000. Warwick, on the Condamine, is the second town of this district. It is also an agricultural neighbourhood; in fact it is the centre of the principal wheat growing districts, and has flour mills. The only other town of any note is Dalby, with a population of about 1,200. It is the western terminus of the railway, which receives here the produce from a large extent of pastoral country.

The Burnett district is between Moreton and Port Curtis, and has been a favourite squatting country for more than twenty years. Its soil is good and adapted for the growth of tropical products. The chief town is Maryborough, situated on the River Mary, sixty miles from its mouth. There are gold-fields on the Mary, which have attracted a considerable population. Sugar, cotton, arrowroot, and tobacco have been successfully grown. It has also very fine forests of timber. The Moreton Bay pine is a handsome tree. The Bunya Bunya grows to a great height, sometimes as high as 200 feet. Its fruit, which resembles the eating-chesnut in flavour, is considered to be a great dainty by the aborigines. It only ripens once in three years, and the natives collect from all quarters to feast on it. The red cedar, the iron bark, the blue gum, box, violet wood, tulip, and forest oak are all abundant and very useful. The iron bark is valuable for railway sleepers, and for all purposes where strength and durability are required. Coal is also found in this district.

Gympie or Nashville, the gold-field to which there was so great a rush some time ago, is situated on Gympie Creek, a tributary of the Mary. It has a population of 6,000.

Port Curtis lies to the north of the Burnett and stretches into the interior. There are several gold-fields in this district. Rockhampton, on the Fitzroy, is the chief town of this and of all the northern ports. It has a population of 6,000. It is the terminus of the Great Northern Railway, which runs in the direction of the Dawson. Gladstone is in the same neighbourhood and has an excellent harbour. A Melbourne firm has lately purchased the marble quarries here, which are highly spoken of, and are being worked so as to prove highly remunerative to the holders of them.

To the west of Port Curtis lies the vast pastoral region called after poor Leichhardt. The Peak Downs are in this district. The gold-fields here attracted a large population in 1865. They are about 300 miles from Rockhampton. The copper mines are likely to be more valuable than the gold-fields. The export of gold from Queensland is, however, becoming an important item. In the month of August last it amounted to 17,798 ounces, of the estimated value of £27,607. The chief town of the district is Clermont, on the Peak Downs. The other townships are Springsure, Taroom, and Nebo.

After this comes an immense country of table-lands and downs, called the Maranoa district, lying westward from the Darling Downs. The town is called Roma, which is 350 miles from Brisbane.

To the north of Port Curtis lies the Kennedy district, including a portion of the northern coast line. It is watered by the Burdekin. It was taken up in 1861 by the squatters. The chief town is Bowen. This country is specially adapted to tropical productions; and there are already several large sugar plantations. A steamer plies weekly between Bowen and Gladstone, Brisbane and Sydney. Bowen has a population of 1,150, and Townsville, the only other town of importance, has 760.

In the vicinity of Cardwell there are thousands of acres of rich land suitable for the growth of tropical produce.

The remaining districts comprise an enormous tract of country, and are being rapidly occupied by squatters. Burketown has been founded at the mouth of the Albert River, which empties itself into the Gulf of Carpentaria.

So great is the extent of Queensland, that in one part or other of it the products of almost any region in the world may be grown. In the Moreton and

Darling Downs districts rapid progress is being made in agriculture, as will appear from the last statistics which have reached us from the colony. The following is the report of the Registrar-General:—

" On the 31st of December, 1867, there were 31,559 acres 1 rood 13 perches of land under cultivation in the colony, being an increase of 7,126 acres 0 roods 26 perches of land over the previous year, and a centesimal increase of 29·17.

" I cannot refrain from remarking upon the great increase that has taken place in the area of land under cultivation of sugar and cotton ; the former showing a centesimal increase of 228·67 per cent. for the year 1867 over that of 1866, and the latter, for the same period, a centesimal increase of 182·56 per cent.

" As regards sugar, with the exception of some few plantations, whose results are most encouraging, some little time must yet elapse before the cultivator can expect a return for his outlay and labour.

" The actual return for last year is by no means unimportant, however, as it amounted to 338 tons of sugar, which may be valued at £12,000, and 13,509 proof gallons of rum ; whilst the average quality of both of these articles appears to have been unexceptionable, and the yield fully equal to those of older colonies, possessed of the advantages of experience and cheap labour, which we have yet to obtain.

" In reference to cotton, as the crop planted in 1867 will not be gathered until 1868, the value exported must not be measured by the total area returned as under crop, the results of which have yet to be obtained.

" The following comparative table shows the quantity as well as the value of some of the more important articles of agricultural produce imported into the colony during the years 1866 and 1867, which might, amongst many others, be produced in it.

	1866.		1867.	
	Quantity.	Value.	Quantity.	Value.
		£		£
Wheat, bushels	5,063	1,573	490	117
Barley ,,	1,591	420	1,199	188
Oats ,,	16,856	5,099	13,608	2,170
Maize ,,	191,059	45,268	57,223	6,726
Hay and Straw, bales	11,281	21,137	3,845	3,687
Potatoes, cwt	78,668	28,503	52,844	10,182
Flour, tons	14,637	261,205	14,412	189,530

"It will be observed that a decrease has taken place in the imports of all the articles mentioned in the above table.

"As this decrease is contemporaneous with an increase in the breadth of land under cultivation, and as there is no reason to suppose that the consumption within the colony of the articles referred to has in any way materially decreased, it is but reasonable to infer that our agriculturalists, besides supporting themselves, are making rapid advances towards supplying the demands of the colony, a result in every way advantageous to us."

The chief fruits which are cultivated with a view to trade are the banana, pine-apple, peach, loquat, guava, passion-fruit, fig, melon, Cape gooseberry, orange, lemon, citron, and mulberry. The pine-apples and some other fruits are largely exported, and can be obtained in any of the colonies for a very small sum. Attention is now being paid to the growth of the vine and the making of wine. A light wine which promises well is made by Mr. Lade, near Brisbane. He had 1,200 gallons from six acres. There is great scope for profitable employment in the cultivation of the vine, and large areas of land in suitable situations are now open for selection. Arrowroot of good quality is cultivated with profit in the Moreton district. An acre will produce one ton and a half, and it is worth about £40 a ton.

The government were anxious to give encouragement to the growers of cotton. And so, in the Land Act of 1860, a clause was inserted to the effect, that during the three following years land orders, to the extent of £10, would be given as a premium for every bale of 300 lbs. of good Sea Island cotton exported to Great Britain. In the following year blocks of land, of not less than 640 acres, were offered to capitalists who would within two years commence the cultivation of cotton on a large scale. And afterwards, £10 for every bale of 300 lbs. produced and exported before the close of 1865, and £5 per bale to the end of 1869, were offered as inducements to its growth. In 1867, 8,194 acres were under cotton. If the soil and climate suit, about a bale and a half seems to be the produce per acre. It is stated that this pursuit can be profitably followed by men having large families, where the children can assist during the picking season. The value of the cotton exported last year was about £60,000. The merchants in the colony give $2\frac{1}{2}$d. a lb. for unginned, and 10d. for ginned cotton.

It is thought that the sugar-cane will eventually become the most profitable object of cultivation. Mr. Hope initiated this branch of industry in 1863, and has been rewarded by a grant of 2,560 acres of land. The sugar sent to market realised from £37 to £40 a ton. It is estimated that there are about 3,000 acres now under this crop. In 1867 there were 186 tons of sugar made, and 13,000 gallons of molasses. The molasses were converted into 10,000 gallons of rum, which is protected by a duty of 3s. 4d. a gallon over that which is imported.

A great variety of tropical plants may be grown by the agriculturist to advantage, even on a small scale. Indigo produces 150 lbs. to the acre, bears two or three crops in a year, and the manufactured article is worth from 4s. to 6s. a pound. Tobacco, if carefully prepared, is found to be a success. Coffee and tea plants are grown in the Botanical Gardens. The tea is pronounced by judges to be very good. During the late visit of the Duke of Edinburgh to Queensland, he was presented with a cabinet, made of handsome native wood, which contained a pound of tea, a pound of coffee, and several pounds of sugar, all the produce of the colony.

In a country capable of growing such a variety of valuable products, and where the new immigrant can obtain good land by paying ninepence per acre per annum, and after five such annual payments is entitled to the land in fee simple, there surely must be great room for the industrious agriculturist. The government also express their willingness to give instruction to those willing to enter upon industries with which they are unacquainted.

The following epitome of the Land Bill is taken from a little publication of much interest, entitled "Queensland as a field for Emigration":—

"Much greater facilities than previously existed for the acquirement of land in the colony have been afforded during the present year, by an '*Act to Consolidate and Amend the Laws relating to the Alienation of Crown Lands*,' which received the Vice-regal assent on the 28th February, 1868. This Act introduces principles entirely new to Australian land legislation, and its operation is calculated to be exceedingly beneficial to the colony. It provides for the classification of lands, and for a considerable reduction in the upset price. Previous to the passing of this Act, the only classification which existed with regard to the unalienated Crown lands of the colony was that which classified them as town, suburban, and country lands; the upset price of the latter, no matter where they were situated, or their intrinsic value to the settler, being one pound per acre. By the new system these country lands are classified as follows: —(1) agricultural; (2) first-class pastoral; (3) second-class pastoral. The upset price of agricultural land is fixed at fifteen shillings per acre; first-class pastoral land, ten shillings per acre; and second-class pastoral land, five shillings per acre. It will thus be seen that the Legislature has effected a radical change in the system which was previously followed in the alienation of country lands. The reduction in the upset price is accompanied by deferred payments on the principle laid down in '*The Leasing Act of* 1866.' By the provisions of that Act, selections could be made on certain lands reserved for that purpose, at an uniform price of one pound per acre, the purchase money being payable in eight annual payments of two-and-sixpence each, which payments having been made regularly in accordance with the rule laid down by the Government, and the selector having observed certain conditions, the imposition of which was considered necessary in order to determine the *bona fides* of purchasers, entitled him to a grant in fee-simple. At the time this Act was passed, it was considered that a large concession had been made to the demand of the public for liberal land legislation, by the admission of the principle of deferred payments. But more than this was required; it was essential that the upset price should be reduced, and that some arrangement should be made for classification. It was not without some difficulty that the advocates of a system of classification were enabled to convince their opponents of the folly of demanding the same high price for the whole of the country lands of the colony, irrespective of their actual value to the settler. The task was, however, performed at last, and legislators who were once obstinately wedded to the opinion that nothing less than one pound per acre should be paid for Crown lands of good, bad, or indifferent quality, lent their assistance in passing the measure to which we have referred. The system of classification is not by any means the most important reform introduced in the new Land Act. The clauses relating to homestead selections are entitled to much more consideration; they consist of an adaptation of the American Homestead Law, by which free grants of land are made to *bona fide* settlers for the formation of homesteads. According to the new Act, the quantity of land to be taken up by homestead selectors cannot exceed eighty acres of agricultural land, or one hundred and sixty acres of first or second class pastoral land. The conditions to be observed before the selector is entitled to the fee-simple of the land are, that during five years an annual rental of ninepence per acre for agricultural land, and sixpence per acre for pastoral lands shall be paid, together with the cost of survey; that he shall reside on the land during the five years; and that either one-tenth of it shall have been cultivated during that period, or the portion securely fenced. Larger quantities of land can be taken up by conditional purchasers, who are called upon to pay the value of the land according to the scale we have quoted in ten annual payments, and to comply with certain conditions, to which no objection can be raised by the *bona fide* settler. The lands thrown open to homestead selectors and conditional purchasers are situated in the settled districts, within a reasonable distance of the coast, and comprise a great deal of country that is well adapted to agriculture and dairy farming. The quantity of land that will soon be available for selection in these districts, comprises several millions of acres in extent."

The new Land Act contains 131 clauses, and is too lengthy to be inserted here. But it is a most valuable document, and has been framed so as to meet the wants of the large or small capitalist, or the man who has little else at starting than his own strong arm. It can readily be obtained from the Agent-General of the colony, at his office, 2, Old Broad Street, London.

" One of the most important features of the Act, and the one to which it is desirable the attention of the intending emigrant should be specially directed, is the provision which is made for granting homestead selections. The clauses of the Act relating to homesteads are adapted from the celebrated Homestead Law of America. It was not considered expedient to adopt this law, pure and simple; and, accordingly, a modification of it was drafted into the Act. The homestead clauses comprise the most liberal provisions of the Land Act, inasmuch as they enable persons to obtain grants of land at a merely nominal price—a price that any person who is not an absolute pauper is able to pay. Anyone who is the head of a family, or twenty-one years of age, can select to the extent of eighty acres of agricultural land, or one hundred and sixty acres of first or second class pastoral land, the conditions being the payment of an annual rental of ninepence per acre for agricultural, and sixpence for pastoral land, shall be paid for five years; that the selector shall have constantly resided on it during that period; and that either one-tenth of it be cultivated, or the whole of it securely fenced. These conditions having been complied with the selector is entitled to a grant in fee-simple. Besides the annual rental, the selector is called upon to pay the survey fee, which is £3 16s., and a deed fee of £1 5s.; so that, for the sum of £20, the payment of which is distributed over a period of five years, a homestead, consisting of eighty acres of first-class agricultural land, may be secured in perpetuity. There are many snug homesteads in the vicinity of Brisbane and the other towns of the colony, the owners of which (who purchased under the old pound-an-acre system) do not possess half the quantity of land that may now be obtained by a homestead selector, yet who have managed, by care and economy, not only to make a comfortable living from their land, but to lay by some provision for a rainy day. The advantages conferred by the Act upon those who become homestead selectors, with the determination to work hard on the land which they are enabled to take up on such liberal terms, must be obvious. The homestead clauses must especially recommend themselves to that large class of English farmers who, by dint of practising the hardest economy and the most unremitting industry, are barely able to make a livelihood, in consequence of the high rent they are compelled to pay for inferior land. No persons can become homestead selectors who have not paid their own passages to the colony, unless they can prove that they have been resident in Queensland for a period exceeding three years."

The colony of Queensland having such a vast territory, and knowing that population is its great want, the government have held out the greatest inducements to allure immigrants to their shores. Free and assisted immigrants are entitled to accommodation for seven days after arrival. They are strongly advised not to be too particular what employment they accept at first. If they have a little money they should not be in a hurry to spend it. Far better to place it in a bank at interest, and go and take some situation for a time, so as to gain "colonial experience," which is invaluable. A year thus spent would not be thrown away. I generally find that those who are disappointed as colonists, and who therefore rail at the colony, are those who have rushed headlong into some speculation of which they knew nothing, or have given way to habits of intoxication. Queensland, rich as it is in resources, cannot help such people. In such a climate especially, a man must be strictly temperate as well as industrious to secure the prize at which he aims—independence.

"The current wages in the colony at the present time are as follow :—

"PER DAY (without board and lodging) :—Masons, 9s.; Painters and Glaziers, 7s.; Plasterers, 8s.; Bricklayers, 9s.; Carpenters, 8s.; Blacksmiths, 8s.; Wheelwrights, 8s.; Farm Labourers, 6s.; Ploughmen, 6s.; Reapers, 6s.; Mowers, 6s.; Threshers, 6s.; Gardeners, 6s.; Quarrymen, 9s.; General Labourers, 5s.

"PER ANNUM (with board and lodging) :—Servants, Married Couples without family, £35 to £40; Married Couples with family, £35 to £40; Men Cooks, for hotels, £40 to £70; Female Cooks, £25 to £40; Laundresses, £26 to £30; General Servants, £26 to £30; Housemaids, £20 to £25; Nursemaids, £13 to £20; Farm-house Servants, £20 to £30; Dairy Women, £25 to £30; Grooms, £40 to £50; Gardeners, £50; Farm Labourers, £25 to £30; Ploughmen, £25 to £30; Reapers, £25 to £30; Mowers, £25 to £30; Threshers, £25 to £30; Shepherds, £25 to £40; Stock-keepers, £40 to £50; Hut-keepers, £25; Generally useful men on Stations, £40 to £50; Sheepwashers, 5s. to 7s. per day; Shearers, 17s. 6d. to 25s. per 100 sheep sheared; Seamen, £4 to £6 per month."

The expense of living is perhaps a little higher than in England. The great thing is to get a house of one's own as quickly as possible. Necessaries are cheap; luxuries are expensive. Subjoined is a list of the retail prices of different articles of consumption :—

"BUTCHERS' MEAT.—Beef, 2d. to 2½d. per lb.; mutton, 2¼d. to 3½d.; veal, 4d.; pork, 6d.; lamb, per quarter, 5s.

"GROCERIES, &c.—Tea, 2s. 6d. per lb.; sugar, 3d. to 5½d.; coffee, 1s. 6d.; chocolate and cocoa, 2s. 3d.; rice, 4d.; oatmeal, 5d.; soap, 3d. Oilmen's stores, &c., at a small advance on English prices.

"WINES AND SPIRITS, &c.—Brandy, 28s. per gallon; Sherry, 20s.; Port, 20s.; Ale and Porter, English bottled, 9s. to 14s. per dozen.

"DAIRY PRODUCE.—Bacon, colonial, 9d. per lb.; do. English, 1s. 6d.; ham, colonial, 1s.; do. English, 1s. 6d.; butter, fresh, 1s. 6d.; do. salt, 1s. 3d.; cheese, colonial, 1s.; do. English, 1s. 6d.; lard, 9d.; eggs, 1s. per dozen; milk, 6d. per quart; fowls, 3s. 6d. to 4s. per pair; ducks 4s. to 5s.; geese, 8s. each.

"VEGETABLES.—Beans, French, 1s. 6d. per peck; cabbages, 2d. to 6d. each; cauliflowers, 3d. to 6d.; celery, 6d. per head; capsicums, 4d. per quart; chilies, 4d.; cucumbers, 3d. each; carrots, 3d. per bunch; eschalots, 3d.; lettuce, 2d. each; marrows, 2d.; onions, 6d. per lb.; parsley, 1d. per bunch; peas, 2s. per peck; potatoes, common, 9s. per cwt.; do. sweet, 8s.; pumpkins, 2d. per lb.; radishes, 2d. per bunch; tomatoes, 4d. per quart; turnips, 3d. per bunch.

"FRUIT.—Bananas, 8d. per dozen; pine-apples, 1d. to 6d. each; passion-fruit, 4d. per dozen; grapes, 6d. per lb.; figs, 3d. per dozen; gooseberries, 6d. per quart; guavas, 1s. per dozen; peaches, 2d. to 1s.; apricots, 1s.; mulberries, 6d. per quart; loquats, 6d.; oranges, 8d. to 2s. per dozen; lemons, 1s. 6d.; apples, 1s. to 3s.; melons, 1d. to 2s. each."

There is no State Church. The English and the Roman Catholics have bishops. The largest body is the Church of England, numbering 37,234; the Roman Catholics, 26,378; Presbyterians, 13,179; Wesleyans, 5,192. There are 60 primary schools, attended by 4,359 scholars, at a cost of £9,334. Grammar schools are fostered by the government.

A Chamber of Commerce has lately been established in Brisbane. The public debt of the colony at the end of 1867 amounted to £3,344,000, the payment of the interest on which was at the rate of £2 4s. 6d. for each person in the colony.

The aborigines are a finer race of men than in others of the colonies.

Still, notwithstanding all that has been said in favour of this colony, arising from its great size, its fertile land, and its liberal Land Bill, what avail all these things in a climate so hot as Queensland is? This is a very natural objection; and it is better to look at it boldly, and to speak of it frankly, than to keep it in the background, and to let the immigrant find it out to his cost on arrival. Queensland is a *hot* country, and there are many persons who are unsuited for it, or to whom it would be unpleasant as a place of residence. Let them seek a cooler residence, or make up their minds beforehand to bear the heat, instead of to grumble at it. In the southern parts the heat is not too great to enable a man to pursue his usual out-of-door employment, and it is a healthy place. The mean temperature of the year at Brisbane is 68·7 ; that of Funchal, in Madeira is 68·5. Rain falls in 108 days out of 365. The atmosphere is pure, dry, and buoyant. "Hot winds" and "brickfielders" (the scourge of the southern colonies) are unknown. Dr. Hobbs, speaking of consumptive cases, writes thus: "Many persons afflicted with this fatal malady have derived great benefit from a short residence in Queensland; and several persons who have arrived in what appeared a dying state, have lived here for years in comparative health and comfort." During a large proportion of the year the weather is fine, the sky cloudless, the atmosphere dry, exhilarating and elastic. The summer months are hot, but not sultry or oppressive. The winter season is exceedingly beautiful. Such a climate is necessarily healthy. The amount of exercise one can take is very great. A friend of mine the other day mounted his horse at Brisbane and rode home, a distance of 106 miles, 60 of which were through a forest, and only got off his horse twice for a short time for refreshment. Men and horses there surely can go through a good deal.

It is the day of small things yet with Queensland, but—

"As in a cradled Hercules, we trace
The lines of empire in her infant face."

LANDSCAPE IN NEW ZEALAND.—*page* 363.

Chapter VIII.

NEW ZEALAND.

NEW ZEALAND consists of three islands. They are officially named New Ulster, New Munster, and New Leinster; but they are better known as the Northern, the Middle, and Stewart's Islands. The one last named is very small and unimportant. They are about 1,200 miles from Australia, and extend 1,100 miles from north to south. Their dimensions are about as follows: The Northern Island, about 500 miles long; the Middle, 550; and Stewart Island, 30. The whole together present an area about one-third less than that of Great Britain and Ireland. These are divided into nine provinces, four of which are in the north and five in the south island.

These islands were discovered and named by Tasman, the Dutch navigator, more than 200 years ago; but it was not until 1769 that Captain Cook took possession of them for England. At his several visits he surveyed the coasts, held friendly intercourse with the natives, and left behind him the potato and the pig. He gave so glowing a description of the climate and the soil, that Benjamin

Franklin entertained the idea of forming a colony upon its shores. About twenty years after the discovery by Cook, whaling ships appear to have frequented the different bays with which the islands abound, and provoked the natives to take a fearful revenge. There can be no doubt that at the period to which we refer they were cannibals. Until the year 1814, there were no white men living on the islands. The venerable Marsden, who is familiarly called the "Apostle of New Zealand," purchased a vessel called the *Active*, and sent it to New Zealand. It returned, bringing several chiefs, and amongst them Duaterra. Marsden went back with them to the Bay of Islands. He took with him a bull and two cows, a few sheep, and some poultry. This was the first introduction of such stock into a country destined within a brief period to rival the settlements on the mainland, and to take a leading position among our great colonies. He was well received by the natives, and the account of his mission, when published in England, was read with deep interest. The first Sunday on which the true God was worshipped in New Zealand since the creation will be for ever memorable in her annals. It happened also to be Christmas Day, 1815. The Old Hundredth Psalm was sung, the service read, and a sermon preached from Luke ii. 10, "Behold, I bring you glad tidings of great joy." Duaterra interpreted as well as he could to the assembled natives. Marsden appears from the very first to have won their entire confidence. He must have been a really brave man to have thrown himself almost unprotected into their very midst, knowing as he did their dreadful propensities and the grounds they had for distrusting the white man. During this his first visit it was that, like Penn, he purchased a large tract of land from the natives for the Church Missionary Society, giving as an equivalent therefor twelve axes. Returning to Sydney, accompanied by many of the chiefs, the governor congratulated him on his safe arrival from so perilous an undertaking. The greatest of the New Zealand warriors at this time was Shunghie, who visited England in 1820, and was received with marked attention by George the Fourth. On his return to his native land, he resolved on obtaining the sovereignty of the whole island. He cruelly murdered a rival chieftain, Inacki, scooped out his eye with his knife and swallowed it, and drank as much of his blood as his two hands could hold. On his second visit to the island, surrounded by such men, Marsden thus describes the way in which he spent the night: "After conversing on several subjects, we had supper, sung a hymn, and then committed ourselves to the Angel of the Everlasting Covenant, and so lay down to rest. A number of the natives lay round about the hut, and some within." This great and good man was spared to make seven voyages to the land he took such interest in. At times he was greatly encouraged, and at other times as much depressed; but he was permitted to see a great change among many of the natives, and the work which he began was carried on afterwards by missionaries of several denominations. On his last voyage he was accompanied by his daughter, to whom at once a powerful chief made an offer of marriage, which the young lady did not seem at all to appreciate. Poor Marsden! His was a trying life; he had a great deal to go through, and much of calumny to endure. But strong in the singleness of his aims, for the glory of God and the good of his fellow creatures, he went nobly on, and finished a long and active life by a calm and peaceful death.

New Zealand settling down once more, after the late unhappy struggles between the two races, into her former busy occupations, promises to become a rich and prosperous country; but however great and prosperous, Marsden's name will ever be cherished by those amongst her sons who can appreciate boldness of character with a simple and earnest desire to preach among the nations the "unsearchable riches of Christ."

We remarked before that the bays were frequented in the early days by the whaling ships; and their crews and the missionaries brought so vividly before the people of England the richness of the soil, the goodness of the climate, and the excellency of the timber, especially the Kauri spars, that in 1838 a number of influential men formed themselves into an association, under the name of

"The New Zealand Company," for the purpose of colonising the islands. On an application being made to the government it was favourably received, because they knew of how great importance it might become if seized by a rival power, and in 1840 a governor, Captain Hobson, R.N., was sent out, who founded the capital of Auckland, on the Waitémata.

The New Zealand Company purchased large tracts of land from the natives, formed the settlements of Wellington, Nelson, Taranaki, and Wanganui, and located in them 5,000 emigrants. But, as was the case in one of the colonies of Australia on the mainland, a misunderstanding arose between the representatives of the crown and of the company; and the shrewd natives taking advantage of this became turbulent, and wished to repudiate the sales of land made to the white men, and anarchy and confusion prevailed for a lengthened period.

Captain Fitzroy had succeeded Hobson as governor, and he in his turn was relieved in 1845 by Sir George Grey, during whose administration of the government the natives were induced to lay down their arms. But it was only an outward peace, for great dissatisfaction was found to exist amongst some of the tribes still. And during Governor Browne's term of office (who succeeded Grey) these disaffected tribes threw off their allegiance to England and proclaimed Te Potatau, (an old Waikato chief,) their king. Governor Browne attempted to take possession of some land in the province of Taranaki, which, although it had been purchased from the native owners, was claimed by the Ngatiawa tribe, and his surveyors were driven back. And things remained in this unsatisfactory state till 1861, when it was thought wise to replace Governor Grey in his old position, inasmuch as he had been very popular among the New Zealanders. But he was not successful in his mission, and the war continued to rage until 1865, at which time it was fondly but vainly hoped that it had died out. Instead, however, of this hope being realized, the sad scenes which have been enacted and the havoc which has been wrought since, present a sad picture, and have carried desolation into many a family and ruin to many a thriving settler. There is now a hope again that things are settling down, and that the rebellion is over. God grant that it may be so. It is not our intention to enter into the question of the withdrawal of the Imperial troops, when their presence was so urgently needed. If the colonists erred, they have deeply suffered. And it must be borne in mind that these native feuds were a legacy bequeathed by the governments of bygone days, when the administration was that of Downing Street, and not a state of things which had sprung up since the granting of the new constitution.

The climate of New Zealand is a very enjoyable

one. The winters are never excessively cold nor the summers oppressively hot. The heat is tempered by fresh breezes, and a fine bright sun is seen and felt during the winter days. It is, however, a country where the winds blow often and strongly, and the changes of the temperature are sudden and great. Fogs are of rare occurrence. It is said that the high winds which prevail in New Zealand are one great cause of its acknowledged salubrity, inasmuch as they dry up the superfluous moisture and disperse malaria.

Dr. Thomson, who was stationed with his regiment for many years in the colony, gives (as we gather from a very useful publication styled "The New Zealand Handbook") the following table of the number of soldiers in 1,000 who annually die from different diseases at various military stations: New Zealand, 8; Australia, 11; Great Britain, 14; Cape of Good Hope, 15; Malta, 18; Canada, 20. There are seldom, if ever, any dangerous thunder storms. To those accustomed to six months of winter in England it must be cheering to know that in the colony under review it only lasts for three, that snow is seldom seen, and that if there is ice, about half an inch is its thickness, and that a frosty night is always followed by a bright sunshiny day without wind. The rosy healthy looks of the children proclaim its suitability to them.

You will perhaps hardly find such capabilities of soil and climate anywhere, excepting perhaps in

Tasmania. For the purposes of production, it has been described by an old settler as one of the finest in the world. Not that there is an uncommonly large area of very rich alluvial soil—such soil as would produce fifty or sixty bushels of wheat to the acre. A good deal of the land is poor. Some of the richest of the land is covered with water, which only requires, however, inexpensive draining to render it available. The native flax land is good, requiring nothing but clearing. Fern land covers a great space and is of very different degrees of quality. In the colder parts of the island a coarse grass prevails, called "tussock grass." The settlers burn this off in the summer, after which a young succulent grass grows up, of which cattle and sheep are fond and on which they thrive well. But very large breadths of land in all directions are being laid with English grasses, which grow remarkably well. Vineyards are planted at Nelson, where the standard peach also is very productive. All the English fruits, vegetables, and flowers grow to perfection. And many things flourish for which England is too cold and the continent of Europe is too hot. The native trees are evergreens. Every thing is covered with perpetual verdure. It is stated that 2,000 species have been collected, from the daisy to the giant pine, and Hooker expects that number to be greatly increased as the progress of discovery goes on.

We shall greatly err if we confound the Maories

of New Zealand with the Australian savage, or with those to be found on some of the neighbouring islands. They are a fine race of men, showing no little mental capacity, and such skill in war that a body of them, numbering probably not more than two thousand, kept at bay for a lengthened period ten thousand well-armed British soldiers. They pull in a boat remarkably well. They have war canoes about eighty feet long, four feet broad, and four deep. Dr. Thomson, in his story of New Zealand, describes these canoes as having fifty paddlers sitting on each side, and three fuglemen standing in the centre exciting the paddlers to exertion by their songs and actions. They have elegantly carved stern-posts fifteen feet high, ornamented with feathers and dyed flax. The crew kneel two and two along the bottom, sit on their heels, and wield paddles from four to five feet long. The steersman, sitting in the stern, has a paddle nine feet long. Over tempestuous seas war canoes ride like sea-fowl. Even when a canoe is upset the crew can bale her out and put her right in the water. The height of the men is from five feet six inches to five feet seven inches. Their colour is a light copper, their heads are broad and low, and their eyebrows prominent. They are very intelligent, and keenly alive to anything affecting their own interests. They are often to be seen in the gallery of the House of Parliament listening attentively to any of the debates which have reference to themselves.

It is not known with certainty whence they came. The general opinion is, that about 400 years ago they abandoned Hawaii, driven thence perhaps by the fortune of war, or urged thereto by the desire of finding a new home, and they landed on the shores of these islands, which were then entirely without inhabitants, although nature had done so much for them. What their numbers were at first it is extremely difficult to tell; but when discovered by Cook they did not exceed 150,000, a number which has dwindled down to about a third, as it is not considered that they now exceed 50,000. And it will be with the Maori, as with all the native tribes when brought into contact with civilisation, that a few years will see them so reduced as to be unable to maintain any distinct nationality. Nearly the whole of the natives are in the Northern island. It has been calculated that there are now not more than seven women and four children under fifteen to every ten men. The number of children is so small as to prove that the race is fast dying out. There does not appear to be any truth in the assertions sometimes made, to the effect that they have been cruelly treated by the colonists. The natives, though energetic in war, are indolent in peace. Governor Grey gained great influence over them, and did all in his power to rouse them and to cause them to take an interest in cultivation, and in the breeding of stock. Any land they liked to sell he bought, and he caused mills to be erected at the public expense for their benefit and use. They were kept well supplied with the luxuries they coveted. This system was denounced as "Sir George Grey's sugar and blanket policy." Wise restrictions were in force against the sale of arms and ammunition to the natives during the time when Grey was at the head of the administration, which being subsequently repealed, it came out in evidence that in three years the Maories purchased arms and ammunition to the value of £50,000, which have been employed against those who had so unwisely permitted them to be sold to them. Their dwellings are still of a very primitive kind. They seem to have learned very little as yet from the presence of the white man. They like to build their little rush huts on the tops of hills. They live on fish, potatoes, maize, and fruit. But their farming and gardening operations are of the rudest kind. They select the best soil they can obtain, and trust more to nature than to art. One who knows them well describes them thus: "They are very teachable, though by no means docile; they learn to read and write more quickly than we do, and in all kinds of trade and manufacture they exhibit much acuteness and skill; but war is their favourite pursuit, and in the art of deceiving and surprising an enemy they have probably no equals. Conscientiousness, faith, hope, and charity are all sadly deficient in their composition. Always accustomed to use language as a means of concealing their thoughts and intentions, they believe nothing that is said to them from any quarter. No amount of kindness is sufficient to secure their gratitude, no extent or degree of consistency can ensure their confidence. They are fierce and cruel, and the steadiness of purpose with which they will for years silently wait for an opportunity to revenge any real or supposed injury or insult, is rendered all the more terrible from the fact that, if unable to reach the supposed offender, they will wreak their vengeance on any one of the same family, the same settlement, the same race, or even the same colour."

Considering all that has passed, and is passing still, to steel the hearts of the colonists against the natives, it is gratifying to read the testimony borne on this subject by the late Bishop of New Zealand, Dr. Selwyn, who was always regarded as the Maori's friend: "In defence of the colonists of New Zealand, of whom I am one, I say most distinctly and solemnly that I have never known, since the colony began, a single act of wilful injustice or oppression committed by any one in authority against a New Zealander."

The mineral resources of New Zealand are great. Gold was discovered at Otago in 1861, and at Hokitika in 1865, and is now being found in large quantities along the west coast, extending for a distance of about 140 miles, and from 60 to 80 miles from the coast. At Coromandel, forty miles from Auckland, there are numerous quartz reefs yielding large returns. And, in fact, we hear of the success of prospecting parties in all directions. Copper is found near Nelson; and at the Great Barrier Island, near Auckland, lead, iron, tin, and plumbago have also been discovered. At present the rush is after gold. In due time, as population increases and new enterprises are taken up, we shall hear more of these. The titaniferous iron-sand found in large quantities on the sea coast yields iron of the highest quality. A "New Zealand Iron and Steel Company," with a capital of £100,000, have issued a prospectus. Nearly all the steamers trading to Greymouth township are supplied with their coal from a mine on the spot, which has a seam about six feet thick. There are besides, the Kawa Kawa and the Wangarei coal-fields, both in active operation. Coal at Auckland is twenty-five shillings a ton. Petroleum of good quality has been found near Taranaki. The native flax (*phormium tenax*) is found in all parts of New Zealand; it grows to the height of about nine feet. Considerable quantities of this are being brought into the market, its value being from £20 to £36 a ton. The forests are very extensive, and the timber forms the most valuable export from Auckland province, and comparatively the only export from Stewart's Island. The Kauri gum is also found in considerable quantities in Auckland province. Formerly the natives had a monopoly of this trade, but now many Europeans are engaged in it. It finds a ready and profitable sale in the London markets.

It is remarkable that New Zealand does not possess a single indigenous wild animal. Like Ireland, too, it has not snakes of any kind. Pigs, from the stock let loose on the island by Captain Cook, are now wild. There are not many birds peculiar to the country. Grasshoppers, caterpillars, sand-flies, and mosquitoes are found in the bush.

In the " Official Record of the Intercolonial Exhibition" the following synopsis of New Zealand's resources is given: " From present appearances, and the great development of the extraordinary resources of this colony, we are led to the belief that it will become the foremost of the Australasias in the future. Long secluded, petty, and almost unnoticed, the settlements in these islands have suddenly sprung into a prominence and importance which recall the rapid progress of Victoria in the first days of the gold discovery. Communications have been quickly built up in those regions which were a hemisphere of mystery to the Old World a few short years ago. The turn of New Zealand is fast coming; within five years or so she has nearly doubled her inhabitants. If the present extraordinary advance of these islands be sustained, they will be soon on the path to that magnificent destiny which, from their geographical position and great natural opportunities, was predicted for them by the thoughtful in England long before the first of our settlements was formed on their shores."

The constitution granted to New Zealand in 1853

is of the character described below. The governor and the judges are appointed from England; a civil list of £20,000 is granted to Her Majesty; the government of the colony is vested in the General Assembly, which meets at the capital, Wellington. This General Assembly is divided into two parts: the Council of thirty-five members, appointed for life by the crown, and the House of Representatives of seventy members. The qualification for voting for or being a member of the Lower House is the owning a freehold of £50 value, or renting a country house worth £5, or a town house worth £10 a year. The above has reference to the *general* government of New Zealand. For the purposes of *local* government, each of the nine provinces is governed by a Provincial Council, the head of which is called "Superintendent," who is assisted by a Council chosen by the electors every four years. Every Provincial Act must receive the assent of the general government before it has the force of law.

Before proceeding to give a brief account of each of the provinces, it may be well that we show the state of the country generally, as it may be most safely gathered from its statistics, a copy of which, to the end of 1868, has been kindly placed at my disposal by the Agent-General of the New Zealand government. The population was 226,618. There are upwards of 40,000 more men than women. During the year there was one birth to every 23, and one death to every 83 persons living. There were 2,085 marriages, 156 of which were by Registrars. 851 vessels of 277,105 tonnage entered *inwards*, and 873 of 287,710 outwards. The value of the imports was £4,985,748, and of exports £4,429,198. There was a considerable decrease in both these items. The gold exported was of the value of £2,504,326, showing a decrease of nearly £200,000. The total value of the gold exported from New Zealand was £17,044,899. The wool for the year reached the large quantity of 28,875,163 lbs., showing an increase of about a million and three quarters of pounds. Its value was estimated at £1,516,548. The total ordinary revenue of the year was £1,195,512, and the total territorial revenue was £425,323. The expenditure was £1,321,872; the total general government debt is £4,260,543. As many as 2,603,077 letters were received, and 2,374,122 were despatched. There are 687,015 acres of land under crop. There are 65,715 horses; 312,835 cattle; 8,418,579 sheep; 115,104 pigs; 323 mules or asses; 11,964 goats; and 676,065 poultry. We find a return of 579 thrashing machines; 736 reaping machines; 12 steam ploughs; and 28 steam harrows. The production of butter was 3,834,252 lbs., and of cheese, 1,300,082 lbs. This is an age of "statistics," and he who reads the above carefully cannot but allow that this colony has made, and is making, gigantic strides towards wealth, notwithstanding the sad ordeal through which she has been lately passing.

THE NORTHERN ISLAND.

This island is divided into four provinces: Auckland, Hawke's Bay, Taranaki, and Wellington, which contain nearly thirty millions of acres. It is a mountainous island, but indented with fine harbours. In summer the days are two hours shorter and in winter two hours longer than in England. It is seven degrees warmer than London. All English fruits grow in it to perfection.

1. Auckland. The capital of this province is also called Auckland. It is the most northern of the districts, and is nearly half the size of England. It was founded by the first governor (Hobson) in 1840. It is 400 miles long, and at its greatest breadth is 200 miles across. It has a population of nearly 50,000. The greater part of the native population is in this province. It has a number of fine harbours, such as Monganui, Hokianga, and Kaipara. The valleys are well watered, and the land is suitable for agricultural purposes. There are thirty harbours on the coast, and its rivers and estuaries are navigable for nearly one thousand miles. The largest lake (Taupo) is here; and there are numerous hot springs. The city of Auckland may be said to stand on two great harbours, the Waitémata and the Manakau, which are only six miles apart. The former of these is regarded as the finest in New Zealand. Every advantage is being taken of its natural situation, and of its water privileges,

to bring the country settlers and farmers into easy communication with the capital. In the immediate neighbourhood of Auckland, the extinct volcanoes, and the scoria with which the country is covered, give it a somewhat dreary appearance. The city has been compared to Folkestone, in Kent, being built up and down the sides of hills. St. John's College stands in the neighbourhood, used by the late Bishop Selwyn as a training college for the natives from the islands of the Pacific. This work is now carried on by the learned and indefatigable Bishop Patteson, who was formerly chaplain to the Bishop of New Zealand. It is called the Melanesian Mission, and is we trust doing a great work. He goes about in his missionary schooner from one to another of the numberless beauteous islands which stud these seas, and in spite of inhospitable shores, dangerous coral reefs always growing, heavy surf, armed savages opposing his landing, and difficulties which can be imagined better than briefly described, this great and good man effects a landing, and in many cases persuades the people to entrust their young men to his care for education. When from different islands he has filled his vessel, he takes them to his home and places them in his college. Here they are taught the arts of civilisation, and are instructed in our holy religion. The hope is, that when thus Christianised and civilised, they may go back to their respective islands and become the native teachers of their fellow countrymen. The bishop's journals are intensely interesting, and the whole scheme is one of deep importance. The different colonies of Australia, one and all, regard this as *their* mission, and are gladly and liberally subscribing towards the necessary funds for working out this great experiment.

The northern peninsula of Auckland is covered with a number of little agricultural communities, who enjoy easy access to the capital by water. Mr. Hursthouse in his valuable work says: "No part of New Zealand is so rich in historic interest as the northern portion of the province of Auckland. Some future Macaulay may relate that here unharmed the missionary fathers first raised the cross among ferocious cannibals; here, the first press was set up and the first Bible printed in the native tongue; here, the early colonisation of the country commenced; and here stood Kororareka, the old 'Alsatia' of the Pacific; here, the treaty of Waitangi, the Maori Magna Charta, was signed by the Queen's first governor and her Maori barons; and here the red cross first fluttered in the breeze and gave to Britain a 'Britain of the South.'" The "East Coast" and the "Waikato" country form perhaps the finest parts of the province, but at present they are mostly in the hands of the natives. Lake Taupo (100 miles in circumference) is situated herein.

By the treaty of "Waitangi," referred to above, the sovereignty of these islands was formally made over to the Queen, the Crown pledging itself to purchase from the natives whatever land was required for the purposes of colonisation; and this agreement has been strictly adhered to.

Land is sold at a fixed price of 10s. an acre. Liberal grants are made to soldiers, sailors, and schoolmasters; and mechanics, servants, and others obtain free grants of 40 acres to adults, and of 20 acres for each child between the ages of 5 and 18. The farmer or capitalist receives also 40 or 20 *additional* acres for each servant or labourer, friend or relative whose passage he may pay. Blocks of land are laid aside also for "special settlements," which have proved a great success. There are no sheep runs in this province, from the circumstance of its being devoid of grassy plains.

"It has been reserved for that Province of New Zealand (says the *New Zealand Examiner*) which has so long been under both a political and commercial cloud to enjoy the most complete flood of 'golden' sunshine yet known in the Southern Hemisphere. The gold that has been hidden at her very threshold is now opened as a vast storehouse of wealth for Auckland. The returns seem almost fabulous, but as the gold does really come home for English goods, we are compelled to acknowledge that all previous finds of the precious metal in the Southern Hemisphere have been completely eclipsed by the Thames gold-fields. We rejoice in Auckland's present great success, not solely on account of this addition to her wealth in gold, but because it will attract to her shores a population that must (as such discoveries have done wherever they have been made) open up a land that only waits cultivation to render it an immense producing country. Our readers need scarcely be reminded of California which before gold was found was little heard of, while it is now one of the great 'agricultural' States of the Union. Already Otago, the first worked New Zealand gold-field, exports corn to the mother country, therefore we cannot but hope that Auckland will quickly follow in its wake. To emigrants of the working kind the Northern Province of New Zealand presents a most enviable field."

2. Taranaki, or New Plymouth. This lies to the south-west of Auckland, and is about 80 miles long by 70 in breadth. Its population is about 4,500. One-third of its three millions of acres is covered with forest, but the rest is rich agricultural land, and is not inaptly styled "The Garden of New Zealand." But the late desolating war has committed sad ravages in it. Its great want is a good harbour. The capital, New Plymouth, was founded in 1841, by a party of gentlemen from Devon and Cornwall. The climate of this province is very pleasant. It is cooler than Auckland. Mount Egmont, an extinct volcano, rises to the height of 8,000 feet. At its base is found the metallic sand, to which a good deal of attention has been paid of late years, and from which razors and surgical instruments have been formed of excellent quality. When once the supremacy of the law has been established, and the native troubles over, this is a most promising land to the agriculturist. Land is surveyed in blocks of from 40 to 240 acres, and is sold by auction at an upset price of 10s. an acre. The same military and naval grants as in the northern province.

3. Hawke's Bay. This was separated form Wellington in 1858. Its capital is Napier. The population is 5,283. It is said that the natives greatly preponderate in numbers. It is an open, grassy and pastoral country. It is described as being " very windy, but bright, cheerful and remarkably healthy."

Rural lands available for agriculture are sold at a fixed price of ten shillings an acre; pastoral land sold by auction, the upset price being five shillings an acre. Naval and military settlements as at Auckland.

4. Wellington. This is the most southern province of the northern island. The population is 21,950, of whom perhaps 8,000 are natives. The city of Wellington stretches along the shore of its magnificent harbour for a considerable distance; the public buildings are good, but are built mostly of wood in consequence of the fear of earthquakes, several shocks of which have been experienced. The city of Wellington was founded in 1840 by the New Zealand Company. It is the capital, and its commerce is very considerable. Being exposed to the high winds which blow through Cook's Strait, as through a funnel, it is said to be the stormiest place on the coast; hence arose the saying that a man from Wellington could be known anywhere, for he was always holding his hat on with his hand. Bishop Selwyn says that, " No one can speak of the healthfulness of New Zealand till he has been

ventilated by the breezes of Wellington, where malaria is no more to be feared than on the top of Chimborazo, and where no fog can ever linger long to deaden the intellectual faculties of the inhabitants." In this province there are also the settlements of Manuwatu, Turakina, Rangitiki, and Wanganui. The last of these is connected with Wellington. In many parts of this province are the stations of thriving squatters, rich in flocks and herds, and numbers of little agricultural settlements.

THE MIDDLE ISLAND.

This is divided into five provinces: Nelson, Marlborough, Canterbury, including the county of Westland, Otago, and Southland. It is about 550 miles long, and contains twenty-eight and a half millions of acres. The temperature is about two degrees warmer than London. The natural pastures of this island are as good as any in the world, and its climate is equally adapted for cattle and for sheep. The average increase on a breeding flock is 90 per cent. There are millions of acres fit for sheep.

1. Nelson Province. This is the extreme north of the island, being 160 miles long and 100 broad. It has a population of 23,814. This province, or in fact the whole of the middle island, has very few natives; it is necessary to bear this in mind. The late troubles in New Zealand were confined to the northern island. The city of Nelson is delightfully

situated, and being protected from the southern gales by a circle of precipitous hills, it enjoys a beautiful climate. It is about a mile and a half from the port. It was founded in 1842 by Captain Arthur Wakefield, under the auspices of the New Zealand Company. The chief agricultural areas are the rich valley of the Waimea and the Motueka. The Dun Mountain mine is about seventeen miles from Nelson, and produces chrome, a substance used by manufacturers of paint; but we hear that this mine is not being worked now. The Coromandel quartz reefs are in this province; Collingwood is the township which sprung up in connection with the quartz reefs. No free grants of land are made; the land is surveyed and an upset price, varying from five shillings to forty shillings an acre, put upon it, and then each lot is put up to auction and sold to the highest bidder.

2. Marlborough. Until within the last few years this formed part of the province of Nelson. It is about 130 miles long by 60 broad. Blenheim and Picton are the two chief towns; it is not certain which will ultimately be the capital. In this province are the celebrated Wairau plains, one of the finest sheep districts in the country. Marlborough is quite in its infancy; its population is only 4,371. There are no free grants of land. It is surveyed, and divided into two classes; an upset price of from ten shillings to twenty shillings an acre is put upon the first class, and from five

shillings to ten shillings on the second, and both are sold by auction to the highest bidder.

3. Canterbury. This province occupies the centre of the middle island, and contains twelve millions of acres, and (including the county of Westland) has a population of nearly fifty-four thousands. This was a Church of England settlement, but, as is always the case with such settlements, it continued so exclusively for a very brief period, and persons of all denominations are to be found there. It had connected with it from the very first an unusual number of the sons of good families in England. Lyttleton is its port, and is about five miles from the Heads. Christchurch is the capital, and stands on the Avon, about nine miles from Lyttleton. It is a bishop's see, and when it was proposed to erect the cathedral, £11,000 were promised towards it within a month. The extent of land adapted for agriculture in this province is estimated at nearly two millions of acres, a considerable proportion of which has already been taken up. There are several shipping places on the coast, and townships are springing up in the agricultural districts. The Grey coal field is about six miles and a half up the Grey River. The upper seam is about fourteen feet thick, and the under one ten or eleven, and they have a dip of about 11°. Very fine gold is found, though in small quantities, all over the west coast. With the exception of reserves for towns and for special public purposes, all the lands in the province are

open for sale at the rate of £2 an acre. Until applied for to be purchased the waste lands may be rented for pasturage purposes. The maximum amount for 20,000 acres is £62 10s. a year. These licenses are renewable yearly till 1870. The settler has a pre-emptive right, but only for a block of from 50 to 250 acres. The high price of land forbids land-jobbing, or buying on speculation to any great extent, but it has been found to work well to the *bona fide* settler. Many capitalists are now turning their attention to grass farming, that is, making paddocks and sowing them with English grasses. It is calculated that this returns a good interest on the capital invested, besides the increased value of the freehold from the improvements. The land now is pretty much taken up for runs. Strangers coming into this province with a small capital, and desiring to turn their attention to sheep farming, would be wise to place so many sheep on a settler's run " on terms," that is being allowed a certain proportion of the wool and of the increase. And if in addition they can get employment for themselves for a time, till they become acquainted practically with the pursuit they intend to follow, the plan will be found safe and profitable. Until lately the prices asked for stocked runs were so high as to be almost prohibitory. Probably now an improved run could be obtained on much easier terms. No free grants of land are made excepting to old soldiers discharged through wounds received in the Russian war, or to the wives of soldiers thus made widows, who are allowed thirty acres. Assisted passages are granted to men of good character, such as agricultural labourers, shepherds, women servants, and tradesmen and artisans, from time to time. The passage money is £17. If the emigrant pays £5, the government gives him £5, and he gives his promissory note for the balance. If he pays one-half, he receives a passage order without incurring any future liability.

4. Otago. This is situated in the south of the middle island, is about as large as Scotland, and contains seventeen millions of acres, ten millions of which are considered available for agricultural and pastoral purposes. The population is nearly 50,000. Of course the climate is decidedly colder than the northern island, but by no means unpleasant even in winter. It has a mean temperature like that of London. Otago was founded by the New Zealand Company, in connection with the Free Church of Scotland, in 1847. The settlement was planted by the late Captain Cargill, in 1848. The harbour is called Port Chalmers. Dunedin is the capital. The land regulations are similar to those of Canterbury. The eastern and central portions of the province contain many agricultural and pastoral districts of great fertility. In the year 1865 New Zealand's first "Great Exhibition" was held at Dunedin, when there were 890 exhibits from the different provinces of the colony, 561 of which were

furnished by Otago. The gold-fields in this district have given a great impetus to trade. Although it was first started as a Free Church of Scotland settlement, the members of the Church of England have increased so fast that it was agreed to form it into a bishopric, the head-quarters of which should be at Dunedin. We give below the latest rate of wages:—

"Male farm servants averaging £50 per annum, with few exceptions; married couples, from £60 to £70 per annum; female cooks, £40; housemaids, £35; nursemaids, £30; laundresses, £40; needlewomen, £1 per week; hotel cooks, £1 to £3 per week; waiters, 30s.; boots, 20s. per week; housemaids for hotels, from £40 a year to £1 weekly; waitresses, 15s. to £1 weekly; barmaids from £1 to £2 weekly; carpenters, 12s. to 15s. per day; painters, from 10s. to 12s.; shearers, 17s. 6d. per hundred, with rations."

5. Southland. Until the year 1861 this province formed part of Otago. It has a population of about 8,000. Its size is small, being not more than twice the size of Northumberland. Invercargill is its capital. It is a fertile district. It contains more than two millions of acres; and Stewart's Island, to the south of it, and which belongs to it, may have about half a million more. The climate on the coasts of Foveaux Strait is wet and boisterous; inland it improves. The winter cold is not, however, greater than that of the south of England; the temperature rarely falls to more than four or five degrees below the freezing point, and the frost

seldom lasts till mid-day. There are many plains which are generally dry and unbroken, so much so that the plough might be driven for miles on any of them without impediment. The hills form dry and healthy sheep runs. Limestone is abundant. It is calculated (says the author of the "Prize Pamphlet on Southland") that the acreage fit for the plough probably exceeds a million of acres. Heavy crops of good serviceable wheat can be raised. Grass succeeds to perfection, after the land has been thoroughly cultivated by two or three years cropping. The *average* agricultural land, with proper cultivation, *but without manure*, will produce 35 bushels of wheat, or 45 of oats, to the acre. Timber of many useful kinds is found in different parts of this province, and in great abundance.

There are no free grants of land. The price for country land is fixed at £2 an acre.

The Chatham Islands are about two days' sail from New Zealand. The largest island is 35 miles long. The coast is very dangerous. The population is 184. Potatoes are the chief produce.

The following "New Zealand Notes" have just been received, and are extracted from the *Argus*:—

"At length there seems a prospect of the near termination of the troubles which have so long impeded the progress of New Zealand. The alarm respecting the general native rising, which was so much feared some few months ago, seems to have died out, and it is satisfactory to note that the new Ministry are endeavouring to conciliate the Maories, and by fair treatment to promote a good understanding between them and the white race. The influence which Mr. M'Lean, the Native and Defence Minister, possesses over the natives, especially on the East Coast, where he long resided as a magistrate, has materially assisted in begetting a feeling of confidence in the new Administration. But while the Government are disposed to act in a conciliatory spirit towards the Maories, they have also exhibited considerable vigour in the field, and the result has been that Te Kooti, the mainspring of the rebellion, has sustained several defeats. The policy of the Ministry in transforming the colonial military force into an armed constabulary has not had a prejudicial effect, as predicted by some, and the re-employment of friendly natives has already produced good fruits.

"The last native news shows Te Kooti—who is now supposed to be the original miscreant of that name—again active, but apparently in a trap. Returning unwillingly and in disgrace from the King's country, he appears to have contemplated a raid upon the country formerly harassed by his compeer, Titoko Waru, with the intention, perhaps, of effecting a junction with the latter, who is—no one knows exactly where—in the fastnesses which lie behind the Wanganui and Patea country. The friendly natives on the Upper Wanganui sent early in September for assistance to their friends on the lower portion of the river, and to the Government. Before these appeals arrived, however, a native force under the New Zealand Government's ally, Henare Tomoana, had been despatched from the East Coast to intercept Te Kooti. At Tauranga—not the Tauranga of Gate Pa celebrity, but a little place near the Taupo Lake—the two parties met, and some smart, but not very decisive, fighting was the result. In the first engagement, which took place on the 9th September, Te Kooti had the worst of it, and fell back on a pa he had built at Tokanu, with a loss of three killed and several wounded. The friendlies had only two men wounded. Two days later there was another brush of a more important character, with the same result. Te Kooti was repulsed, and five of his men are reported killed. A few days afterwards Colonel M'Donnell, who has been re-instated by the present Government, and Lieutenant-Colonel Herrick, with a strong force of friendly natives, effected a junction with Henare Tomoana. Te Kooti fell back on Moerangi, but was pursued by the colonial forces, and on Saturday, September 25, an engagement took place. Te Kooti, with a force of from 250 to 300 strong, attacked Tokano, a position occupied by Colonel M'Donnell's troops. Severe fighting took place, which resulted in the defeat of the enemy, with considerable loss, estimated at 30. Colonel M'Donnell says that the enemy had plenty of ammunition, and that 30 and 40 rounds were found in some of the pouches taken. The colonial force, which consisted of 249 natives, and two or three European officers, had only seven wounded. All appear to have behaved well. A general attack was to be made on the Monday following this engagement, but the result is not yet known. Te Kooti's position at the present time is a very desperate one, and as he is almost surrounded by forces numerically superior to his own, and is probably short of supplies, he will scarcely be able to make a very effectual resistance.

"Three of the leading rebel prisoners, late allies of Titoko Waru, have been found guilty of treason-felony and murder by a jury, in the Supreme Court at Wellington, and are sentenced to death. Eighteen other prisoners have been liberated, as no evidence could be found against them. Tauroa, the chief of the West Coast prisoners, was not amongst those tried. Dorrington, the watchmaker at Parnell, who was arrested on two charges of selling arms and ammunition to the natives, has been acquitted on both charges. The three natives implicated in the same case pleaded 'Guilty,' and were sentenced to three years' imprisonment, together with a fine of £5 each.

"Another successful occurrence, which is to be attributed mainly to the influence of the present Ministry among the natives, and the confidence they are disposed to place in Mr. Fox and Mr. M'Lean, is the purchase of the Kaimanawa country, described as a block of land of enormous extent, reaching from Ruapehu to this side Ruahine, and from Taupo to Napier and the Puke track. The country is said to include all the reputed auriferous land south of Lake Taupo. The terms on which this purchase has been arranged have not yet been made public, but are said to be most satisfactory, both as regards the commercial nature of the transaction, and, what is of still more importance, as respects the effect which will be produced on the natives by the future monetary interest which they will have in the heretofore valueless soil. The present pay, direct money, is only £60. But that is a mere earnest of the bargain—the great point to which the natives look being the income secured to them from one-half of the amount derived from miners' rights.

"There is some hope, too, of an early opening of the Ohinemuri district in Auckland province — known as the Upper Thames. Mr. M'Lean, the Native Minister, has gone on a visit to the King with the object of obtaining his permission to carry the line of telegraph through the Waikato. If he succeeds in obtaining this concession, the advantage will be incalculable; for if once the telegraph wire is fairly carried through the country, roads, settlement, trade, cultivation, and gold-mining would follow, and the end of the Maori war would be seen. The Upper Thames chiefs declare that if the King agrees to open up the Waikato, Ohinemuri must follow.

"His Excellency Sir George Bowen lately visited Wanganui, and was presented with an address by the tribes of that district, requesting him to build a house in that part of the country, so that he might reside there during some months of the year as he did at Auckland. His Excellency, in reply, congratulated the natives on the improved state of affairs since his last visit.

"The Parliamentary session closed early in September. A great number of bills were passed, but few have any general interest. Machinery has been provided for the establishment and maintenance of public libraries, and the initiation of a system of state life assurances and annuities similar to that lately inaugurated in the mother country. Two other acts are also worthy of a passing remark. The one provides an endowment for the order of the New Zealand Cross, and the other incorporates the New Zealand Law Society. The superintendent of Otago has obtained powers to found special settlements at Martin's Bay and Preservation Inlet, on the Western Coast.

NEW HOMES.

If this project is successful, the new settlements will be the nearest inhabited portions of New Zealand to Victoria.

"The intelligence of an industrial character is very encouraging from all parts of the islands. The many flax companies which have been started of late promise that New Zealand will soon take her proper place as a great flax exporter, for that article which grows in such abundance there is of specially good quality. The smelting of the steel sand found along the Taranaki shore has been successfully commenced. It is calculated that a profit of £400 a week can be made. A colony of Welshmen is being established in Canterbury, with the view of forming a blanket manufactory in that great wool-bearing province. A lecture recently delivered by the well-known explorer, Dr. Hector, shows how various are the localities in which extensive coal-fields exist. The gold-diggers in the provinces of Auckland and Otago are largely supplied with fuel from the coal mines in those regions. The Thames gold-field still maintains its reputation for unparalleled richness, but the amount of speculation going on there is naturally bringing about disastrous consequences. A collapse is impending in the share markets at Auckland, and no wonder, when the advertised capital of the companies started since the beginning of the year amounts to £2,000,000. Within a period of three months no less than 86 applications were lodged for the registration of new companies on this gold-field, the nominal paid-up capital being £1,532,552. Two statements, recently made on good authority by an Auckland paper, will afford some idea of the rapid advance in the price of shares at the Thames. From a share-list published, it was found that amongst a total of 87 companies there was capital to the amount of £1,270,201, and the advances on the selling rates of shares amounted in one week to over £534,175. Many people are of opinion that the richness of the Thames is over-estimated; but several Ballarat gentlemen, who have recently returned from New Zealand, express an opinion that it is really a permanent and first-class gold-field, and predict that in 12 months it will be the most wonderful gold-producing place in the world. The claims at present are being worked in a very wasteful manner in the majority of instances. The long drive lately crushed 300 lb. of stone, which yielded 4 oz. to the lb. This gives a dividend of £2 8s. per scrip. The yield of the Golden Crown for the month of August was 2,345 oz.; for the year, 26,343 oz.; value, £68,368. Two full shares in the Coromandel have been sold for £12,000 each. Capital from all parts of the colonies is being invested there, and as an instance of how the fame of the gold-field is extending, we may mention that a French gentleman, living in Paris, has authorised his agent to invest a considerable sum of money in some of the best claims for him. Encouraging accounts are received from several of the other gold-fields. The Virginia claim, at Coromandel, has yielded nugget specimens surpassing anything obtained at the Thames. Numerous prospecting parties are out in all parts of the country.

"Mr. E. W. Stafford, late Colonial Secretary, and Colonel Haultain, late Defence Minister, have declined the honour of knighthood of the order of St. Michael and St. George. Colonel Whitmore, late in command of the Armed Constabulary Force, to whom it was also offered, promptly accepted it, as an acknowledgment on the part of 'the Queen and country' of the services he had rendered.

"Several large fires have occurred during the month. Quick's coach-factory at Auckland was burnt. The loss is estimated at £6,000; and Messrs. Jacobs and Isaacs' store at Christchurch was totally destroyed. The building and stock were insured in the latter instance.

"The story recently published concerning a cave at Raglan containing 38 petrified Maories is pronounced to be a miserable and silly fabrication."

We have thus very hastily run over the whole of New Zealand. Every year will see its advance among the new group of colonies. It has had, and may have again, many a hard struggle; but its natural resources are so varied and extensive that when once the *native difficulty* is got over, as we heartily trust it may be, and a clear and definite line laid down and acted upon between the colonists and the Maories, its onward progress will equal, if it does not surpass, many of the colonies on the mainland of Australia. Each and every one of the colonies in this part of the world has great capabilities, and if they are but united they will some day form a mighty confederation.

> We rejoice to see, with England's flag unfurl'd,
> A new Britannia in the Southern world.

And now our task is well nigh done. We cannot but feel that the sketch we have given of each colony is a very imperfect one. And yet enough perhaps has been said to give the intelligent reader an idea of the places referred to. I know full well that the American colonies have a great advantage over Australia in their proximity to England, thereby lessening the cost of transport. But I believe that this is their *only* advantage over her. And it may be that the difficulties which stand in the way of an extensive exodus to Australia and New Zealand, may to a certain extent be overcome by the hearty co-operation of the very large and influential body of men in England who are deeply interested in those lands. We hail with peculiar satisfaction the formation of the "National Emigration League," the members of which are so numerous and so influential that their efforts will, we do not doubt, be crowned with a large amount of success. Sir W. Denison's idea was, that a large system of colonisation should be undertaken, and if possible 100,000 people sent away yearly. This, he said, could only be done with the aid of the government, who should make all necessary arrangements for their transmission, reception and allotment of lands. Mr. Torrens despaired of the present emergency being met by charity. He regarded the League as a political body in the highest and wisest sense, having no considerations of class, party or creed. It was their duty to put before the government the task of providing a remedy for the existing distress, and suggesting that the best and most wise way would be by sanctioning and conducting a continuous stream of colonisation and emigration. They should impress upon the Premier the absolute necessity of the measure, in consideration of the lives of the people, the good order of society, and the maintenance of the law.

In the year 1830, the following paragraph appeared in the "Quarterly Review":—

"Government, for instance, might either undertake at once the expense and arrangements for conveying labourers to the colony, or leaving this to trading importers, only become answerable for repayment of the passage money, either at once or by instalments. An office might for this purpose be appointed in the colony, at which every labourer as he arrived should be registered—the cost of his passage, with that of insurance on his living long enough to repay the sum debited to him, and he might then be allowed to work where and how he chose, on the sole condition of paying a certain sum, weekly or monthly, to government, towards the debt incurred by his importation. The collection of these instalments from labourers scattered over the colony could be effected by the same machinery as, and would hardly be more difficult than, the collection of any other tax; and, at all events, would be far more easily effected by government than by individuals, who cannot enforce their claims but by borrowing, in an awkward manner, the aid of government. But should this plan be supposed impracticable or unadvisable, there are other indirect ways of levying the same sum, in such a manner that it shall be unfelt, perhaps unsuspected by the labourer as he pays it."

It has been proposed to ask the government to utilise some of the vessels in the navy, in these piping times of peace, by employing them as transports. This would of course remove a great difficulty, as the cost of transmission would thus be much lessened. One great thing must we think be kept carefully in mind. The different colonies (at least I can speak for the Australian colonies) are ready and willing to receive emigrants; but they must be men of the right stamp, and such a class as is required in the respective colonies. And it would not do to send them out too many at a time. It is a *continuous stream* that is required. No persons know the wants of each country better than the Agents-General of the respective colonies, resident in London. And it might be well that if the scheme succeed, their co-operation should be sought in carrying out the plan. The colonies have been aiming for years past to frame such Land Bills as to place "homes" at the disposal of the industrious; and now that so much has been done, it only requires assistance from this side to make those homes available to the people. That the distress in England is very great no one can doubt, and he is no friend to his fellow-men who does not seek, by every legitimate means, to remove that distress effectually by a wise and well-considered scheme of emigration.

Many of the colonies are holding out great inducements to the capitalist, in granting him land for all the labourers he takes out. If this plan were pursued it would help to relieve the pressure at home.

I know that some persons doubt the willingness of the people to leave their country; but this is not *generally* the case. Vast numbers are I know only looking out for an opportunity of escaping from the sad state of things which unfortunately exists here. There are I am aware some who think a great deal of the voyage; but all fears on this head are foolish, and would be dissipated within a week on board ship. The voyage to Australia is one of the safest known; in fact it is frequently undertaken as a kind of pleasure trip. I know of more than one party who have made it a "wedding tour," and the other day I heard of a friend in Melbourne, who holds a high appointment, and who wished to come and see a sick relative, but who said that if he came by the January mail he could only stay in England a *fortnight!* A voyage round the world, and to stay a *fortnight* at home!

And let the emigrant of every class bear in mind that he is not now going to a wilderness, whichever colony he may select. The day of privations and isolation is rapidly passing away. He will find everywhere English towns, English people, and English civilisation. Railways are connecting places that used to be remote, and the electric telegraph is about to connect Australia with England.

It is to be regretted that the postal regulations are not keeping pace with the times. By a most ingenious process, the mails are so arranged that you cannot answer your letters without great loss of time, or without an expense to which the emigrant should not if possible be put. Thus, for instance, this month, which is but a sample of all the months, the mail *viâ* Southampton *goes out* on the 22nd, and the letters by Marseilles *come in* on the 24th (or two days after the Southampton mail has gone). The Marseilles mail *leaves* on the 28*th*, and the Southampton mail *arrives* on the 29*th*. So that unless you get your letters always by Marseilles, which route costs 10d. for a letter instead of 6d., and is therefore a great tax upon the mass of the people, you cannot answer at all without waiting *nearly a month*. I took the liberty some time ago of addressing the Postmaster-General on the subject, and received a courteous reply to the effect that the arrangement had been made after due consideration for the *convenience of the public!* I am afraid it is a convenience which the public do not appreciate. To my mind it seems that it was just made to fit in with the Indian mail, without any regard to the wants of Australia.

The careful reader of the above pages will see that in going out now his children can be educated almost if not quite as well as in England; churches and chapels are scattered over all the countries; the Lord's day is observed quite as well if not better than it is in England; and the tone of society has so greatly improved of late years, that he must be fastidious indeed who cannot find those with whom it would be a pleasure to associate. All the new books are just two months later than you have them in England; and for the information of the ladies, I may say this applies to the "fashions" too.

In fine, my advice to all those who from circumstances are led to think of seeking "new homes" is—"Go to Australia." If I had a dozen sons, slenderly provided for, or unprovided for, and they had "sound minds in sound bodies," willing to work and disposed to be sober, I would say—"Go, and, God blessing you, you will prosper." (I have but two sons, and they are both in Australia.)

A project which promises to be of great value to all the colonies, but specially to New Zealand, has just been put forward, viz. : for a steam and railroad service from Milford Haven to Portland (Maine) in nine days; from Portland to San Francisco by rail in seven days, and thence to Australia and New

Zealand in 23 days, thus bringing the colonies within 40 days of England.

The news from New Zealand is of such importance, and is of so hopeful a character, that it is thus commented on in a late number of the *Standard:*—

"The New Zealand news is of an important character, and seems to convey positive evidence of future tranquillity in the Northern Island. An interview has been held between Mr. M'Lean, the Minister of Native Affairs, with the principal chiefs of the Waikato and Ngatimamopoto tribes, at which, although the 'Native King' himself was not present, Rewi, his chief man of war, who has succeeded the late William Thompson as 'Mayor of the Palace' and real head of the Maori Confederacy, has, after five years of sullen neutrality, spoken words of peace, if not of friendship. According to the interesting report of this meeting, which is given in the *New Zealand Herald* of the 15th of November, the proceedings were characterised by the absence of many of those ceremonies which have hitherto been held essential to polite diplomacy. The songs and speeches of welcome which form so important a part of these meetings, and in which the dark-skinned warriors take so keen a delight, were not forthcoming to greet the representative of the Pakehas. In their stead 'Prayers in the Hau-hau form' were offered—an evidence that the Kingites at least have completely broken away from the teaching of the missionaries, and an ominous sign of the extent to which they had sympathised with the anti-European rising. In other respects the proceedings were satisfactory, as indicating that there is at least an earnest desire among the neutral tribes of the interior for peace. In response to a speech from Mr. M'Lean, Rewi stood up and declared that his word was peace, and that there should be no more fighting. He made three requests, which it is important for us to note, as showing that the grievances of the Maories are something quite other than their fanatical friends at home are wont to represent. He did not complain of any of those things with which Lord

Granville has charged the settlers. He did not protest against their 'greed for land' or their policy of confiscation. He did not desire the 'restoration of the island,' or even the independence of the Maori population. He asked that the European occupation at Taupo should cease. He asked that Te Heu Heu, who had been 'foolish,' should be liberated. He pleaded for Te Hura, as one who had been punished sufficiently for his fault. It is gratifying to know that Mr. M'Lean was able to satisfy all these requests. The land at Taupo had not been taken, and was only occupied temporarily by the troops for the protection of the friendly tribes and the punishment of crime. Te Heu Heu would be released. And Te Hura, although a convicted murderer, would also be made over into Rewi's hands, on condition that the chief became security for his good behaviour. On his part, Rewi promised to show no further countenance to Te Kooti and the insurgents, and the meeting ended with expressions of mutual good-will.

"We congratulate the Colonial Government on the wisdom and tact with which they have managed this most difficult negociation, more difficult by the assistance rendered from the Imperial authorities. It is obvious that the colony of New Zealand has narrowly escaped a very great peril, and it is important to note, once for all, that the peril would have been vastly increased had Mr. Fox's Ministry acted by the advice given them by Lord Granville, or had they been deprived of the presence of the battalion of Queen's troops which Lord Granville insisted on recalling. The colonial press, without exception, attribute the improved temper of the King natives entirely to the moral effect produced by the retention by General Chute of the 18th Regiment, contrary to Lord Granville's orders. So long as any Imperial troops remain in the island, so long will the natives continue to believe that the Queen has not abandoned the country —a belief which for many years to come will be the best pledge of peace in New Zealand. It remains to be seen whether Lord Granville will permit the good results already obtained to be neutralised by an obstinate adherence to his most unwise and cruel order for the withdrawal of the 18th Regiment."

The policy of the present Government with regard to the Colonies forms the subject of an admirable article, from the pen of Mr. Froude, in the last number of "Fraser's Magazine." The article is too long to transcribe, but a faithful epitome of its contents is given by the *New Zealand Examiner*:—

"Mr. Froude has contributed to the current number of 'Fraser' an article which treats the great questions of Colonial policy with so much breadth and vigour, that we can do our readers no better service than to present, in a very brief form, the leading ideas he enunciates. Mr. Froude is so far behind the age that he believes in patriotism, and thinks that England may have some greater claim to the regard of posterity than that of having given birth to America. While, of course, entertaining the sincerest desire for friendly relations with all other countries, Mr. Froude does not deem it a matter of indifference whether the increase of material prosperity which in every age, in this working world, befals some one or other (and, if we examine the matter, ever the worthiest) shall fall to our own share, or to that of some other nation. Above all, Mr. Froude grudges that any large portion of England's best wealth, the living men who are crowded so thickly on her own shores, should be cast off as forming no valuable part of the body politic. Every industrious and honest man is a source of well-being to the community to which he belongs, and Mr. Froude is alarmed at the notion that it is a matter of indifference whether such a one, finding no room for him at home, betakes himself to the United States, or continues to be an Englishman in one of our own Colonies. For it is not a metaphor, but a plain fact that these Colonies are essentially a part of England, and, as events are progressing, it will soon be palpable that England would no more be England without them than, three hundred years ago, she would have been England without Norfolk or Cornwall. The notion that England is to become one huge cotton mill, and that other countries will be proud to grow corn for her, and acknowledge her the mistress of creation, Mr. Froude believes to be a fallacy. A factory is not a nation, and man does not live by calico alone. No nation, he points out, ever became or continued great without an agricultural population proportioned to that of the towns. He traces many of the evils which we deplore to the growing disproportion between the two elements; physical deterioration, an increasing consumption of intoxicating drinks, trade feuds, general impatience of honest work, and indifference of honest dealing. If there was not too great a proportion of country to city in the time of Henry VIII., there must be a vast disproportion the other way now. The obvious way is to seek new Norfolks beyond the sea to balance our new Manchesters, and, doubtless, to create Manchesters and Liverpools of their own; which, in turn, will require still farther colonisation. In this light a colony is something very different from what colonies originally were—penal settlements for convicted or unconvicted scamps, the great recommendation being that hardly any one came back from them. The same mechanical progress which has brought Canada almost as near to London as Edinburgh once was, has brought Australia and New Zealand proportionately near, and a man who emigrates no more abandons home ties than he does by removing to another county in England. Two members of the present Government gained their political education in Australia, and in every circle of a few score men in almost any grade, we may rely on finding some who have acquired experience, if not wealth, in some of our Colonies. To use a well-worn simile, the blood now flows towards the heart, as well as from it. If we look to the essential bond of union, New Zealand and Australia were never more truly an integral part of England than now, and we cannot, even for the sake of peace and quietness at the Colonial Office, allow it to be proclaimed that they have no claim on us, or that we have no benefits to seek from them. The one thing the Colonies ask from us—in addition to abstaining from mismanagement—is that we will send them the men who, in a certain sense, are superfluous and even mischievous here. The thing needs to be done boldly, once for all; and it must be remembered that, once done, it would not soon need to be repeated. For every emigrant, as experience shows, is but too glad to bear the cost of bringing new hands—whether his own friends and relations or others—to share the work that he finds ready for him. The cost of a couple of iron-clads yearly for the next seven years; or, still better, a New Zealand expedition fitted out with the same promptitude, and at half the cost of the Abyssinian one, would repay the outlay by the diminution of pauperism, and the stimulus given to trade in every direction. But, as Mr. Froude puts the case, it is not a question whether this undertaking will turn out immediately profitable or not. The tendency of civilised men in these days is to aggregation into great states, and if the Colonies cannot be integral parts of the British Empire, they would prefer to become united with some other power, rather than continue isolated, and, for the present, insignificant communities. Even from a Manchester point of view, it is worth while to remember that the Colonists are our customers to the amount of more pounds per head than the people of the States are for shillings. And let us not doubt that if we cannot hold the Colonies, the American Government, which ruled California when the route to it lay round Cape Horn, will be able to render them substantial accessions to her power. And with the Stripes and Stars floating all over the world, it is doubtful, according to Mr. Froude's view, whether our trade, to which we should have sacrificed everything, could survive many years, and morally certain that we could not hold our Indian Empire. Moreover, if these considerations are not serious enough, there is another which may have more weight with the British Legislature. If there is no more land to be had to cultivate—if England is not to be enlarged according to the growing needs of her people, how long may we expect the present land laws to last? Mr. Froude is disposed to think that the number of years may be counted on the fingers of one hand; and even if we do not adopt this view, it is patent that the question of land tenure in England is the next great subject but one for consideration by the British Parliament, and it will be well to avoid any new errors that may embitter the discussion. Let it be understood that this is no party question; but that the statesman, be he who he may, who first takes in hand this great Colonial difficulty, holds the key of the future."

In my first chapter I spoke of the voyage out as it was performed in days gone by, and purposed, after a trip to and examination of each colony, to describe the voyage home by steam. Just as I was about to join the ship which brought us to England, I had to travel 150 miles from my son-in-law's station. He lent us his carriage, horses, and coachman. We entered on a dreary plain extending for forty or fifty miles without a house—without a tree. Presently the man told me that the tire of one of the wheels was coming off, and he (being a new hand in the country) had come away without nails, hammer, rope, or straps of any kind. I was at my wits' end. A month might elapse before any good Samaritan might pass that way. At length my wife said, "Let me have my dressing case." She opened it, and took out a pretty delicate looking little thing with a pearl handle—a *stiletto;* not the Spaniard's deadly weapon, but a lady's stiletto, which they use for—I really do not know for what. She told the coachman to break the handle off, and to drive the little instrument into the weakest point. He did so. I was appointed to watch the wheel as it slowly revolved, and it actually held together and brought us safely to the end of the day's journey.

I have had the greatest regard for stilettos ever since.

And now, after more than thirty years' hard work, let me get on board the *Great Britain* steamer, and take at least a holiday for a time at home. Nine hundred souls were congregated on board this magnificent steamer, the main-sails of which contained 3,000 yards of canvas. We passed through a vast field of icebergs; rounded the Horn—that region of storm and darkness; gradually got towards the north into fine weather; on the Equator witnessed a total eclipse of the sun, a sight which, seen under such circumstances and in such a place, none of us will ever forget, for it was awfully grand. We had regular services in all parts of the ship, in which poor Mr. Draper, who was lost in the *London*, regularly took part; we spent a life just like that in a large floating hotel, enjoying every comfort and many a luxury. We had a fine German brass band, which discoursed sweet music during dinner and dessert; concerts or dances, or something of the sort, on deck, occupied the evenings. We had no death and but one birth—a little boy, the son of poor parents, who was duly baptized by the names of "John Gray Britain." The lady of the stiletto took an interest in the youngster, and was seen about in all parts of the ship with a long sheet of paper; this turned out to be a subscription list of threepences, sixpences and shillings. Ten pounds was the result, and this sum was deposited for the little fellow's benefit in the Liverpool Savings' Bank, so that when he arrives at man's estate he will have a little fortune to receive.

And thus passed the days, until, in God's good time, we sighted old Ireland's shores, and were shortly afterwards safely landed in Liverpool. The same day took us through the beautiful valley of the Trent to London, the whole country looking to us like one vast garden and the pretty trees like shrubs.

But here I must stop. But before doing so, if I were asked what great lesson I have learned by mixing with men of so many nations, and travelling to far distant lands, I would say emphatically, a lesson of *liberality*. People who live all their lifetime in the same spot are apt to become exclusive and narrow-minded; they are split up into little sectarian parties, and are apt to be illiberal and uncharitable towards all those who differ from them. I have learned that there are good men of all shades of opinion, and in religious matters I would not quarrel with people who cannot exactly see with my eyes, and I endeavour to respect even their prejudices. It was formerly said, "See how these Christians *love* one another," but really so narrow-minded are many of us that it might almost be said, "See how these Christians *hate* each other." Now, we are all children of the same Father, redeemed by the blood of the same Saviour, trusting to spend an eternity of happiness together in serving the same God and Father of us all. Let us then give the right hand of fellowship to all those who "love the Lord Jesus Christ in sincerity" instead of "falling out by the way."

THE END.

www.ingramcontent.com/pod-product-compliance
Lightning Source LLC
Chambersburg PA
CBHW051733300426
44115CB00007B/547